FROM BUST TO BOOM

By JOHN FIELDHOUSE

GREAT NORTHERN

Great Northern Books
PO Box 213, Ilkley, LS29 9WS
www.greatnorthernbooks.co.uk

ISBN: 978 1 905080 59 5

Design and layout: David Burrill

Printed in the UK by CPI William Clowes Beccles NR34 7TL

CIP Data
A catalogue for this book is available from the British Library

CONTENTS

Foreword I:
Justin Whittle

I remember the day I signed for Hull City. I've never had so many people questioning my sanity.

It was towards the end of November in 1998 and the approach came pretty much out of the blue.

At the time, I was at Stoke when the manager Brian Little came in and said Hull were interested.

Not knowing much about Hull, I looked at the league tables in the paper and it wasn't hard to spot them. They were in bottom place . . . in the bottom division. I think they'd got nine points on the board and the season was almost half-way through.

People told me I was mad to even consider going to Hull. I know this sounds like a cliché but all I wanted to do was play football. I drove up to Hull, met manager Warren Joyce and his assistant John McGovern, and decided to sign.

Everyone said Hull were heading for relegation but 'Joycey' was always very upbeat and very enthusiastic. He was determined to put together a side to get the club out of trouble. He was particularly keen to build a strong defence.

I was one of the first of the new arrivals and others followed . . . lads like Gary Brabin, Jon Whitney, Jason Perry, Steve Swales and Andy Oakes.

They were all characters and I've always said that while we didn't win too many awards for pretty football, not too many opposition sides argued with us. Basically, we fought our way up the table.

My debut was against Carlisle United at Boothferry Park. We won 1-0 with Craig Dudley scoring from a corner in the last few minutes.

To be honest, no-one liked coming to Boothferry Park to play us. The pitch was fantastic, one of the best in the league. The stadium, though, was pretty much falling apart. It reminded me of Stoke's old ground, before they moved to a new stadium.

The turnaround that first season at Hull was amazing. Long before the final game, we'd made certain of staying up.

If we had gone down, the club would probably have gone bust. There would probably have been no saviour, no takeover, no promotions and no prospect of Premier League football.

People always ask me what the secret was that season. 'Joycey' deserves tremendous credit. It was his first job as a manager and he was still playing as well. He was a surprise choice as manager but he was determined to prove he could do the job. He was a good bloke, honest and straightforward. He just wanted us to go out every week, play with passion and give 100 per cent.

The spirit within the squad was brilliant . . . the best I've ever known in my career. Yes, we had plenty of laughs along the way but we knew when - and how - to be serious. We knew what was at stake.

One game that stood out was the home match against Scarborough. I think we were safe by then but the point from a

1-1 draw made absolutely sure. I remember the official attendance was around 13,000 but there must have been at least five thousand more crammed inside Boothferry Park.

I didn't play in that game. I was injured. I had to sit and watch from the back of the Main Stand. Every time the ball hit the roof, you'd be covered in rust and bird-muck. It was quite an experience but I think all the season-ticket holders were used to it.

I didn't miss many games in the second half of that season although I very nearly didn't play against Brighton. At the time, Brighton were playing their home games at Gillingham. We'd stayed at a hotel the night before the game and everyone expected us to leave for the match at about one o'clock. Apparently, though, there was something of a problem over the bill so we left early. I had no idea and was still in my room. I strolled into the reception area at about ten-to-one and couldn't find anyone. When I went outside, the coach had gone.

Fortunately, one of the directors had stayed behind. I jumped into his car and we sped off down the road. We caught the team coach up a couple of miles from Gillingham, flagged it down and I climbed on board. No-one had noticed I was missing! Fortunately, we drew 0-0.

The following season was disappointing. 'Joycey' lost his job, largely because everyone expected us to win promotion. That was totally unrealistic.

It wasn't long before off-the-field problems started to kick in. As players, you keep your head down and try to focus on football. It wasn't always easy, especially when you hadn't been paid for a couple of months.

They were dark days for the club and we kept reading and hearing the next game would be the last one. The fans were amazing. At times, they kept us going with their various collections. Some players left. The thought never entered my head.

Somehow, we reached the play-offs only to lose to Leyton Orient. Ironically, Brian Little, the manager who had sold me to Hull, was in charge then.

It took the arrival of Adam Pearson - and the appointment of Peter Taylor - to really turn the club's fortunes around. Mind you, I don't think Adam thought the club would be heading for the Premier League so quickly.

I did get to play at the KC Stadium and let's just say it was a bit different to Boothferry Park. There weren't too many rats in the dressing rooms. Don't get me wrong, I'll always love the old ground and whenever I drive past now, I always have a little look. It was, though, time to move on.

On a personal note, it was sad when I had to leave Hull City myself but that, as they say, is football.

Since then, it has been once success after another and credit to everyone involved. The fact the club has progressed so far - and in such a short space of time - is hard to believe.

I'll never forget that Great Escape season . . . the way everyone pulled together and united a whole city.

Today, of course, Hull City is a Premier League club and hopefully it will stay that way for a long time to come.

I attended quite a few games at the KC last season and it was amazing to see Hull playing the likes of Liverpool, Arsenal, Manchester United and Chelsea.

It was all a bit different to 10 years ago when the big games were derbies against Scarborough, Scunthorpe and York.

Was it really only 10 years ago?

How times have changed . . . and for the better.

Foreword II:
Ian Ashbee

It's seven years since I signed for Hull City.

The manager at the time was Jan Molby and we met at a hotel in Birmingham.

It was the pre-season of 2002 when he came down to see me.

I drove up to Hull a couple of days later to sign a contract.

I remember coming along the A63, past South Hunsley School and the Humber Bridge.

To be fair, I didn't know much about Hull, only what Jan had told me.

I had played at Boothferry Park before so I knew what the place was like . . . the letters missing from the sign outside, the Kwik-Save off to the left-hand side of the ground and the 'Portakabins' in the car park which served as the offices for the chairman and the football secretary.

I'd just left Cambridge and although the clubs were in the same division, Hull was much bigger.

Not that it was nailed on that I was going to sign.

Just before Jan contacted me, I was very close to joining Oxford and there was also a chance to go to Northampton. Both those clubs were doing well at the time. They were both closer to my home city, Birmingham, so in many ways a move to either Oxford or Northampton made sense.

But I'd listened to what Jan had to say - and to what the chairman Adam Pearson had to say - and there wasn't any doubt in my mind really about what - and where - I was going to do.

To be honest, the chairman really sold Hull as a club - and as a place. He outlined his plans - including the new stadium - and I wanted to be part of them.

The chairman was very ambitious and so was I. At the end of the day, that's why I signed.

From the very start, I always knew the club had potential. I always knew it could go all the way to the top but whether it would happen in my time was a different matter.

To progress to where the club is now is a truly unbelievable story.

I still remember my debut . . . a game against Southend at Boothferry Park, August 2002. We drew 2-2 and I was sent off which wasn't a great start to be honest.

If someone had said back then that seven years on and I'd be playing for Hull in the Premier League, I'd have looked to the nearest white van and straight-jacket!

Unfortunately, Jan didn't last long - something like 13 games - and it was a difficult time for everyone, because there were such high expectations.

I was one of five or six new signings but basically, Jan had inherited players who had been at the club under previous manager Brian Little. I don't think Jan exactly endeared himself to those lads and it was very difficult for the new players to settle in.

When Jan went, Adam brought in Peter Taylor. Again, things didn't start too well and we finished that season in mid-table, behind clubs like Cambridge, Kidderminster, York, Torquay and Oxford. If I remember correctly, Rushden and Diamonds won the league that season.

Peter took some stick from the fans . . . often because he wasn't always in Hull on a Monday. He used to drive up from his home near London.

The following season, we were promoted and I don't think anyone can argue with what Peter did for this club. He brought in some tremendous signings and three or four of them are still here now.

Looking back, that first promotion was very important and the game where we made sure - at Yeovil - will always mean a lot to me. We'd messed it up a few times in the weeks leading up to that game and it was definitely 'squeaky bum' time. Fortunately, it all came right at Yeovil and I managed to get one of the goals . . . top corner if I remember!

Twelve months later, we were celebrating again. Suddenly, we were in the Championship.

The back-to-back promotions were special but if I had to name a high point during my time at Hull, it would be Wembley when we won the play-off final to seal promotion to the Premier League for the first time in the club's history.

Everything about Wembley . . . the build-up to the game, the parties after, the civic reception . . . was brilliant. I'd gone through the two promotions before but nothing was quite like Wembley. The before and the after was absolutely massive for everyone involved, not least the fans.

There was also the honour - and the privilege - of leading the team out in our very first Premier League fixture against Fulham.

If you looked at my face as I walked out of the tunnel that day, I had to blink a few times just to make sure it was actually happening.

To win that first game - and to stay in the Premier League - was another tremendous achievement.

Because we'd started off the season so well and then tailed off, I don't think we got the recognition we deserved.

In the end, we were all relieved that we'd achieved what we set out to do. Hull City is still a Premier League club.

Is staying in the Premier League more important than Wembley? I'll let you decide.

Whatever you think, it's another incredible chapter in the Hull City story.

It's hard to take in everything that's happened at the club.

Hand on heart, I can say I loved Boothferry Park . . . even if my missus didn't like coming to the ground because the place used to stink of urine!

Now . . . we're playing in the best league in the world . . . in one of the best stadiums in the country.

So, what next? What will the next ten years hold?

I'm sure the club will continue to evolve, to build for a very exciting future.

I'm proud to have played a part in the story.

It's been an incredible journey . . . and one that is not over yet.

Ian Ashbee is believed to be the only player who has captained the same club from the bottom division of the Football League to the top. In all, he has made 224 league appearances for Hull City.

Preface:

A night at the pantomime

Shit, shit, shit. It was all going wrong. The instructions had seemed so simple. 'The players know when – and where – to meet the coach. You've no need to worry about anything. We'll be there about six o'clock, so see you at the hotel. Any problems, you've got my mobile number. Oh, and if you've got the time, work out who's sharing a room with who.'

That was the basis of the telephone call I'd received from Warren Joyce. He was the Hull City manager. A great guy; someone you'd do anything for. He'd been appointed manager on the very day I started covering the club for the Hull Daily Mail. Initially, he was sceptical. He said he didn't like – or trust – journalists. Within weeks, we'd become good friends. He told me I wasn't like a proper journalist. I think he meant it as a compliment. No one was more chuffed than me when, against all the odds, Joyce guided City to their now famous Great Escape in his first season in charge. When he'd taken over, in November 1998, City were nine and then 10 points adrift at the bottom of the Football League. It was a club in crisis. A club without a future. Forget the Premier League. Everyone said the only place City were heading was the Conference – or the bankruptcy court.

There again, they'd been saying that for years . . . almost 100 years, in fact. The club was formed in 1904 by a bunch of cricketers who wanted something to do in the winter months. There was never any shortage of ambition – 'We believe we can become one of the top clubs in the country,' said its first President, Alfred E. Spring. The closest Hull came was in 1910. They failed to win promotion by just 0.29 of a goal. It was an era of just two divisions. City looked certain to go up until losing 3-0 at Oldham on the final day of the season. Oldham went up, and one of their scorers was Alf Toward, a player City had sold to Oldham earlier that season for £350 and a couple of iron turnstiles.

During the next 90 years, City never really came to the top flight again. There were occasional glimpses, but financial problems were never far from the surface. In 1992, City became the first English club to go into administration. After that, it was a long – and predictable – slide towards the bottom of the Football League.

The fortunes of the football club echoed what everyone thought of Hull: a frozen outpost on the east coast of Yorkshire. The stench of fish being off-loaded in Hessle Road docks has long since disappeared and the fishing industry, which had propped up the local economy for years, was dead. But you could (almost) see the rusting, abandoned trawlers from Boothferry Park. The city topped just about every nefarious list going – from being burglary capital of England to most teenage pregnancies. Locals didn't need the smug presenters of

Location, Location, Location to tell them it was the worst place in the country to live. In the late 90s, you could still buy a terrace house for £50,000, and get a bit of change. True, thousands of people passed through Hull on the way to North Sea Ferries, the gateway to Europe. Very few stopped off. Even the railway line stopped in Hull. Anything east of the city boundaries was located in a land time had forgotten. Hull was supposedly a rugby league city. Just to prove the point, the main duel carriageway into Hull was named after Clive Sullivan, a revered figure who played for both Hull FC and Hull Kingston Rovers.

Against this background, Joyce performed a miracle. From that seemingly impossible position, he steered City to safety. He did it the hard way – as player-manager. It was – and remains – a remarkable achievement. He made possible what happened later. At the end of that first season, he handed me his shirt. It was sweaty, dirty and there were some old stains where blood or snot – or a combination of both – had run down the front. 'Thanks,' he said. What had I done? Eleven years on and I'm still not certain of the answer.

There is no doubt that we'd forged a strong alliance. From the very start, he told me things he didn't want to appear in the newspaper. We'd been through numerous scrapes together. I was very close to the team – and to Joyce. Too close perhaps. He let me into the dressing room before and after matches; mind you, someone had to push the skip containing the team strip.

I like to think he trusted me. When he took over, he was desperate for some training facilities – any training facilities. I tapped into a few 'old' contacts and managed to get City use of Hull Ionians' ground at Brantingham Park. It was a rugby union set-up, but it didn't matter. There was a pitch, a car park and the showers worked. Then, when Joyce wanted a hotel for a few of his new signings to stay in, I managed to get him a special mate's rate at nearby Cave Castle. In short, I think I believed in Joycey at a time when very few people shared my optimism. That first season proved to be an unforgettable experience. Joyce did more than keep Hull City in the Football League. He kept them in business. That was the reason why I was in my present predicament. And why everything seemed to be going wrong.

Joyce had telephoned me at home on New Year's Day 2000. I'd just spent a miserable evening seeing in the Millennium on Scarborough beach. City were due to play at Leyton Orient on January 3. The team coach was infamous. It was grey and green; rumour said it was actually two vehicles welded into one. On away trips, we'd often joke that you could see the welding work running down the central aisle.

It was supplied by one of Stephen Hinchliffe's seemingly never-ending list of companies. Hinchliffe effectively owned City. He was the leading shareholder. He couldn't be the chairman, or even a director for that matter. He was barred from holding any official position because of an investigation into his affairs by the Department of Trade and Industry. The Football League was taking a special interest in the coach, and in Hinchliffe himself. He was, to say the least, a larger than life figure. He was well over six feet tall with a ruddy face topped by suspiciously light-coloured hair. It suggested he made regular visits to a salon. He wore well-cut suits and smart ties. Even in hot weather, he was usually wrapped in a huge fawn overcoat. His business empire was in ruins. To get around that DTI ban, he claimed to be 'advising' the club. The League was not convinced. Earlier that season, Hinchliffe had written a prominent article in the match-day programme for a Worthington Cup tie at home to Liverpool, City's highest profile game for years. Several high-ranking League officials were at the game. By writing the article, Hinchliffe appeared to be sticking two fingers up at the League's hierarchy. He signed it 'vice president'; honorary, of course. You could describe Hinchliffe as many things. A shrinking violet was not among them. In fact, I could almost imagine the huge grin on his face as he penned that programme piece. The League didn't like Hinchliffe. He couldn't give a stuff.

So, why was the League interested in that coach? Well, if you believed the rumours, it had cost the club the thick end of £80,000. They'd paid for it just 24 hours after receiving a loan from the Professional Footballers' Association, supposedly to cover the players' un-paid wages. Coincidence? Perhaps. No one dared approach the subject with 'Hinch' who was built like a second row forward and had some bigger friends. Often he turned up to matches in a Rolls Royce or a Bentley. His 'business partner' at City was Nick Buchanan, the club's chairman and also built like a brick out-house. He told me he'd played in the second row for Sheffield Tigers Rugby Union Football Club. 'We didn't win many games,' he said, 'but we never lost a fight.' You didn't argue with Buchanan either, but he was good company.

Hinchliffe and Buchanan liked the good life: expensive Cuban cigars, red wine, meals at Mr Chu's, John Prescott's favourite Chinese restaurant on the riverside in Hull. To be hauled before them was a bit like being summoned to meet the Mafia. When it happened, I knew I'd written something they didn't want to read. I'd always spot the burly minder waiting by their car. Once inside the restaurant, they'd put an arm round me – if they were in a half decent mood – and whisper a few words of advice in my ear along the lines of: 'Naughty, naughty, don't do it again.' They always said they had the best interests of the club at heart.

Before Joycey called, I'd been expecting a leisurely trip to London and an overnight stay at a decent hotel with dinner thrown in. Then he delivered his hammer blow. He'd told me that virtually the club's entire back-room staff – including his assistant John McGovern and goalkeeping coach-cum-kit-man Rod Arnold – had gone down with flu. Youth team coach Billy Russell was in Scotland. At such short notice, I was the only non-player available. My job was to ensure the coach – and the players – arrived safely at the team hotel.

Along with half-a-dozen of his squad, Joyce travelled from his home in Merseyside on a daily basis. His car – a people carrier – also served as his office. He used to ferry half of City's squad to games and to training: Gary Brabin, Steve Morgan, David Brown, Jamie Wood, Gerry Harrison. All of them lived close to Joyce, so this group would make their own way to matches. The rest of us – those based closer to Hull – were on the team coach. Or at least, they should have been on the coach. We'd actually left Hull on time, one o'clock. Justin Whittle was waiting at the Duke of Cumberland pub in North Ferriby, a large village 20 minutes down the road to the west of Hull. We'd stopped at Newark Services on the A1 as scheduled too. We'd arranged to pick up the Lincoln 'boys' Jason Perry and Jon Whitney. Sure enough, Pez and Whits were there on time. All of us piled off for a quick toilet break, except for Theodore Whitmore and Ian Goodison, who were laid out on the back-seat. I have to say that 'laid out' is an apt description: the two Jamaicans were so relaxed, they were in danger of falling over. They'd played in the World Cup. They were legends in their own country. So no one could quite understand what they were doing in Hull. They kept themselves to themselves and interviewing them was a nightmare. An occasional nod of the head – or a grunt or a 'yeah man' was the best I could hope for. When they did speak, their accent was almost impossible to understand. Whitmore, in particular, was happy for me to 'make up' his quotes for the paper. As he was already linked with a £1m move to Chelsea, he was Hull City's gold-plated investment. It seemed only a matter of time before his big money move to the Premier League came along. Goodison was reckoned to be the 'makeweight' in the deal that had brought the pair to the club. Still, he was worth a few bob in the transfer market. But neither of them were about to lose any sleep over transfer speculation – or anything else for that matter. On away trips, Whitmore and Goodison – Teeo and Ian – occupied the back seat of the coach. Usually, they had a couple of heavy duty over-coats draped over their track-suits for warmth. They also had huge head-phones over their ears and would nod their heads to the beat of what we all assumed was their favourite Reggae music. They didn't speak. At times, they rarely seemed to breathe. In fact, it was difficult to say whether the pair were awake or asleep. Still, I checked them as we filed off the coach. There they both were, absolutely flat out.

'You okay?' I asked.

'Yeah, man, we're chilled.'

I explained we'd be stopping for ten minutes and then setting off again. Fifteen minutes later, we were back on the coach heading down the A1. We'd travelled another 20 miles when there was a shout from Steve Swales. 'Hey, where's the Jammies?' I walked up to the back of the coach. Whitmore and Goodison were nowhere to be seen. Panic set in. I checked the emergency exit door. It was 'rusted' shut. Superman couldn't have opened it. Where were they? Hull's most valuable assets for 100 years had gone missing; AWOL. And I'd lost them. What would I tell Joycey? After the initial shock, the reality set in. I must have left them behind at the service station. I asked whether anyone seen them since we'd left it. There was a synchronised shake of heads. Had anyone seen them get off the coach? Another synchronised shake of heads. George, the driver, performed a hand-break turn and cups, books and papers went flying. Cars screeched to a halt as George calmly took a turning across the central reservation and back up the other carriageway, heading north again. About half an hour later, we pulled into the service station. As we reached the car park, I saw Whitmore and Goodison perched on a wall outside McDonald's. The coach came to a halt and its doors opened. The pair sanguinely nodded their heads and stepped back on the coach, as if nothing untoward had occurred. They strolled up the aisle to the back seat, laid down again and promptly went to sleep with their headphones on. 'I think we're all on this time,' Swalesy told me. Whitmore and Goodison didn't stir themselves into life until we reached the outskirts of London, where we had another problem. I couldn't find the hotel. We'd stayed there the previous season. The problem was that George hadn't been driving the coach back then, and I'd gone down by car. I knew it was close to Epping Forest; Epping Forest, however, is a big place. As we inched along the North Circular Road in the rush-hour no one could remember the way. Remember, this was well before cars and coaches had satellite navigation systems. George didn't have directions either. He never used them.

I rang the hotel. The receptionist spoke about three words of English – yes, no and okay. Later I discovered she knew how to say: 'Your bill sir?' Somehow, she managed to pass on some instructions. By now, we'd pulled up at a set of traffic lights. Left, right or straight on? I told George to go right. I was wrong. A minute or so later, and George was performing another U-turn – this time on a side-road. A gaggle of mothers, waiting to pick their children from a nearby school, didn't look over-pleased, and a startled Lollipop Lady had to step out of the way smartly before our front wheels ran over her toes. We finally made it to the hotel about an hour late. Joycey was already there, and he wanted to know if we'd had any problems. No one said a word.

Soon, the focus was on the room-sheet, and who was sharing with whom. When I looked around at the faces, I was surprised to see goalkeeper Nick Culkin among them. Culkin had signed on loan from Manchester United. But Joycey had told me that he'd been recalled by United and consequently wouldn't be playing at Orient. Well, at least that's what the headline in the Hull Daily Mail had said the previous day. Joycey had forgotten to tell me that Alex Ferguson had agreed to let him stay. No one, however, had packed a shirt with Culkin's name on it. The only goalkeeper's shirt in the skip was Steve Wilson's. Culkin had to play with 'Wilson' across his back.

Soon we were slipping around again on the black ice of farce. Joycey travelled the few miles from the hotel to Orient's Brisbane Road ground in his car. The coach set off shortly afterwards. But where exactly was Brisbane Road? I knew it was tucked away on a side-street off Leytonstone High Road. According to Swalesy, you turned off beside a kebab shop. There was one problem: every single shop sold kebabs. And every shop – and every side-street – looked exactly the same. I decided we'd be better off trying to spot Orient's floodlight pylons. I remember that George had employed the same tactic before in the search for Peterborough United. I also remembered that the groundsman at Peterborough Rugby Union Football Club had looked a little surprised when we pulled into a deserted car park.

At last we found Orient's ground. When I got there, Joycey had already filled in the team-sheet. I rushed it off the coach and into the referee's room just two minutes before deadline. At the same time, I was phoning live copy back to Hull for the Saturday evening Sports Mail. We drew the game 0-0, and Culkin as 'Wilson' had a blinder. On the return journey, we were joined on the coach by Buchanan and Hinchliffe, which meant a detour to an off-licence because they never travelled anywhere without their cigars, red wine and champagne. It was a long journey back to Hull, but at least we didn't leave anyone behind.

*   *   *   *

Away trips on coach always seemed to be fraught. My first had been to Torquay the previous season. This time, it was the middle of December and we were booked into a hotel right on the sea front. Hull's Great Escape had yet to take shape. Joycey hadn't even started digging the tunnel, let alone thinking about a full-scale break-out. He said he'd invited me on the trip to 'get to know me.' It was his fifth game in charge and my fifth game covering them, and we were six points adrift at the foot of

Division Three. As ever, he'd travelled the bulk of the way in his own car. We met up with him at Strensham Services on the M5. I'd shared a seat with Joycey's assistant, John McGovern, who regaled anyone within listening distance about the tales of his European Cup triumphs with Brian Clough and Nottingham Forest. He kept a photo in his wallet. It showed him lifting the European Cup. The photo of his wife and kids was behind it. I lost count of the number of times I saw that Cup winning picture.

McGovern was the total opposite of Joyce – old school, and a disciplinarian. He met up with the coach at a service station near Sheffield. When he saw me, he almost choked on his bottled water. He wasn't happy that a reporter was on the coach. 'It wouldn't have bloody happened in my time,' he said. Thirty minutes later and he was bringing out that photograph. Apart from the driver, he didn't have anyone else to talk to. McGovern became a good friend. We once played air guitar together in a pub in Exeter. We regularly shared a few glasses of his favourite tipple – Rioja. It still narked him, though, that Joycey was content for me to wander in and around the dressing room area.

On the Friday afternoon in Torquay, Joycey decided it would be good for everyone to attend the local pantomime. He'd already booked the seats. He waved away the moans and groans. There were no excuses, he said. We were all going. So there we were, a party of 20 men, sat amongst hundreds of eight year-olds waiting anxiously for a performance of Cinderalla; or was it Jack and the Beanstalk?

City's physio Mick Matthews tipped me off that Joycey had spoken to the theatre staff and told them that it was my birthday. His plan was to get me on stage, and everyone would sing 'Happy Birthday.' I took decisive action. I had a quiet word with the theatre manager, who was a Torquay season ticket holder. I told him Hull City's players were in the audience. I just happened to lie that it was Joycey's birthday. Half-way through the show, the cast stopped and the star, Bernie Clifton, asked if there was a Mr Joyce in the audience. Joycey had to stand up and then walk on stage. The poor guy couldn't disappoint the kids who were applauding him. On stage, he then listened as the whole place sang a rousing rendition of 'Happy Birthday, dear Warren.' He declined Bernie Clifton's offer of a free autograph, though I think he got a peck on the cheek from one of the Nolan Sisters. The players pissed themselves laughing. Joycey glanced in my direction. If looks could kill, I'd have been incinerated on the spot. The bonding exercise didn't work, either. City lost 2-0.

A few weeks later, we were on the coach again bound for an FA Cup tie at Aston Villa, who were then top of the Premier League under John Gregory. City were 92nd and hopeless. It was a surprise when Joycey's team beat non-League Salisbury in the opening round, and no one predicted a 2-1 win at Luton in the second round either. The club couldn't afford the cost of an overnight stay in Birmingham. But we did have a pre-match meal of pasta and chicken in a four-star hotel on the northern outskirts of Birmingham. And then we set off for Villa Park.

Again, George couldn't find the way. We pulled up at some traffic lights on the main A38 into Birmingham. There was a newsagent at the junction, and Joycey told me to nip in and ask for directions. I clambered over the railings, walked into the shop and found an Aston Villa fan, claret and blue scarf and all. He walked outside with me, and saw the coach and the huge 'Tiger' in the front window. 'Wait a minute,' he said. 'Is that the team coach?' 'Yeah,' I replied. 'We seem to have taken the wrong turning.' He told me it was best to avoid the main road route – 'the traffic is murder' – and head down the side-streets because 'it's much quicker.' He drew the route on a page torn out of my notebook. Twenty minutes later we pulled into Villa Park via the back entrance. We travelled the last half mile the wrong way down a one-way street. The players piled off the coach and McGovern and I were the last two to leave. As I stepped off, a mean-looking police commander – peaked cap and silver-topped walking cane – was waiting. 'Who's in charge of the coach?' he barked. McGovern look straight at me: 'He is,' he said. 'Right sonny,' said the policeman, 'what the hell have you been doing? I've had four out-riders and two police cars waiting back on the motorway to give you an official escort . . . and you've come the wrong way up a one-way street. I should bloody arrest you now.' For once, I was lost for words, and McGovern was nowhere to be seen. I escaped with a five minute lecture about wasting police time and resources. 'And don't expect an escort after the match,' was the parting shot from the copper. 'You can find your own way back to the motorway.'

I still had to fulfil my official duty: pushing the skip containing the strip into the dressing room. On the way in, Villa's management, including John Gregory, lined up to shake my hand. So did Doug Ellis, the Villa chairman. 'Pleasant journey?' he enquired. City lost 3-0. In the post-match press conference, I met Gregory again. 'Haven't I just seen you pushing a skip?' he asked. 'Don't ask,' I replied.

Buchanan and Hinchliffe promised that some of City's share of the receipts from a near 40,000 crowd would go into signing new players. Months on, and Joycey was still waiting.

The club was depressingly skint. There always seemed to be

a transfer embargo in place. Like Joycey, I had trouble keeping up with them all. On more than one occasion, I waited with him at his office on North Road, next to Boothferry Park. The office was on the top floor of a run-down house. The first job was always to remove the piles of pizza boxes and other assorted rubbish from the porch. Upstairs, there was a desk, a couple of chairs and a telephone. It was always cold in there. The state of the kitchen would have struck the fear of God into a council health inspector. As for the toilet . . . well, don't even mention it. Once, we were expecting striker Graeme Jones. Apparently, terms had been agreed and the money was supposed to come from those Villa receipts. Jones never showed up. Another embargo had been put in place. Potential transfer target Colin Alcide didn't turn up either. He'd arrived at the reception area, on the other side of the stadium from North Road, and was told to walk to the manager's office. I found him 35 minutes later, lost in the pitch dark in the corridor beneath the main stand. Alcide did sign – once his eyes had become accustomed to daylight again. And he played an important role in that Great Escape.

*   *   *   *

After the heroics of that season, City were duly tipped to challenge for promotion. The pressure on Joycey was extraordinary and totally unrealistic because the financial problems had mounted. Boardroom squabbles had also increased, and so did my official 'invites' to meet Buchanan and Hinchliffe. Things often turned awkward, and sometimes downright nasty. I began to watch my back whenever I walked down those ominous dark and unlit corridors that seemed to exist at every lower division ground. I even received a sinister phone call at home. The warning was blunt: 'Print that story and you'll be floating down the Humber in a concrete coffin.' I didn't recognise the voice at the other end of the line.

By now, City's affairs were being investigated by the Football Association's trouble-shooter Graham Bean, an ex-police officer. He'd got to hear about the concrete coffin threat. He asked if I would be interviewed as part of their on-going enquiries. I declined. Was it the right decision? I honestly don't know. But, as I considered the various options, that image of the Humber – and a coffin – kept appearing in front of my eyes.

Things went from bad to worse, and the marvellous memories of the Great Escape were soon forgotten. The seriousness of City's sad plight was evident. Joycey was sacked in April; ironically after a hat-trick of wins against Carlisle, Leyton Orient and Mansfield Town. City scored seven goals in those three games . . . and didn't concede one.

One of Joycey's last away games in charge was at Halifax. As a cost-cutting measure, City had stopped travelling by coach. Instead, the players were ferried to away games in cars. For the Halifax trip, my old Ford Sierra – dog hairs and all – was pressed into service. My passengers were Mick Matthews and Gary Bradshaw. About ten miles from Halifax, the M62 ground to a halt. Three solid lanes of traffic with kick off an hour-and-a-half away. I rang Joycey. Bradshaw was due to start the game – another story that the manager had forgotten to mention to me.

Joycey suggested driving along the hard shoulder. I turned on to it just in time to see a police car and couple of officers about three hundred yards ahead stopping drivers and handing out tickets. They couldn't believe their luck. 'Try it,' said Joyce. 'They might let you off. Anyway, the club will pick up your fine.' I stayed in the queue, eventually the holdup cleared and we arrived at Halifax's ground less about 45 minutes before the kick off. But the steward – shaven head and studded ears – wouldn't let me in the car park. 'I've got a Hull City player in the car,' I pleaded. 'Pull the other one,' he said. Bradshaw not only played, but scored the only goal in a 1-0 win.

Within a week, Joycey had been sacked. He rang me straight after he'd been told about the decision. He had to take his hire car back to Boothferry Park. He asked if I'd mind picking him up and running him to Leeds United where he was about to start work on their Academy coaching staff. There was another car waiting for him at Elland Road. I don't mind admitting that I was blinking back the tears when I heard he'd lost his job. We travelled to Leeds, talking about the memories of the last 18 months.

It was almost another year and a half before Buchanan eventually resigned, and disappeared off the radar. At the same time, Hinchliffe also disappeared, but at the bequest of Her Majesty's pleasure. He was jailed for five years in March 2000 after pleading guilty to a series of fraud and corruption charges.

The legacy of their reign was this: the club almost went bust. There were all kinds of allegations about dodgy deals and missing money. It is important nevertheless to state that neither the Football Association nor Humberside Police's Fraud Squad could find enough evidence to press charges against any City director or shareholder from that era.

I lost Joycey's shirt. My editor claimed it as his prerogative, and I gave in meekly. After all, he signed my expenses. There's only one thing I kept asking myself about that period. Whatever happened to the team coach?

Chapter One:

Living in the dark ages

August, 1997-May, 1998

David Lloyd was shorter and chubbier than I'd expected. He had a pigeon toed walk and he didn't look you straight in the eye when he spoke to you. The first time I met him he was also wearing a brown suit with a pair of black shoes. Somehow, he didn't look like a successful multi-millionaire. Lloyd was attending his first ever match as Hull City's new owner. He would never confirm or deny it, but rumour had it that the previous day he'd driven to the city for the first time. He spotted some floodlights from the A63 on the way into the city. He followed them and arrived at the Boulevard, the home of Hull Rugby League club. Lloyd thought the Boulevard was Boothferry Park and couldn't believe he'd just paid a fortune for it. Someone pointed out the shape of the posts, and sent him in the direction of Boothferry Park.

It was mid-August, and City's opponents in a Third Division game were Notts County. Lloyd didn't lack ambition – or money. He didn't lack vision, either. He believed he could transform City into a credible Premier League side, based at a state-of-the art stadium, costing many millions of pounds. For a while, he had us all believing that dream; and believing he was the man to make that dream happen. When he took over, City was a club in crisis – again. Their much-loved home ground, Boothferry Park, was crumbling. One side of the ground was shut because of safety fears. Weeds grew between terraces still in use. The Main Stand was built out of corrugated sheets seemingly held together by endless coats of paint. Every time the ball hit the main stand roof, the patrons below were showered in rust. Lloyd was the new saviour, the answer to the prayers of every long-suffering City fan.

We'd spoken on the telephone several times, but this was my first face to-face interview. I remember waiting patiently, just outside the boardroom door. I glanced down at the carpet. It was worn and dirty. No doubt it would be replaced. The paper was peeling off the walls. The door had notices on it relating to the previous year. There again, City was a club living in the past; and not a very glorious past at that. I was ushered into the boardroom to be met by a crowd of faces. I recognised some of Hull's more influential businessmen. I cringed as one of them asked me if I was going to question Lloyd about what it was like to be married to Chris Evert. I pointed out it was Lloyd's bother, John, who married the former Wimbledon champion and that the marriage had been dissolved in 1987. To be fair, it was hardly surprising people knew little of Lloyd's background. Born in Essex in 1948, he was one of Britain's most successful tennis players throughout the 1970s and 80s but rarely threatened the world's top 100. He was the star of several Davis Cup campaigns and, after his career finished, he went on to captain the British side as well as occupying a number of high profile posts within the Lawn Tennis Association. His business empire flourished. He initially launched the David Lloyd Tennis Club, and then the David Lloyd Leisure Group and the Next Generation chain of fitness clubs. He coached Tim Henman and was a regular pundit for the BBC at Wimbledon. But tennis, it has to be said, was hardly the most popular participation sport in Hull. I'd been summoned so that Lloyd could outline his plans for the future of professional sport in the city. He guided me into a quiet corner. There was a whiff of cigar smoke in the air. The half full glasses of red wine – disfigured by stubbed out cigarettes floating in them – were shoved to one side. Lloyd was only too pleased to talk. Already, there had been a good deal of scepticism about why a successful Essex-based businessman – with a tennis background – wanted to write a large cheque in Hull, where rugby league and football reigned supreme. My first impressions? He appeared genuinely passionate about the future. If I'm honest, the interview was rushed. He warned me that he didn't have much time. Kick off was less than an hour away, and there were plans for him to walk out on to the pitch. It was a chance for the fans to see the new Messiah. Inevitably, my first question was about how much money Lloyd was prepared to stump up. 'You can't buy success,' he said. 'You have to build it. Coming to Hull is a business decision and has to be a long-term project. The potential here is enormous, especially if we can get everyone in the city pulling together. In that respect, Hull has an advantage over somewhere like Manchester, which will always be split because they have United and City. I'm not here on an ego trip. I don't need that, but I am excited by the prospect of building something special in Hull.'

I'd heard the word 'potential' before. Every single Hull City owner had been saying the same thing since the club was formed in 1904. Lloyd acknowledged that 'something special' was a new stadium, incorporating sporting and leisure facilities. He added: 'It is a complicated jigsaw, but if we can fit the pieces together it will be a fantastic end result - and not just commercially, but for sport.'

At the time, City were struggling in the bottom Division, and Lloyd played down expectations that he would fling money at them. 'If Hull City are to be successful,' he said 'we must spend out of profit, rather than just pump money into the club. That is what the really successful clubs do. We are still going through the accounts and trying to work out exactly what state the club's finances are in – and what our break-even attendance will be. I do believe the cash being thrown about by many clubs now is not sustainable and not in the long-term interests of the game. Only five out of 92 Football League clubs made a profit last season. That can't last. We have to find a different way of doing business.' Those words didn't encourage supporters who had watched City finish 17th in the basement Division – their lowest position in their history. Under manager Terry Dolan and chairman Martin Fish, the Tigers had tumbled down the Leagues. It was almost a decade since they'd spent any decent money on a player. When they had, it almost bankrupted the club. To be fair, most of the details behind Lloyd's plans were already well known. But people – and the media – were fascinated by his presence. But how did Lloyd come to be involved with City? It started in 1996 with a game of golf.

The venue was the exclusive Wisley Golf Club, just outside London. Aside from Lloyd, one of the central characters was

Tim Wilby, a former rugby league player with Hull FC. Wilby was what you would term a journeyman pro – his career including spells at Leeds and Hull FC, and then in France and Australia. The highlight was an appearance in the 1980 Challenge Cup final at Wembley: Hull v Hull KR. He scored Hull's only try in a 10-5 defeat. Once he'd hung up his boots, he'd briefly toyed with coaching but became – I was told – a successful property developer. I knew Wilby, and he could have sold sand to the Saudis. However, he'd spent enough time in Hull to realise the untapped potential for sport. There had been a time in the 1980s when Hull FC and cross-city rivals Rovers had dominated rugby league. Now, though, that crown had gone to Wigan. Hull FC – and Rovers – were struggling to catch up. Wilby nonetheless recognised that there was a massive fan base for professional sport in Hull, and precious little competition for miles around. His own vision involved merging Hull City and Hull FC – and quite possibly Hull Kingston Rovers as well – and moving them into a new stadium. There was just one problem. Wilby lacked the financial resources. He needed a major investor. Enter Lloyd.

After his retirement, Lloyd had opened his first tennis and fitness centre in 1982. He'd then built up a 16-strong chain before selling out to the Whitbread Group for £201m in 1985. Lloyd's profit was £21m. He had other successful business interests at home and abroad too. Cynics questioned his absence of a football background, though rumour suggested he was a Spurs' fan. Privately, he admitted he didn't know much about football – and even less about rugby league. He'd never visited Hull before either. Wilby, though, supplied all the background Lloyd needed. I thought it was like a spider enticing a fly into its web; and a well-spun web too. From those tentative talks in the clubhouse at Wisley, the pair formulated their plan. It involved buying Hull City and Hull FC, and Lloyd went public with it in April 1997.

A spokesman for one of his companies, Bridgestate Developments Limited, said: 'David is an astute businessman and when he sees opportunities, he is always willing to investigate them.' Within weeks, he'd bought the rugby league club. In June, he agreed a deal with Hull City. City's major shareholder was Christopher Needler, the surviving head of local dynasty that had tried, without success, to make City a powerful and credible force. After the Second World War, the Needlers had invested heavily in the club and in the construction of Boothferry Park. Harold Needler, a successful builder, initially spearheaded the family interest in City's affairs. He served as chairman with brothers John and George also on the board of directors. A long list of managers, from the much loved Raich Carter in the early 1950s to the short-lived Stan Ternant in the early 90s, had failed to reward the Needlers' considerable backing with a place in the top Division. Harold Needler – known as Big Aitch – died in 1975. Shorn of his inspired leadership and always open chequebook, City's fortunes plummeted. Twenty years on and his son, Christopher, became chairman. Unlike his father, he was not a football man. He was more than happy to take a back-seat role and allow Martin Fish to take on the day-to-day running of the club. Fish, a local accountant, was likeable. However, two relegations – and his backing of manager Dolan – made him a hated figure among City fans. There were many protests against Fish who, among other things, had smelly old cod-heads shoved through the letter box of his home. Dolan hadn't fared much better. Denied money for new players, he struggled to keep City afloat on the pitch. Fish had a similar struggle off it. That's when Lloyd made his move.

Fish recalled: 'Wilby came in and said: 'We could be interested in this.' I remember saying 'Who's we?' and he said: 'David Lloyd and I.' The talks were lengthy. On one specific day, Fish remembers, he was in discussions in Hull, Herefordshire, Hull again and finally in London. Lloyd paid around £1.1m – 25p for every share. Needler's shareholding had previously been valued at almost £6m. Minor shareholders did not receive a penny. To many City fans, Lloyd's takeover was a God-send. They were glad to see the back of Fish. As soon as Wilby was installed as chairman, he sacked Dolan.

As Lloyd was buying two clubs (the football club and Hull FC) the agreement still had to be sanctioned by the Monopolies and Merges Commission. That, inevitably, led to a delay and the takeover was put on hold. So, when City's players reported back for the start of pre-season training in July, Fish technically remained in charge. One of his first tasks was to reinstate Dolan. The deal was finally approved on July 11. That finally ended a mind-boggling two weeks in which Dolan was sacked, re-instated and then sacked again.

The new regime swept into the club. Rob Smith, then a member of City's commercial staff and now the club's marketing manager, recalled: 'On the first day the new regime met the staff. Tim Wilby breezed in wearing knee-length khaki shorts and white trainers. He set up camp in my office and wasted no time in making himself comfortable. He put his feet on the desk and began calling people in one-by-one. It became obvious that they had done their homework. One of the people who came in with them was Frank Killen, who was a well-known figure on the Hull sporting scene. From the start, certain faces did not fit in their long term plans.' Commercial manager Simon Cawkhill was one of those summoned, and Wilby politely asked him to return with a certain set of figures immediately – or 'fuck off.' 'Simon was almost reduced to a crumbling mess by Wilby and I just remember him (Wilby) sitting there, feet on the desk without a care in the world,' says Smith. 'Simon didn't know what to do and we never saw him again.'

Working alongside Wilby as chief executive at the rugby club was Peter Tunks, a former Australian Test player. Wilby and Tunks had previously run greyhound operations at another rugby league club, Oldham. Ian McMahon took on a similar role at Hull City, but lasted slightly less time than it took for the paint to dry on the nameplate on his office door. No one denied that City needed shaking up, but as the new regime made their presence felt, Smith says all the staff feared for their jobs. 'Wilby took us all from Boothferry Park to a local pub,' says Smith 'When we got there, I only had a pint-and-a-half because I was driving, but I just thought: 'What the hell do I do? These are the new owners. Should I stay all night?' Fortunately, Wilby took on instant trust whatever I said to him. I think they needed people who knew how things operated, and I was fortunate. I'd built up a good knowledge of how the football club ran. At that stage, of course, we hadn't actually met Lloyd. As other members of staff were ousted, my own level of responsibility increased dramatically day-by-day. Suddenly I was looking after contract work for the players, which was never in my remit. But if you weren't willing to do something, you were out.'

When the new season kicked off, fans became aware of a key part of Lloyd and Wilby's blueprint. They intended to sell Boothferry Park and move City into the Boulevard. It would be a temporary move in preparation for the brand new stadium. The City Council was another key player. Lloyd wanted them to provide the land and financial support. In return, he promised to re-invest the proceeds from the sale of Boothferry Park and, in time, the Boulevard.

Hull is almost unique in that sports fans are either football or rugby league followers. The rivalry is long established. The thought of City moving to the Boulevard would normally have been greeted by wide-scale protest and derision. However, Wilby had told City fans that was the scenario at a packed public meeting – and was cheered. It was a bizarre event. There was Wilby – a former rugby player – telling football fans that they would have to leave their traditional home and move to a rugby league ground. I'd have expected him to be hung, drawn and quartered. But, because City fans had endured years of misery and broken promises, they were prepared to accept anything and anyone. It was standing room only at that public meeting, held at the City Hall. Hundreds more fans listened as the speeches were relayed by tannoy outside. He promised new players and a big-name manager. He had the majority of the crowd eating out of his hands. Long-time City fan Mike Farrar said: 'To be honest, Wilby could have told us anything. We were fed up to the back teeth of lies, lies and more lies – and shocking football. Mickey Mouse could have stood in front of us that night and we'd have believed him. All we wanted was a better football club and Wilby and Lloyd were the only people who were willing to put their hands in their pockets. We kept hearing about these groups of local businessmen, but when it came to doing something, they seemed to run away. Now we had some hope. Lloyd certainly had money, and it made sense to build a new stadium.' Not everyone was convinced, though. Former City stalwart Pete Skipper – who made more than 300 appearances between 1978 and 1988 – was in the audience that night. He said: 'Some of the things just didn't stack up. I remember shaking my head and thinking: Why aren't people questioning some of the things he's saying.'

Wilby lapped up the occasion. As he spoke, it was all too easy to be drawn by the emotion. The general feeling seemed to be anything – and anyone – was better than Fish and Dolan. In retrospect, some of the non-committal answers, as well as Wilby's promises, ought to have set alarm bells ringing. I was no different to anyone else. Lloyd seemed the way forward. The alternative was administration, probable closure. I spoke to Lloyd a couple of days later. He moved quickly to dampen growing optimism of half-a-dozen high-profile signings. In fact, he always seemed to err on the side of caution when it came to discussing possible recruits. He did suggest that he wanted to bring a big name manager and, once again, the speculation mounted. The Lloyd/Wilby partnership was still very new and the fact they didn't always seem to be saying the same things hinted at possible problems. There is no doubt Wilby relished his hero status. I saw him stroll around Hull as though he owned the place. Lloyd also seemed happy with his own profile. Rarely a day went by without his name featuring on the front pages, the back pages or both. Hull suddenly became national news.

Having actually acquired both clubs, the key now was the

super-stadium or, as Lloyd described it, an American-style leisure city. It would be home to City and the two rugby league clubs. Hull KR were in as big a financial mess as their two neighbours. They could not withstand a Lloyd-led takeover. For the moment, though, Lloyd was happy with his two purchases. He hoped the stadium part of his leisure city would be ready in only two years. There was talk of a massive retail development: new roads, cinemas, restaurants and a hotel. The list went on. Someone even produced some plans. No one questioned where they had come from. 'I think it will be the best centre for sport in the north of England . . . if not the whole of England,' said Lloyd. Any criticism of Lloyd's vision was brushed aside. No one was interested in negativity. Lloyd said Wilby was already holding talks with the city council about the plans and a suitable site. Several potential venues were put forward, including land close to the Humber Bridge. There was a problem, though, in that much of it belonged to East Riding Council rather than Hull City Council. Kingswood, a rapidly developing area just to the north of Hull and within the city boundary, became the early front-runner. Lloyd merely continued his PR offensive. He said: 'We are looking at 10 years here – minimum. At the end of the day, if people want to throw stones at me they can, but we are trying to produce something that will be for the good of them. We are going to put Hull on the sporting map and no one is going to stop us.' Expectations soared higher still.

There were protests and sceptics. But anyone questioning Lloyd was in danger of being deported. Paul Harrison, a freelance journalist covering the story, said: 'There wasn't a lot of substance to back up what Wilby and Lloyd were saying. The trouble was everyone appeared to be behind them: the council, the business community and the media. I wrote a couple of pieces basically outlining my suspicions – not least the cost of everything. The City Council didn't have much money back then. They were shutting schools and hospitals. So how could they justify the type of investment Lloyd was talking about? Boothferry Park wasn't in a great area. The council had invested a lot of money a mile or so down the road re-developing St Andrews Quay. A lot of things didn't add up to me, but I got a very negative response.'

The Lloyd bandwagon rolled on, and City hadn't even kicked a ball yet. More mouth-watering visions were revealed. Apart from the stadium itself, his 'leisure city' would feature a centre of sporting excellence and shopping malls complete with fountains, hotels and a museum. When the talk returned to football, Lloyd admitted the Premier League was the ultimate goal – and within four or five years too. As far as the chase for a high-profile player manager . . . well, former Newcastle and England legend Peter Beardsley was the name on most lips. Lloyd and Wilby did deliver a former England international. It wasn't Beardsley, but Mark Hateley. Hateley had won 34 England caps and played for some of Europe's biggest sides, including Glasgow Rangers and AC Milan. However, his management experience was nil. His appointment took everyone by surprise; not least City's own staff.

Rob Smith remembers Wilby 'breezing in' to boast: 'We've got Mark Hateley as manager. We're meeting him tonight – and you're coming.' We met at La Perla, a local Italian restaurant. I couldn't believe I'd been invited. Mark strolled in and obviously the deal had almost been signed, sealed and delivered. I'm not so sure what he knew about Hull. He was very casual about the whole thing. Hateley arrived with Scotsman Billy Kirkwood, who became his assistant. The pair of them were introduced to the media the following day, which increased the sense of optimism around Hull. Again, it was all too easy to look past Hateley's total lack of management experience. I met Hateley shortly afterwards. He agreed to write a weekly column for the Hull Daily Mail and we sat in his office in that run-down house just off North Road. If you peered through the years of grime on the upstairs' window, you looked out on the back of the Main Stand at Boothferry Park. After so much as a light shower, the rain dribbled down the rusty corrugated sheeting. Some of the windows were broken. Others were boarded over. A few were covered in plastic sheeting blowing in the wind or left open to the elements. The entrance was usually strewn with litter and discarded takeaway meals. Quite what Hateley – more accustomed to the palatial surroundings of the San Siro and Ibrox – made of it all is open to question. The look on his face that day seemed to sum everything up. It was as though he couldn't quite believe he was in Hull. His sparsely furnished office, tucked away on the top floor, was freezing cold. Kirkwood sat in a corner listening to our conversation. In his new trainers, and with a gold chain around his neck, Hateley leaned back in a chair, his feet on the only desk in the room. There were three mobile phones in front of him, and one of them was always ringing. It become obvious that conversations were taking place with his contacts in Scotland. City were linked with several potential Scottish signings, notably Hateley's former Rangers' strike-partner Ally McCoist. It was the first in a long list of red herrings.

City did sign some Scottish players, such as goalkeeper Scott

Thompson, who were hardly in the McCoist class. Hateley freely talked about his career. He was less than forthcoming when it came to discussing Hull. Rob Smith got to know Hateley better than most. 'I don't think he ever felt at home,' he says. 'That house on North Avenue was a shit-hole. He'd turn up in a really flash two door Mercedes – aqua marine and the latest model. It was the first and only one in Hull. We'd never seen one before. All the players were turning up in battered Escorts. Mark always seemed to have a mobile phone in his hand – even when he was training.'

Hateley discovered the delights of Hull's nightlife. Smith recalled: 'If we went out in Hull, Mark always seemed to have a tartan suit on. If we were going to a club – and it cost a fiver to get in – Mark wouldn't pay. He'd rather get in a taxi and go home. He always said: 'I don't pay to get into clubs.' We'd offer to pay for him, but he wouldn't have it.' Hateley was appointed less than a month before the new season. City's first game was at Mansfield on August 9. Mark Brattan was one of an estimated 2,000 fans who made the trip to Field Mill and expected nothing less than a victory. 'For years, we'd watched Dolan's style of football. And it wasn't very pretty. My mate used to say Dolan's philosophy was 'if it moves, hoof it and if it doesn't move, hoof it even harder.' Any half-decent player was sold. Now, we had a former England international in charge. Okay, he had a big bald patch and a pony tail. His sun-tan was definitely suspicious. It was bright orange. But we also had a multi-millionaire as owner of the club, and there was the new stadium and the Premier League in just five years time. We couldn't fail, could we?'

City lost 2-0 at Mansfield. They hardly got a kick. The City side that day at least contained a few new 'names': Thompson,

Steven Boyack and, not least Hateley. However, it was worryingly close to the line-up that had struggled in the same Division the previous season. Still, Lloyd, Wilby and Hateley labelled the defeat as no more than teething problems. Hateley didn't even travel back with the team. City improved to draw their next game 0-0 at newcomers Macclesfield in the first round of the Coca-Cola Cup. Hateley accentuated the positive. He said the clean sheet was a bonus. Four days later, Notts County came to Boothferry Park.

Because of Lloyd's arrival, the crowd was 7,462 – almost double City's average from the previous season. They'd come to see him. Accompanied by Wilby, he was given a standing ovation. However much he boosted the attendance, Lloyd didn't lift the players. City were stuffed 3-0. Lloyd wasn't panicking. 'Mark will sort things out,' he said.

City lost their next League game 2-0 at Peterborough, beat Macclesfield 2-1 in the second leg of the Coca-Cola Cup and then the goals flowed in the last fixture of the month: a 7-4 win over Swansea with Duane Darby scoring a hat-trick. The game set a record for the most goals scored in a League game at Boothferry Park. It was a rare success for Hateley; City failed to win any of their next six League matches. They did, however, topple then Premier League side Crystal Palace in the next round of the Coca Cola cup. Darby scored the only goal in a 1-0 victory at home and then defender Ian Wright restricted Palace to a 2-1 win at Selhurst Park. City went through on away goals. Their reward? A plum third round tie against Newcastle at St James' Park. Predictably Newcastle were just too strong; City lost 2-0. Still, the performance was encouraging and Lloyd could at least count on the share of the gate receipts from a crowd of nearly

36,000.

By then it was October and ominous cracks had started to appear in Lloyd's master plan. In fact, Wilby's services had been dispensed with a couple of weeks earlier. A national newspaper carried out an exposé, which suggested he wasn't a property developer, but a caretaker of a block of council-owned flats in London. Westminster Council were none too happy about Wilby's infrequent appearances at his day job. What did they expect? He was running a football club and a rugby club 250 miles away. More speculation followed. There were supposed to be more stories about Wilby relating to his private life. A clearly embarrassed – and clearly rattled – Lloyd took decisive action. Wilby was sent on a scouting mission to Australia, explicitly to identify new talent for the rugby league club. He was never seen – or heard of – again (though I once bumped into a Hull FC fan who said he bumped into Wilby backpacking in Panama).

As Wilby headed out of Hull, so did Tunks. He lost his post as chief executive at Hull FC. Again, there were allegations about his business affairs. Lloyd also had other problems. His back-room staff in Hull included Bryan Calam, a former high-ranking local police officer who wasn't popular with City's fans. A few years before Lloyd's arrival, Calam had been in charge of policing City's home games. When promotion-chasing Bradford visited Boothferry Park, he'd decided to turf City's fans out of the South Stand and hand it over to Bradford supporters instead. It was a PR disaster. Another high-profile member of 'Team Lloyd' was financial expert Michael Appleton, who had a influential role at both the football and rugby club. Like Lloyd, he was a talented tennis player and had appeared for his county. However, he developed a reputation at Hull as being aloof and arrogant. He hardly endeared himself to the Hull FC faithful by selling star player Tevita Vaikona to rivals Bradford Bulls. Hull journalist Richard Tingle remembers: 'He made a huge mistake. There was an uproar after the sale of Vaikona and I think it was the first time people had started having a go at Lloyd. I remember asking Appleton what he thought about the fans reaction to the club selling Vaikona. He replied along the lines of: 'What's it got to do with them?' I went away and printed it. Again, there was an outcry. Lloyd was in the firing line as well. He tried to calm things and instructed Appleton to go out and make a big signing. Hull paid a staggering £150,000 for Alan Hunte, Steve Prescott and Simon Booth. They doubled Hunte's wages to bring him in from St Helens. The fans still weren't happy, though, and even after those signings there was a feeling that the damage had been done. There had always been scepticism about Lloyd. Now the fans didn't trust him.

Things were hardly going well at City either. Rob Smith recalled the fall-out from Wilby's departure and Appleton's arrival. 'Appleton was in charge of the football side of things and Calam the rugby. They definitely tried to integrate them. In fact, all the staff and the City players went to the Boulevard to watch a rugby game and we all thought: 'What are we doing here?' We went into the bar after the game for a beer. Wilby was still at the club then, and he got into a fight with a fan. In fact, when we kicked off the football season at Boothferry Park, he'd go across to the Three Tuns pub with the supporters and he'd get into fights there as well.'

On-the-field, there was the occasional decent result, but generally City struggled. Lloyd did sanction the arrival of ex-England international David Rocastle on loan. He scored on his debut in a 3-0 win over Scarborough, but would eventually be dragged down to the low level of his team-mates. Glyn Hodges, a Welsh international, formerly with Wimbledon and Newcastle, also arrived, but was frustratingly inconsistent. Chris Bettney was recruited from Sheffield United, a deal which prompted no rush at the turnstiles. Lloyd stumped up around £25,000 to buy Matt Hocking. He wasn't the big name signing City craved. Neither was Hateley's former Rangers' team-mate Brian McGinty, who arrived on loan. On top of everything else, City fans were outraged that Lloyd had spent around £200,000 on the three new signings at Hull FC.

Off the field, the headache for Lloyd was the presence of Kwik Save on one corner of the Boothferry Park. The supermarket's main entrance was alongside City's reception. Indeed, on more than one occasion, unsuspecting visitors had walked through the wrong door and found themselves looking at mountains of fruit and vegetables and frozen turkeys. It was assumed Lloyd would persuade the City Council to move the supermarket to another site. But, following the Wilby affair, the Council was starting to back away from the Lloyd-led regime. And Kwik Save had a 107 year lease and didn't want to move from a residential area. It seemed incredible that Lloyd – such a successful businessman – had bought the football club without identifying the lease issue. The store always looked run-down and the illuminated sign and trolley park was a nightly target for local vandals. It was, though, popular with shoppers – the second most profitable store in the North East of England. Lloyd claimed Kwik Save were demanding a multi-million pound compensation deal to terminate the lease. They also wanted a guaranteed site for a new store, preferably in the same locality.

When Lloyd turned to the City Council, he found they were looking the other way.

With the proper planning permission, some reports suggested Boothferry Park could be worth as much as £10m. But the City Council had become nervous about Lloyd and questioned his motives. In February, 2008, the inevitable happened. With City on the verge of a relegation battle, Hateley was faring worse than Dolan. And with the City Council refusing to intervene in the Kwik Save debate, Lloyd announced that he was no longer prepared to help fund the new stadium project or find the cash to strengthen City's team for the following campaign. Lloyd tried to recover lost ground, stressing his commitment to the football and rugby clubs.

The collapse of his stadium plan was greeted with relief in some quarters. John Cooper was stadium manager at Boothferry Park. He holds the same post at the KC Stadium today. Just after Lloyd's takeover, he was ordered to prepare the Boulevard for League football. The deadline was November 6. Cooper decided to do everything he could to delay it because he thought the proposed move had nothing to do with sport and everything to do with commerce. 'It was a time when everyone was still getting their stadiums up to standard after the Taylor Report which was produced following the Hillsborough disaster. I concocted a plan to take sure that the work would take far longer than anticipated. I was talking to the Football League. My contact there told me the criteria for entry. It wasn't just the quality of the playing surface. You had to have a certain percentage of seats, and then there were all the various safety requirements. The floodlights even needed work.'

To enable the work on the pitch to go ahead, Hull FC's home

games in the Rugby League play-offs that summer had to be switched to Boothferry Park. That, in turn, led to a loss of vital revenue for the RL club. Cooper says he spoke to the RL club's directors, who were increasingly concerned. 'They knew the football club was the prime asset and that the RL club was a tool to get the whole thing to a new stadium. Boothferry Park was worth millions. The Boulevard wasn't. It was a case of let's get to the Boulevard and let's sell Boothferry Park off. If that had happened, I feared we'd have stayed at the Boulevard for a long time. In fact, I don't know what would have happened to the football club. That was my biggest worry all the time, especially if the new stadium hadn't gone ahead. What would Lloyd have done then?'

Hot weather meant Cooper was forced to delay vital drainage work on the Boulevard pitch, which gave him breathing space. At the same time, Cooper was pulling out all the stops to make sure the pitch at Boothferry Park was one of the best in the League. 'We had to get the pitch absolutely pristine. Lloyd would be walking on it and he couldn't fail to be impressed. We had to get it like the centre court at Wimbledon. Sure enough, after he walked on it, he turned round to me and said: 'We'll stay here until we get the Boulevard totally right.' Suddenly, there was no pressure. It was a stay of execution. The Boulevard went back to being a RL ground. But if City had gone there, we would have stayed there.'

*   *   *   *

As early as October 1997 – with the dust still settling on Wilby's sudden departure – Lloyd had a spat with Hateley. The venue was in a car-park after a League game at Cambridge. City had won 1-0, Hull-born Mark Greaves scoring the only goal of the game. It proved to be City's one away win of the entire campaign. Lloyd, though, was in no mood to congratulate his manager. Instead, he was fuming about the cost of the hotel City's players had stayed at prior to the Cambridge game. The disagreement, witnessed by players and fans, soon came to the attention of the media.

And the low point of City's campaign came in November – humbled 2-0 at home by Hednesford Town in the first round of the FA Cup. It was the first time since the Second World War that City had lost to Non-League opposition. City did win two League games in November – against Exeter and rock-bottom Doncaster Rovers. They lost four others, though, including a 4-1 drubbing at home to Shrewsbury. City fans were used to poor results, but in the excitement of Lloyd's takeover they had never expected a battle against relegation and a shock cup exit. Nor could he use 'teething problems' as an excuse.

There was no sign of a recovery during December and January. It was just as well that Doncaster and Brighton were in an even worse predicament than City. In February – when Lloyd delivered his double whammy about abandoning his plans for a super stadium and not making any funds available for new players – morale hit rock bottom. City lost 2-0 at home to Rochdale and 5-1 at Torquay. Defeats followed against Barnet, Scarborough and Shrewsbury.

The season trudged on into March, and off-the-field events captured the headlines again – this time with potentially damaging consequences. The annual meetings of City and Hull FC were held on the same day at the Willerby Grange Park

Hotel. City's meeting passed off without major incident. Lloyd revealed he had spent almost £3.5m on the Tigers – and £1m on FC. Those figures included £50,000 on ground improvements at Boothferry Park and double that amount at the Boulevard. More worryingly, he said he was losing £12,000-a-week and warned that he was not prepared to lose more than £5m in total – half his personal fortune – for the sake of his family. It didn't take a financial genius to work out he was very close to that £5m figure. He'd asked his bank manager to extend his overdraft to £500,000 to pay City's players for the rest of the season. He listed nine players City had signed during his regime, though a shareholder quickly countered that the majority of the signings were either loans or free transfers. Hateley sat alongside Lloyd on the stage and looked surprised when Lloyd revealed he'd promised his manager funds for new players before the start of next season. He insisted that his plans for a new stadium were not dead in the water. Lloyd revealed he was looking at re-developing the Boulevard as a downscale 'super stadium.' Calls from some City shareholders for Boothferry Park to be re-developed instead were quickly dismissed. Lloyd was adamant he needed the money from the sale of the football ground to fund any development programme at the Boulevard. The thorny issue of Kwik Save came up again. Lloyd said he was willing to negotiate but would not – and could not – pay a huge compensation fee.

Lloyd clearly showed signs of losing his patience: 'You seem to think I am some mysterious body that will rape you and take all your money when I am the only person for a long time who has actually put his hands in his pocket.' Lloyd went on to deny ever promising Hateley 'one penny' for new signings. 'I wasn't even a director then,' he said. I assumed the remark was a dig at Wilby's wild promises at that public meeting at the City Hall. Wilby, of course, was no longer around to defend himself. The atmosphere was tense and Lloyd left knowing that shareholders and fans alike weren't happy with his regime. As Lloyd held the bulk of the shares, the views of a very small minority of other shareholders hardly mattered. The fans, though, were a different matter. Public opinion was stacked against him.

Hull FC's meeting was far more hostile. Lloyd came under increasing fire regarding his proposals to under-write a £500,000 share issue. He claimed that was the amount of money he'd loaned Hull FC to strengthen their squad following a successful campaign to secure promotion back to the Super League. Lloyd also said he'd always made one thing clear: that loan would have to be re-paid. Former Hull FC chairman Roy Waudby, a hugely influential figure, led the opposition. Waudby claimed Lloyd was trying to take control of the club 'on the cheap' with ten million shares priced at just 5p. He said that would de-value the shares bought by supporters at £1 each. Lloyd lost his composure. He shouted: 'That's it, I'm off,' and stormed away from the stage. For a few minutes, no one knew what was happening.

I was whisked into a backroom. Lloyd was drinking a cup of tea. He looked relaxed. Then, the fireworks started. He asked if my tape recorder was switched on and then ranted: 'I've had enough. The people of Hull are crap. They are living in the dark ages and they always will.' I asked whether he was sure he wanted me to print that. I knew the damage it would cause. He told me to go ahead and do my job.

From that moment on, the scepticism among supporters

turned into hate. It wasn't just fans of Hull City and Hull FC either. It was everyone: from the City Council to the people who swept the terraces at Boothferry Park – and the Boulevard – on match days. However fierce the provocation, Lloyd had gone too far. He probably wished he'd never set eyes on Hull. And the feeling was mutual.

Over the next few weeks, Lloyd became increasingly unpredictable, and hostile. His words might have sold newspapers, but they also opened up an ever deeper split between him and local people. Lloyd, however, could not afford to walk away. Almost £5m of his own money was tied up in both clubs. In April, he hatched a plan to bring homeless Premier League club Wimbledon to play in Hull. Wimbledon had failed to reach an agreement with their local council for a new stadium and attracted fierce opposition from the football authorities after announcing plans to move to Dublin. Lloyd's plan would have effectively meant Wimbledon replacing City, though it was unclear which Division the 'new club' would perform in. The Premier League was opposed to the idea and The Football League was hardly in favour either. Lloyd confirmed he had spoken to Wimbledon owner Sam Hamman and added: 'In my opinion if we had a team in Hull that was winning, the support would be fanatical. A stadium of 30,000 would fill every match.' The scheme never went any further. For many, the end of Lloyd could not come quickly enough. Thanks to their home form – ten wins, seven draws and just six defeats – City finished in 22nd place with 41 points. Doncaster (20 points) and Brighton (35 points) were so poor that City could not go down, and so the pressure was largely lifted from the shoulders of Hateley and his players. They lost only one of their last five games.

Eleven years on, and I still find it difficult to believe Lloyd agreed to buy Boothferry Park, knowing Kwik Save had that 107-year lease. Early on in his reign, Lloyd was compared to Sir John Hall, whose millions had rescued and rebuilt Newcastle. Unlike Hall, though, Lloyd had no previous links, either emotionally or physically, with Hull or Hull City. There's no doubt he spent at least £4m. There is no doubt either that he didn't always get a fair hearing from leading figures in Hull. In the end, though, Lloyd effectively slit his own throat.

The fans thought things couldn't get any worse. How wrong they were.

Chapter Two:

A race against the clock

June, 1998 - October, 1998

After the drama of the closing weeks of the previous season, the summer of 1998 was relatively quiet. Having threatened to walk out on both Hull City and Hull FC at those stormy annual meetings, David Lloyd stayed put. 'I could have gone,' he said, 'but that would mean the end for both clubs and that is the last thing I wanted.' While cynics said he was only protecting his investment, Lloyd argued that he still had unfinished business in Hull. It soon became apparent that he hadn't given up on the idea of a super stadium. Relationships with the City Council, which at best were rocky, had virtually broken down. So all hope of building the stadium on a council owned site at Kingswood was off the agenda.

Instead, Lloyd revealed he was going to submit planning applications for Boothferry Park and the Boulevard. He wanted to sell Boothferry Park for re-development and build a new 30,000 seater stadium at the Boulevard with the proceeds. The council was wary. So were fans of City and Hull FC. No one had taken kindly to being labelled as 'crap' or as 'living in the dark ages.' The Boulevard, surrounded by low-cost housing, seemed an unlikely setting for a state-of-the-art stadium. American style shopping malls and fountains would have looked out of place. Lloyd, though, had scaled down his initial ambitious project, perhaps realising that financial backing from the council wouldn't be forthcoming. However, he was unrepentant: 'All the money from the sale of Boothferry Park will go back into both clubs to provide facilities and players. I want to make it clear that I am not in this to cream off millions of pounds. I've spent millions already. I've put my hand in my pocket when other people wouldn't. Without me, there wouldn't be a Hull City, but I need to re-develop Boothferry Park. I don't have a bottom-less pit. Anyway, I can't sell one ground and just walk away with the money. That was a condition of the original contract I signed last summer.'

Lloyd's revelation about that original contract effectively tied him to Hull. He could have sold Boothferry Park and moved City to the Boulevard, subject to Football League approval. But it wasn't clear who would want to buy Boothferry Park anyway, especially with Kwik Save trading, and the City Council was unlikely to give permission for any large scale re-development. Lloyd was still losing money. Hull FC were competing in the Super League that summer and were now known as Hull Sharks. According to Lloyd, they were just about breaking even. As for City, the summer months meant bills had to be paid, but Lloyd had no gate receipts to help towards the costs. As his losses mounted, Lloyd wanted positive action – and quickly. He was aware of the growing opposition to his plans and, indeed, his presence in the city. He warned that if the new stadium proposals were not given the go-ahead, he would walk away from Hull, putting the future of both clubs in serious doubt. He explained: 'If it (the stadium) is going to happen, then it has to be in a year's time. I can't hang around any longer. The rugby league club will make money – not much – but enough to cover itself. However, the football club is losing £750,000-a-year. It will cost me £1.5m in two years. I can't afford to lose any more. By the end of next year, I will have spent over £5.5m. That's big money in anyone's book. If I can't turn it around by the end of next year, something has to give.'

Just a few months earlier, Lloyd had said that for the sake of his family, he couldn't afford to spend more than £5m. He'd now gone £500,000 over that figure. The losses were set to continue – at least for the foreseeable future. It was thought that redeveloping the Boulevard would cost at least £20m. The sale of Boothferry Park – even with enhanced planning permission – might bring in £10m. Then, there was the compensation for Kwik Save of perhaps £3m. The sums did not add up. Lloyd's threat to walk away from both City and Hull FC hardly endeared himself to fans of either club, or to the council. The council favoured a new stadium. Proposals had been on the drawing board for at least five years. However, as Lloyd ploughed on, the council seemed to distance itself from his proposals. Of course, Lloyd could have cut his losses and shut down both clubs.

However, there were whispers from within City Hall that the council would not be held to ransom. Ray Tupling, a stalwart City fan, summed up the mood at the time. 'Quite honestly, I'm disgusted at the thought of selling our main asset and ending up at the Boulevard. I think this talk of a super stadium could all be pie in the sky. Boothferry Park is our number one crown jewel.

If we let that go with nowhere else to go we could be left high and dry. It would be diabolical if we were left at the Boulevard.' The Boulevard still did not meet Football League requirements. If Boothferry Park was sold for re-development, and the Boulevard essentially knocked down to make way for a 30,000-capacity stadium, where would the two clubs play?

Lloyd had arrived in Hull 12 months earlier with the best intentions. Now everyone started to question his motives. No one seemed to trust him and his decision to criticise Hull constantly came back to haunt him. As the summer went on, Lloyd revealed he was still negotiating with Kwik Save. He was 'hopeful' of reaching an agreement. In addition to solving the Kwik Save problem, he would need planning permission for any re-development at Boothferry Park and the stadium proposals. The odds were stacked against him. There were rumours of a McDonald's drive-though being built on the front car park at Boothferry Park. Others suggested the site could become a huge B&Q store. B&Q, though, had just ploughed millions into a new store a mile or so away from Boothferry Park at St Andrews Quay. And what of the residents living close to Boothferry Park? They were unlikely to want a major retail park on their doorstep. Residential development was another possibility, but it was hardly an area to start building executive-style four or five bedroom detached homes. It was evident only low-cost housing was likely. I couldn't accuse Lloyd of lacking optimism or belief in his proposals. He was, though, spending increasingly less time in Hull and was reliant on people such as Bryan Calam and Michael Appleton. The whole planning process threatened to drag on for months; possibly years. As far as City fans were concerned, there were more pressing matters: the start of a new season.

To say Hateley had suffered a difficult start to his managerial career is putting it mildly. Hateley pointed out it was difficult to manage against the backdrop of off-the-field problems. Certainly, the early promise of significant investment in his squad had never materialised. Excuses, though, would not wash with City fans. They'd shown commendable loyalty throughout a difficult campaign, but their side didn't score enough goals at one end of the pitch and conceded too many at the other. Hateley had only made nine appearances and appeared to have become a frustrated and disillusioned figure. Many people wondered how he'd survived. 'You could say I was given a false impression when I accepted the job,' he said. 'I was told there would be £3m available for new players and there was also talk of a new stadium – but then the rules kept changing as the season moved on. It would have been easy to walk away, but that has never been my style. The majority of the fans seemed to appreciate the restrictions I was working under, but they were still pleased with the way the team tried to play football. I might have been asking for too much from some players at times, but now I believe that we have improved the quality of the squad.'

Under pressure from Lloyd, City trimmed their playing squad from 46 to 22 professionals. There were five new signings: Dave D'Auria (Scunthorpe), Jon French (Peterborough), Steve Hawes (Sheffield United), Neil Whitworth (Kilmarnock) and David Brown (Manchester United). The majority of those deals were completed for very little outlay and there was no sign of the big name to lift the morale – and confidence – of supporters. The list of players heading out of the club was headed by Duane Darby, a popular striker whose 13 goals had provided one of the few highlights of the previous season. Scott Thompson, who will hardly be remembered among the best goalkeepers in City's history, returned to Scotland, along with Steven Boyak. Hateley's assistant Billy Kirkwood summed up the situation: 'It is difficult for any manager when there is no money to spend. Hull City was like a runaway ship when we arrived. We had to put the brakes on and try to turn it around. That will take time, but the amount of time available is not in our hands. Last season was a disaster but we are working to a three-year plan and I believe we are heading in the right direction.'

At least, Hateley assured me he was fully fit for the new campaign. However, there were signs all was not well, as D'Auria revealed. The Welsh-born midfielder had spent the previous season captaining Scunthorpe. He was lured to Boothferry Park by the attraction of a bigger club. But the move very nearly didn't happen. 'I was sharing a house with Gregor Rioch, who played for Hull City. He was – and still is – a great mate. Typical of him, he was full of what was going to happen at Hull with Mark Hateley in charge and David Lloyd as chairman. I listened to everything and thought I wouldn't mind a piece of that. Don't get me wrong, I was happy at Scunthorpe but Hull looked to be a better bet. Financially, it was a good move, but that wasn't the only reason. I genuinely thought I was joining a club on the up.' D'Auria believed the deal had been sorted out and even rejected a chance to stay at Scunthorpe. But, as the start of pre-season training approached, he still had not signed. D'Auria added: 'One morning, Gregor packed his kit and headed off earlier than usual. I asked him where he was going and he said it was the start of pre-season training. I genuinely hadn't heard anything. I got him to phone Mark

Hateley and ask what the hell was happening. When Gregor asked him about me, he basically said: 'Dave who?' Then he must have remembered because he told Gregor to bring me to training and things would be sorted out. It was crazy, really. Totally unprofessional.' D'Auria duly signed a contract, but it didn't take him long to work out something was wrong with the set-up at Hull – and not just with the manager's memory. He said: 'I couldn't believe how badly City was being run from the very top right down to the bottom. I'd come from a smaller club where everything was very organised and very professional. At Hull, it was a total shambles. No one knew what was going on . . . least of all the players. The training was terrible. No one had any idea. Mark was okay as a person, but he spent more time on his mobile than he did doing anything else. I should have sensed then that something was seriously wrong before I signed. I put my trust in a club – and I was let down.'

D'Auria did score on his debut, but City lost their opening game of the season 3-1 at Rotherham. The following week, Lloyd attended the first home game against Darlington. City lost 2-1 and their owner was not impressed. He was critical of the team and the fans. City had to wait until the third game for their first point: a 2-2 draw at Chester. Hateley was on target in that game and again the following week. He scored the only goal in a 1-0 victory against Peterborough at Boothferry Park. The side had also progressed through the first round of the Worthington Cup after seeing off the challenge of Stockport on goal difference. Did improved times lie ahead? Fans desperately wanted to believe City could challenge for promotion. But off-the-field problems were never far away.

Lloyd confirmed he could no longer afford to maintain two

grounds. Talks with Kwik Save had reached stalemate. City were losing £15,000-a-week and Lloyd insisted they could have to move to the Boulevard. In a letter sent to all staff at the start of September, Appleton wrote:

'There has been considerable speculation and comment in the press recently regarding a possible sale of Boothferry Park and relocation to the Boulevard or an alternative playing venue. I therefore felt this was an appropriate time to write to you and explain what our current plans are and how this might affect your future employment with the club which I know many of you are concerned about. Hull City is losing money on a day-to-day basis. We have tried to reduce the amount of loss over the past year but are still faced with monthly payments which exceed our income. It is a pity that this situation is on-going especially when we have huge backing from our supporters with regard to season ticket sales. It is a situation however which is not exclusive to Hull City – many other Third and Second Division clubs are losing money. However, it is fair to say that some clubs are actually making money by prudent management and keeping costs firmly under control.

In the light of the on-going losses we have had no choice but to put a salary freeze on the company this year and we have also tried to look at ways where additional savings can be made. A solution that has been reported in the newspapers, but one which is not that easy to implement, is to try and sell the ground at Boothferry Park and negotiate a ground rental/share agreement with Hull Sharks. We would then be able to utilise the Sharks' existing office and administration facilities, the pitch, seating and restaurant facilities and would supplement the set-up with our own staff and administration support, where appropriate. It would also enable us to look into the possibility of a full scale merge of the two companies at some future date, something that was muted over a year ago. The dream is still a possibility.

Due to the fact that Hull City and Hull Sharks are two quite distinct companies however it is essential that all negotiations between Hull City and Hull Sharks are carried out on an 'arms length' basis and that a fair deal for both parties is negotiated. In the light of this I have asked Bryan Calam to deal with matters relating to Hull Sharks and I will deal with matters relating to Hull City. I would hope that some form of deal can be done but this is by no means certain and it is possible that Hull City may have to look at other possible solutions instead. If a deal is done, it is not likely to start until the end of this current football season: ie summer '99. I will keep you informed of any developments as they arise but felt it was appropriate to let you know the current situation as early as possible so you are kept in full in the picture.'

If the letter was meant to ease any fears, it failed. Rob Smith said: 'We were all worried about our jobs and every time Lloyd seemed to speak in the press he was threatening to shut City down. Now we had a letter saying we could be moving to the Boulevard but there was no guarantee about our jobs. And, there was also the question of if the Boulevard didn't come off, what did the 'other possible solutions' mean? Closing the club down? Moving to another town or city.'

Calam confirmed that City had contacted the police, the council and the Football League about the possibly of moving to the Boulevard. He said: 'We have to make a move sooner or later

IN ITS PRIME: Hull City's Boothferry Park ground pictured in the mid-1980s when it was still a match for most stadiums in the country and the subject of various expansion plans - none of which came to fruition.

FULL STEAM AHEAD: When it first opened in the 1940s, Boothferry Park had been one of the first stadiums in England to have its own railway 'halt.' It soon fell into disrepair and was shut down, long before the club's financial problems started to 'bite' in the 1990s.

LOOKING WORRIED: Former chairman Martin Fish (centre right) looks on from the directors' box at Boothferry Park in one of his final games at the helm. Fish, a local accountant, had become embroiled in an increasingly bitter campaign, instigated by the club's disgruntled fans.

THE SAVIOUR: David Lloyd (right) and chairman Tim Wilby applaud the club's fans before the kick-off of the home game against Notts County at the start of the 1997-98 campaign. It was Lloyd's first visit to the club on a match-day.

SUITED
AND BOOTED:
Tim Wilby in a typical
pose for the cameras,
shortly before his sudden
exit from the club, amid a
series of allegations
about his personal and
private life.

REMEMBER,
REMEMBER?:
Ian McMahon who
was appointed City's
chief executive after
the David Lloyd-led
takeover. His stay at
the club was shorter
than Wilby's.

A WAITING GAME:
John Cooper who schemed behind the scenes to delay Lloyd's plans to move City from Boothferry Park to the Boulevard, the home of Hull Rugby League Football Club. Cooper still works for City and is the stadium manager at the KC Stadium.

POINTING THE WAY:
Michael Appleton (right) who was brought in by Lloyd as his financial expert to control the affairs of Hull City and Hull RLFC. Appleton was not a man to cross.

A WARM WELCOME: Player-manager Mark Hateley (right) welcomes ex-England international David Rocastle to Boothferry Park. Rocastle, who was signed on loan, was one of the few high-profile players to arrive during the Lloyd era.

GOAL: David Rocastle (left) celebrates a rare goal in a league game against Scarborough at Boothferry Park. Note the empty East Stand in the background. It had been closed because of safety problems.

THE FINAL TIME: A track-suited Mark Hateley looks on as he takes charge of one of his final games at Boothferry Park before being replaced by Warren Joyce.

IN CHARGE: Tom Belton, the Lincolnshire-based farmer, who took over as chairman under the regime led by Nick Buchanan and Stephen Hinchliffe.

ALL SMILES:
Nick Buchanan, the South Yorkshire-based businessman, who, along with Stephen Hinchliffe, became City's leading shareholder after Lloyd moved on.

HAPPY DAYS:
Nick Buchanan (centre) and Tom Belton are at least on speaking terms in the directors box at Boothferry Park - before a damaging and very public split that led to Belton's sacking and the threat of legal action.

A FAMOUS FACE: East Hull MP and Deputy Prime Minister John Prescott (left), together with Nick Buchanan, holds up a new Tiger-style wall decoration for the Boothferry Park boardroom. In the background are directors Richard Ibbotson (right) and Philip Webster.

ON THE BALL: Warren Joyce in action for Hull City before his appointment as the club's player/manager.

THE DREAM TEAM: Warren Joyce (right) and assistant John McGovern, the former Nottingham Forest and Derby County captain, look on from the sidelines in a home game at Boothferry Park. Against all the odds, they steered City clear of almost certain relegation from the Football League. A few months later, they were sacked.

HELLO, HELLO, HELLO: Three of Joyce's first signings for the club (from left to right) Steve Swales, Andy Oakes and Justin Whittle who all played key roles in the 'Great Escape.'

CAPTAIN MARVEL: Justin Whittle who proved to be in inspirational captain and defender in some of the City's most worrying times. Today, he's a part-time postman.

ACTION MAN: David D'Auria, City's captain in the 'Great Escape.' He was eventually sold, against his wishes, because of the club's mounting financial problems.

DON'T MESS WITH ME: Former nightclub bouncer Gary Brabin shows off his six pack as he celebrates a win at Boothferry Park alongside team-mate Brian McGinty.

I'M HERE: Colin Alcide, the striker who was one of the heroes of the 'Great Escape' even though he 'lost' his way in the gloomy corridors beneath the West Stand on the day he signed for the Tigers.

IT'S PARTY TIME: Delighted fans invade the Boothferry Park pitch after the home game against Scarborough that ended any fears of relegation from the Football League. Note the fact that the East Stand has been re-opened.

TAKE THAT: Liverpool's players appeal in vain for offside as City players - led by Mike Edwards (centre) - celebrate a goal in the first leg of the Worthington Cup tie at Boothferry Park. City lost 9-3 on aggregate but the revenue from the two games kept the bank manager happy.

WE'RE HAPPY: These lucky Hull City fans are all smiles after securing tickets for the Worthington Cup tie against Liverpool at Boothferry Park. Some fan queued overnight . . . only to discover the tie wasn't a sell-out.

THEY'RE HERE: Jamaican internationals Theodore Whitmore (left) and Ian Goodison (second from right) with two 'mystery' friends after signing for the Tigers.

A LOT OF BOTTLE: Jamie Wood who was picked to play for the Cayman Islands . . . even though he'd no idea where they were!

END OF THE ROAD: Warren Joyce (left) and John McGovern (centre) discuss tactics with Jon Schofield just days before they were sacked after failing to secure promotion.

and we want to be positive about it. We are looking towards the amalgamation which is what David Lloyd has said from day one. Boothferry Park is running at a loss and we cannot sustain that debut for ever and a day. In simple business terms, we cannot run two stadiums. Boothferry Park is worth a lot more money than the Boulevard, even with the supermarket not playing ball. A lot of work needs doing at the Boulevard such as fencing, crowd segregation and crowd monitoring. The Football League has told us what is required and seem in favour of us going there. It will be a sad day to leave Boothferry Park – and it will be another sad day to leave the Boulevard in the future – but it will be exciting to see the team run out at a new stadium.' Calam was identified in some reports as City's chief operating officer. Appleton, though, had indicated he was in charge of City, and Calam of Hull Sharks. It was another sign of the increasing confusion and chaos.

Lloyd tried to appease fans and revealed: 'Our plan was to win promotion in three seasons. We consolidated last season and now it is knocking on the door time.' It only added to the pressure on Hateley, still struggling to put together a squad capable of finishing in the top half of the table, never mind the promotion positions. Hateley desperately needed experienced players and was busy trying to persuade Lloyd (or Appleton, or both) to release funds to sign former Scottish internationals Andy Goram and Steve Nicol. Goalkeeper Goram had been handed a free transfer by Rangers; former Liverpool legend Nicol had been released by Sheffield Wednesday. Nicol spent a few days training with City. That was as close as he came to Boothferry Park. Neither deal came off. By now concerned fans had prepared their own battle-plans.

The Tigers' Co-operative became an increasingly effective protest group. Headed by the formidable Angie Rowe, it vehemently opposed moving to the Boulevard. Members also increased the pressure on Lloyd. Results scarcely indicated City were ready to 'knock of the door', as Lloyd had put it. City were floundering in the League and a 4-1 hammering at Barnet signalled a new low in the club's fortunes. Three days after the Barnet game, Lloyd received a crystal-clear confirmation – if any were needed – that the fans had lost faith in him. City headed to Bolton for the first leg of Worthington Cup tie on September 15. Bolton were then riding high in the First Division. City were next to bottom in Division Three. It was a David v Goliath clash and, as such, attracted interest from the media. However, it was City's fans who took centre stage. The kick-off was delayed after fans hurled hundreds of tennis balls on to the pitch – suggesting former Davis Cup star Lloyd should stick to what he knew best. Ground-staff quickly cleared the pitch only for more tennis balls to appear. The fact City lost the game 3-1 was almost incidental. The fans message was obvious. They'd had enough of Lloyd. And Lloyd felt the same about them. Within hours of that Bolton clash, he'd put the club up for sale. Potential buyers quickly appeared on the scene. One was a consortium of mystery businessmen – headed by former Scunthorpe chairman Tom Belton, who confirmed the consortium's interest but admitted a proposed deal had fallen through at the 11th hour. Calam responded: 'They (the consortium) are messing us around. They try to get into a deal which we accept and then they try to whittle it down. The club has been for sale for a long time, but no one will put their money in. It's alright the fans shouting 'Lloyd out' all the time but if he pulled out now, the club would fold.'

Belton said he was confident his consortium could do business. He also said he feared Lloyd would accept an offer from a developer to turn Boothferry Park into a retail outlet, even though the City Council had indicated they were opposed to any such idea. Such a scheme would, of course, have meant the end for the club. The Tigers Co-operative called a series of meetings, and Rowe said: 'I am gutted by what has happened. I feel the last two years have been a waste of time. Mr Lloyd has the power to just shut the club down and the fans have been frightened by what might happen.' Lloyd went on the offensive. With no sign of a deal to buy City being struck, he warned on October 7 that unless a buyer came forward, he would shut the club down. He said: 'I am the only person in the history of Hull who has put his hand in his pocket and paid the bills. I have had my fill of certain people in Hull and I am going. Make no mistake, this is not a threat. It will be the end of professional football in the city and it will never come back. When I asked the fans about moving to the Boulevard temporarily, they didn't want it. That is why Hull is living in the dark old ages. I have been pushed too far and now I'm going. I will not put the club into receivership or administration. I don't have to because it is my money – my debt. Unless someone comes forward with £2m to buy the club by the end of the week I will be walking away.'

The Tigers 2000 group were stung into action. They wanted to buy a stake in the club but lacked the funds to make an offer. Rowe urged Lloyd to put City into receivership, and said: 'He is being a bully and totally unfair. How can he expect anyone to raise such money in so little time?' The Football League was monitoring the situation, and yet said they were powerless to prevent Lloyd from liquidating the club. Lloyd continued his rants, claiming Belton's consortium did not have the money to buy City. Even Hateley was caught in the black-lash. Lloyd said the former England international was one of the best paid managers outside the Premiership. Lloyd gave figures too: 'Mark is on a quarter of a million quid, which is an absolute fortune, and he lives in a house which is worth £250,000. I know that because I bought the house.' Hateley batted his words back at him: 'I think the chairman has been misinformed. I took a huge wage cut to come here, and I am earning only slightly more than the previous manager did. I am a professional and I try and keep a professional outlook, but all this speculation is bound to affect the players.'

While the spat was going on, City had lost their last four games and slipped to the bottom of the Football League. There was a fear that the next match – at home to Cardiff in October 9 – would be their last. Apparently Lloyd spent the week leading up to the Cardiff game playing golf in Spain. He did nonetheless give an interview in which he appeared to back-down from his threat to shut City down. 'After the abuse I've taken in the last 18 months,' he said 'all I am saying is that I'm not putting any more money in. But when the bank says: 'Pay the interest on the overdraft', as it will do in the next few days, somebody had better come in with some money. Anyone who comes in with £2m can have the whole lot.'

Apart from the Belton-led consortium, there was reported interest from at least three other groups. Kevin Phelan – an Irish based businessman – acted as a go-between Lloyd and one interested party. There was also interest locally but, as Lloyd put it, no potential buyer was willing to show the colour of their money. Former chairman Don Robinson also wanted to buy City. Robinson, a successful Scarborough-based businessman, had emerged as City's saviour in the early 1980s when the club, then losing £9,000 a week, went into administration. Under his leadership, Robinson guided City to within striking distance of the top flight before resigning and passing control back to the Needler family. This time around, Robinson's only stipulation was that he was refusing to pay Hateley's wages. Robinson said: 'Having spoken to Mr Lloyd, I feel a deal is 80 per cent agreed. There is no way everything can be finalised by the deadline he set but I am sure he understands that and will reconsider his position. When I first came to Hull, the club was facing bankruptcy but we moved forward and we were never in the red again. These days, the club is losing £7,000 a week and the manager is on £5,000 a week. I am sure Mark Hateley is a nice person but anyone can see this is not the way to run a successful business and, if I am successful, I will run the club on a tougher and tighter budget and make sure it makes a profit.'

As the Cardiff game approached, the Hull Daily Mail launched a campaign to encourage supporters to turn out in force. The match was staged on a Friday night. It was wet, miserable and bitterly cold. More than 8,500 fans – more than double the attendance for the last home game – answered the call. For 20 minutes before the start, they chanted: 'Say No To The Boulevard.' City lost 2-1 and stayed rooted to the foot of the table. And still the speculation about a new owner dragged on. City's next game was at Scarborough. Robinson stressed he was still hoping to complete a deal and went as far as to rule out a move for Scarborough manager Mick Wadsworth as a replacement for the increasing under-fire – and under pressure –

Hateley. However, on the very day of the Scarborough game – October 17 – Lloyd disclosed that he'd agreed to sell his interests in both City and Hull FC to Phelan, an agent for Gameplan International, who had been negotiating on behalf of two anonymous investors based in the Midlands. It seemed City had been saved. Or had they? Three days later, the takeover had still not been completed and few details of it were emerging. Phelan was determined to protect the identity of the proposed new owners. He also indicated their plans were ominously similar to Lloyd's. They intended to sell Boothferry Park and the Boulevard before moving both clubs into a purpose-built new stadium. A possible site was identified: the Costello athletic stadium. Their plans included provision for a new retail development, which might have tempted Kwik Save to leave Boothferry Park. If the reports about the takeover were correct, Lloyd was ready to write off his losses of more than £4m and sell for less than £1m. As a prelude to the deal, Appleton quit as chief executive. Hateley offered to work unpaid for a year to help the takeover go through. 'I have this year, plus next year, to go on my contract and I have been offered an extension on that for another year, which would give me two and a half seasons, and I will do that last year for free,' he said. 'I feel confident the new owners will come in. There is unbelievable potential in Hull with nearly a million people living in the city.' Lloyd was keeping a low profile. Reports suggested he had flown to Dublin to seal the Phelan-brokered takeover. As ever, though, there was a final twist to the saga.

The deal with Phelan collapsed; apparently on the issue of staff salaries. The speculation started again. This time Paul Caddick, owner of Leeds Rhinos RLFC and the Headingley sports complex, emerged as a possible buyer. He'd teamed up with Robinson in what was perceived to be a last-gasp bid to save City and Hull FC. Their bid would be fronted by former Hull FC chief executive Stephen Ball. As Caddick could not effectively own and run two RL clubs, his role would be restricted to building a new super-stadium, leaving Robinson free to concentrate on running City. Caddick also expressed an interest in buying Hull KR, who were in administration. I was invited to meet Caddick at the headquarters of one of his businesses based near Selby. He was a confident and imposing figure. He seemed genuine and rolled out his plans for a new stadium. They looked impressive. Unlike Lloyd, his PR was second to none. No one could argue with Caddick's record at Leeds or his success as a businessman. His right-hand man, Ball, still lived in Hull and had all the right credentials and contacts. It looked like the perfect arrangement for all concerned. It was, though, nearly the end of October, and Lloyd was losing patience. Money for wages was also running out. 'There is no more money to put in and maybe the footballers need to play for nothing until this is all sorted out,' he said. 'I am talking to every single person in the world who wants to take over this football club but no one has put a penny on the table.' Forty eight hours later, Lloyd claimed he was confident a takeover would be agreed. Amid yet more convulsions, Gameplan were back in as the likely buyers rather than the Caddick/Robinson-led consortium.

City had been saved. Again.

Chapter Three:

The Great Escape

November, 1998 - May, 1999

November 3, 1998 and Hull City finally had new owners. David Lloyd called a halt to the saga. He announced he had agreed to sell the club, though not to Gameplan. Forget Irish millionaires. Forget Don Robinson. Forget Paul Caddick. Forget the various groups of assorted local businessmen and ex-players. City were now under the control of a Lincolnshire-based pig farmer, Tom Belton, and his 'mystery' backers. As the Lloyd regime cleared their desks, Belton was immediately installed as chairman. Slowly details emerged of the other figures behind the successful bid. They were headed by Sheffield-based businessmen Stephen Hinchliffe and Nick Buchanan. Between them, Hinchliffe and Buchanan controlled over 60 per cent of City's shares. Hinchliffe owned 37 per cent and Buchanan 28 per cent.

Initially, they were joined on the board by Richard Ibbotson, a Sheffield-based solicitor, Doncaster-based David Bennett and Philip Webster, an accountant from the village of Cherry Burton near Hull. The new owners were, we were told, 'football people' – unlike Lloyd. Belton was a former chairman of Scunthorpe United; Hinchliffe and Buchanan had links with Sheffield United, as did Andy Daykin, who had been appointed as City's new commercial manager. After the increasingly confused situation of the Lloyd regime, the new owners said – and did – the right things. They stressed they had no links with Lloyd, an all-important quality as far as long-suffering City fans were concerned. Yes, there was money for new players. No, City would not move from Boothferry Park. Fans had fresh optimism. The fact the consortium had bought the club for around £200,000 was almost pushed into the background. It also emerged Lloyd had retained ownership of Boothferry Park. Lloyd said he had paid off almost £1m of City's debts to enable the takeover to go ahead – a clear indication of his determination to get out of Hull. In a letter sent to City staff on November 3, Lloyd said: 'As from today's date, Hull City AFC has been taken over by Mr Nick Buchanan and his consortium. I would like to thank all the staff for their support and hard work during the past 18 months. Bryan Calam will act on my behalf to ensure a smooth transition at the changeover and any problems should be directed to him. Once again, thank you for your support and I wish you all the best for the future.'

I was summoned to meet the new regime at Boothferry Park. At the time, the reception desk was being staffed by Martyn Hainstock, a part-time actor who had appeared in Coronation Street and Heartbeat amongst others. He also doubled up as the club's PA announcer. I'd got to know Hainstock pretty well and I remember walking into the front office. He was surprisingly quiet. I tried to break the ice with a joke. Then I asked: 'What are new owners like?' He kept his head down and said nothing. It was most unlike him. I later found out that one of the dividing walls between the reception area and Belton's office contained a two-way mirror and, allegedly, hidden microphones. Hence Hainstock's silence. I was quickly ushered into the inner sanctum – or Belton's new office. The new owners were all waiting. At first, I felt like I was back at school. Actually, it was more like meeting the Mafia. The lighting was very low. It was all black suits, cigar smoke and bottles of red-wine . . . at ten o'clock in the morning. I glanced into a corner, half expecting to see a few violin cases. I'm often asked what Belton was like. My answer is simple. He looked anything but a football club chairman. He spoke with a slightly posh northern accent, so quiet that at times I struggled to hear what he said. He looked like a person who would be more at home in a Working Men's Club than a football club boardroom. He liked the odd glass of wine, but he always preferred beer in a half pint glass. He always seemed to have a cigarette in his hand. The guy could have chain-smoked for Britain. Although Belton was the chairman – the public face of the consortium – it soon was clear that the real power behind the throne belonged to Hinchliffe and Buchanan. Apparently, the new directors had got to know each other during pheasant shooting parties on Belton's land. To be honest, no one scrutinised the new owners too closely. Why? Well, quite simply, they had to be better than the previous regime. City fan Mike Duggan admitted: 'There were a few rumours about Hinchliffe in particular but anything was better than Lloyd and Co.'

Hinchliffe was soon in the spotlight. Just two days after the consortium completed their takeover, he was disqualified from acting as a company director for seven years after accepting the

Department of Trade and Industry's case that one of his companies – En Tout Cas – had paid more than £1m to other companies he controlled and then gone bust, owing creditors £3m. It also emerged that the Serious Fraud Office (SFO) was conducting an investigation into another of his companies, Facia. It wasn't long before the SFO charged him with corruption and conspiracy to defraud. It wasn't long either before City were drawn into the investigations and Hinchliffe was, eventually, jailed. In the very early days of their time at City, Buchanan and Hinchliffe adopted a low profile. Belton was the friendly, approachable face. He did most of the talking – at least in public. In one of his first interviews, he told me: 'I was involved at Scunthorpe for more than 20 years. I've a lot of experience at the lower levels of football and I know what is needed. I'll be involved financially. I'll be running the show on a day-to-day basis from the front. My experience makes me the obvious choice.' He basically told me that if I was straight with him, he'd be straight with me. That was Tom Belton. In that initial interview, Buchanan and Hinchliffe sat in the background, nodding their heads in agreement. They were both big men used to getting their own way. They rarely interrupted. Belton stressed the new owners were not interested in Hull Sharks, another vote winner as far as City fans were concerned.

In many ways, Lloyd's decision to run both clubs had proved to be his downfall. Whatever he spent on City, Sharks fans thought he should spend on them – and more. It was that age old argument: Is football or rugby the major sport in Hull? Belton's consortium knew all about the problems Lloyd had run into in trying to sell Boothferry Park. He was non-committal about the club's long-term future there and hinted the consortium would not be opposed to moving to a new stadium. That led to more approving nods from Messers Hinchliffe and Buchanan. If Lloyd did sell Boothferry Park, I'd heard that the new owners had secured a deal with Lloyd to compensate them financially. Belton – as he always did when asked an awkward question – shrugged his shoulders and smiled. At the time, the majority of city's fans were more interested in football than off-the-field problems. Again, there was positive news. Belton added: 'We will be trying to strengthen the squad. There is money available. We want Hull City fans to back us. It is about time this club started to realise some of its potential. It should be in the First Division at the very least.' More nods from the major shareholders. Meeting the new regime was – I've got to admit – a fairly positive experience. The atmosphere was a little intimidating, but Belton came over as a friendly, helpful person. He was, after all, the main point of contact. Belton quickly met the Tigers' Co-operative and no doubt won them over with his almost man-next-door charm. Nothing seemed to upset him. Lloyd could often be a loose cannon – a joy to quote but a nightmare to deal with. Belton was the exact opposite. I seemed to have pages of notes after talking to him. It's only when I analysed those notes that I realised he'd actually said very little worth printing. I remember thinking he was the type of man you'd love to meet . . . if you were about to ask permission to marry his daughter.

One of the consortium's first decisions regarded the future of Hateley. At first, Belton appeared to give him a vote of confidence and added: 'In fairness, his position is secure at the moment and I think everyone realises he hasn't had money to spend on new players. I haven't really had the chance to sit down and talk to him yet, but I will be doing so and we will be discussing just what we can do to get the club moving up the Third Division table. City's first game under new ownership was at home to Leyton Orient on November 7. They lost 1-0. By the date of the next game – at home to Brighton on November 10 – Hateley had been sacked. Or, as Belton put it, 'relieved of his duties.' The chairman said simply: 'Mark Hateley will not be attending the club until further notice, pending further discussions.' Hateley, the last management link with the Lloyd regime, had gone. At least Hateley's frustrations were at an end. Not surprisingly, he's never managed another League club. David D'Auria wasn't surprised by the change in management. He recalled: 'The table didn't lie. We were shocking. There were no tactics, no ideas and no leadership on and off the field. We all thought we were heading in one direction – and it wasn't the next Division up the Football League ladder either.' Speculation immediately turned to a replacement.

Russell Slade, then youth team manager at Scarborough, was linked with the post, along with the usual list of suspects including Mick Wadsworth and Neil Warnock. In fact, just about anyone with a Sheffield connection was mentioned. The final choice, though, stunned everyone: Warren Joyce. Joyce had spent the previous two seasons playing for City. He was one of the more consistent performers in an under-achieving side, but he was not exactly popular with the club's fans. There was a reason for that: 18 months earlier, he had publicly backed manager Terry Dolan before the Lloyd takeover. At the time, Joyce was club captain, so in fairness he could scarcely have done any differently. The fans, though, were not impressed. They despised Dolan – and anyone who supported him. The relationship between Joyce and the fans deteriorated even further when he scored two goals and celebrated in front of a deserted (it was closed down for safety reasons) East Stand. But he had been working as Hateley's assistant after the departure of Billy Kirkwood. When Belton was asked about Joyce's appointment, he replied: 'There's just something about him that I like.' Joyce was a vastly experienced player who had done some coaching in the junior set-up at Manchester United. He was, though, a managerial rookie . . . just like Hateley. His first match in charge was that Brighton game. City had made two recent loan signings, a 19-year-old striker Craig Dudley from Notts County and goalkeeper Paul Gibson from Manchester United. Ominously, the rest of his squad were the players who had been unable to prevent the club from sliding to the foot of the table. Ironically, Brighton's boss was Brian Horton – one of City's most successful and popular managers. Joyce had little time to influence affairs before it. Hateley had apparently cleared his desk on the very day of the game. He said his farewells to the players just before the kick-off. City produced a battling display, but still lost, 2-0. New manager and new owners, but City were firmly entrenched at the bottom of the table. And time was not on City's side.

While that game was Joyce's first as manager, it was my first match as full-time City reporter for the Hull Daily Mail. I'd stood in for absent colleagues on previous occasions and – as chief sports writer – had covered most of the major stories through the latter stages of the Lloyd era. As such, I did know Joyce. In fact, it was me who'd asked him the 'loaded' question about his backing for Dolan. Joyce hadn't forgotten. He was never at ease dealing with the media, although to be fair he was an almost impossible position after that Brighton game.

At the time, the Hull Daily Mail's only competitors were Radio Humberside. Fortunately, Joyce disliked their sports producer Dave Gibbons more than he disliked me. All the media wanted to know was how Joyce planned to turn things around. After that Brighton game, though, he didn't say much, and who could blame him? He'd only been in the job a matter of a few hours. He didn't know the new owners and he didn't know whether he would be the manager for a week, a month or the rest of the season. The day after the Brighton game, Joyce invited me to Boothferry Park. I was back in that freezing cold office at North Road. Unlike interviews with Hateley, there were no flash new trainers, no feet on the desk and no mobile phones. Joyce seemed awkward, hesitant. He was dressed in a track-suit. His desk was littered with sheets of paper containing lists of possible signings. As I walked up to shake his hand, I almost 'missed' a figure perched on a chair in the corner. It was McGovern, the former Forest captain, a true and trusted disciple of the legendary Clough. Joyce told me to sit down. 'Listen,' he said. 'You are new to the job. So am I. You can help me . . . I can help you. We're going to have to work together so let's start from scratch. You okay with that?' 'Fine,' I said. 'No problems.' McGovern, apparently no lover of the media, grunted. Only later did McGovern reveal one thing: he couldn't believe that Joyce had invited me into his office with the list of possible signings in front of him. He said: 'I'd have spoken to you in the bloody car park – if you'd been lucky.' I can remember thinking that the car park was warmer – and probably drier – than the office. In fact, it wasn't long before Joyce was conducting most of his business elsewhere. I don't blame him. If the whiff of damp at the North

Road house didn't get you, then the smell of rotting donner kebabs, dumped in the front garden did. That house was systematic of a lot that was wrong with City and with Boothferry Park. It was old and unloved. It needed money spent on it to bring it up to date.

Joyce had played for City long enough to know he need to strengthen the team. 'Have you met the directors?' he asked. 'Yeah,' I replied. 'They seem like a pretty decent bunch.' Joyce just smiled.

McGovern grunted – again.

*   *   *   *

City's next match was an FA Cup tie at non-League Salisbury. You'd think non-League opposition would be straightforward. However, it was a real banana skin of a game. Joyce actually invited me to travel on the team coach, but I'd already made other plans; plans that I couldn't get out of. 'Never mind,' he said, 'there will be another time.' Salisbury were playing at least two Divisions below City. However, given City's position – and record (they had won just one of their last 12 games) – many people made the non-League side favourites. City won 2-0. Gregor Rioch smashed in a 30 yard screamer and Brian McGinty forced home the late match-clincher from a corner in the dying minutes. In those days, I had to phone 'live' copy back to the Hull Daily Mail for their Saturday evening Sportsmail. I remember the copy-taker at the other end of the phone asked me to repeat my first few words when I used a sentence containing the words: 'Hull City' and 'victory.' I have two abiding memories of that game. One of was the sound of a light aircraft, taking off from a nearby airfield midway through the second half. The pup-pup-pup noise of the engines suggested it wasn't exactly a Boeing 707. The passengers on that plane were City's directors. Apparently, they'd hired the plane to travel to the game in style. As they were coming into land at Salisbury, the pilot informed them he'd have to take off at four o'clock for the return flight – before it got dark. Take-offs were only allowed in daylight hours. It was the middle of November. So, while the game was still in progress, the directors headed for home. After the match, Joyce invited me into the dressing room. The look on McGovern's faces said it all. 'What the fuck are you doing in here,' he barked. 'The manager says he wants to see me,' I replied. 'That's Mr Joyce – or gaffer to you,' said McGovern. I strolled into the dressing room. Joyce, who had played the full match, was perched on a wooden bench at the far end. Before I had time to say well done, I was drenched in water from head to foot. The players thought it was funny. So did Joyce. McGovern even laughed. My brand new tape recorder threatened to crackle into life and then went up in smoke.

Joyce was delighted with the win – and rightly so. I conducted my interview while he was in the bath. He kept Radio Humberside waiting outside. Hateley – and Dolan before him – had always been keen to restrict access to players. Joyce told me I could talk to anyone. I duly headed in the direction of Rioch, who was talking about his goal to anyone who would listen. I could have filled a book with his version. As he talked me through what happened, the distance the shot covered increased from 20 to 30 and then 40 yards. 'The goalkeeper never stood a chance,' he said, a smile on his face. The atmosphere in that dressing room was a massive improvement and Joyce was certainly a popular figure among his players. A Cup win was welcome, but League points were the priority. Joyce had to try and turn things around – and quickly. A week after Salisbury, City headed for Glanford Park and a derby clash with Scunthorpe. The directors opted to travel by car this time. City's performance was a big improvement, but they suffered a cruel 3-2 defeat. Sadly, the game was marred by a serious injury to Neil Mann, one of the nicest pro footballers you could ever wish to meet. He was also one of City's better players. The injury was something Joyce could not afford. Mann will never forget the date: November, 21, 1998 – two days after his birthday. He said: 'The day before the game, Joycey called me into his office and offered me a new contract. I'd been on the list under Mark (Hateley) but when I asked why, they said they were just trying to give me a gee-up. When Mark was the manager, they were difficult times for everyone. He'd come in as a big name, a massive name . . . what a player. Maybe certain things were said to him that didn't materialise. We made a few decent loan signings but maybe they weren't conducive to playing in the bottom Division. We'd have won a five-a-side League with our ability, but it's all about getting the right balance. We were beaten far too easily. We couldn't grind out results. I was as disappointed as anyone that we were at the bottom of the table but all I wanted to do was play and do my best for Hull City.' The injury wasn't how Mann had planned to celebrate his new contract, or his birthday for that matter. 'We knew it would be a tough game. Scunthorpe were riding high in the table. It was a massive local derby. I was playing left back. A free kick came in to our box and was headed back across me. I swivelled to try to kick the ball off the goal-line. I was looking down at the ball when one of their players (Jamie Forrester) nipped in and headed it. I was committed. I kicked Jamie across the chest and I'm watching my leg as it kind of crumbles under me. I'm down. In the six yard box. My bone has fallen away from where it should be. I knew straightaway that something serious had happened.'

Mann had damaged his knee. He was out for the season. Some people said he'd never play again. City had to battle on. A week later, Dudley scored the winning goal in a 1-0 success at home to Carlisle. A happy dressing room after the game included Buchanan and Hinchliffe, glass of red wine in one-hand, Cuban cigar in the other. It was Joyce's first League victory and the mood among fans was lifted again when City announced they had agreed a £50,000 deal to buy centre forward Leo Fortune-West from Lincoln. The big, raw-boned front-man was just the bruising striker City needed. The signing never went ahead and Joyce quickly learned one of the golden rules of management: there is a world of difference between being told you can sign a player, and the money actually appearing to enable the deal to go ahead. After that Carlisle victory, normal service was restored. City lost 2-0 at Torquay after our visit to the pantomime failed to produce a positive spin-off. Two home games followed and City lost them both: 2-0 to Swansea and 2-1 to Chester. The club was marooned at the foot of the table. We were heading into December. City – and Joyce – needed a miracle.

Even though the deal for Fortune-West had fallen through, Joyce was beginning to make changes to his squad. Justin Whittle was recruited from Stoke for £50,000. Whittle, a former soldier, quickly earned the nickname 'Sarge.' A rugged centre half, he'd started his career at Celtic without making an appearance for them. Whittle recalled: 'I suppose it was a bit of a gamble going to Hull. Everyone knew Hull were struggling but at the time. I was in and out of the Stoke side. Hull made their approach, but I never spoke to Joycey. Instead, it was his assistant John McGovern. He said: 'Son, we're in trouble. We need your help and we need to get some players in.' I thought about it and decided: Why not? The club seemed desperate for me to play for them. I'd enjoyed every minute of it at Stoke, but it just seemed the time was right to move on and start playing a few games.' Whittle wasn't the only new face. Fellow defenders Jason Perry – a former Welsh international – and Jon Whitney arrived from Lincoln. The duo soon made an impression on their team-mates with their tendency to kick lumps out of each other – and anyone else – in training. Joyce also recruited full back Steve Swales from Reading for an undisclosed fee. Whitby born Swales – his dad ran a fish-and-chip shop in the resort – had been linked with a big-money move to Arsenal just 18 months earlier. His career had stalled. Like Whittle, he needed a new challenge. 'I'd been at Stoke a long time and seen them move into a new stadium. It was a lot different to Hull but I knew what to expect when I came here. Boothferry Park was an old stadium but it wasn't a shock to me. I remember one of my first games for Hull was at Shrewsbury. We lost 3-2 and I gave one of the goals away. I thought I was a footballer, tried to bring the ball down in my own box and let their centre forward have a tap in.' The signings effectively meant Joyce had re-built his entire defence. Utility player Gareth 'Gripper' Williams also signed on the dotted line from Scarborough. There was a new goalkeeper as well: Andy Oakes, recruited from non-League Winsford Town. Oakes went into the side as a direct replacement for the unfortunate Gibson. Joyce's contacts at Old Trafford meant he'd secured Gibson's services for the rest of the season. An hour later, the goalkeeper was on his way back to Manchester after breaking two fingers in a pre-match warm-up. It was typical of City's luck.

City's performances did improve, but when they lost that game at Shrewsbury – their last match of 1998 – the prophets of doom had a field day. With the side nine points adrift at the foot of the table, many people thought Joyce should be sacked. I felt that was totally unfair. I always had confidence Joyce could turn things around. I just couldn't quite work out why. Fortunately, the directors did not panic, though Belton later admitted they had seriously considered replacing Joyce with a more experienced manager. That, however, would have cost money. By now, I had Joyce's full trust. He was a pleasure to work with – even if he often forgot to tell you the basics. And it helped when he switched his mobile phone on. I lost count of the number of times he'd either make a change, or lose a player through injury, without telling me. Fortunately, I was regularly giving Mick Matthews – former player who was now the club's physio – lifts to away games. Matthews would keep me up to date with injuries. Unfortunately, he was not particularly good at navigation. Even though he'd played at virtually every football League ground in the country, he just couldn't seem to find any of them.

Shrewsbury was a classic example. Matthews said: 'I'm sure you turn left here, then go straight across at the round-about. Now, take the next left. No, sorry, next right and we're there.' We duly pulled up in Sainsbury's car park on the wrong side of town. Eventually, we made it to Gay Meadow with only minutes to spare. Matthews calmly unpacked all his gear and strolled off towards the dressing room. 'See you back here after the game,' he'd say, 'for the trip back home.' 'Do you know the way?' I asked. 'Sure,' he said. 'No problems.'

*　　*　　*　　*

The end of the year was a worrying time for City. Whittle recalled the feeling among the players: 'Everyone outside the club thought we'd go down, though we never really talked about relegation. The number of new players – and the type we were bringing in – meant we thought we could turn things around.' Apart from optimism, one thing had probably kept Joyce in a job. While City struggled in the League, they progressed in the FA Cup thanks to an against-the-odds win at Luton with goals from Rob Dewhurst and local youngster Ben Morley. Dewhurst was one of the survivors from the Hateley regime. Morley was one for the future and everyone thought his superbly taken goal at Luton was going to lead to a big money move to the Premier League. That Luton victory earned City the third round tie at Aston Villa on January 2. City were handed an allocation of 6,000 tickets and the club sold out in under an hour. After the trials and tribulations of that journey to Villa, the atmosphere inside the ground was amazing. City were well-beaten 3-0 as injuries – and the fact most of Joyce's new signings were cup-tied – meant fielding a weakened side. The result, though, was almost inconsequential, a fact Joyce recognised. 'It was a great day out for the fans,' he said, 'but, frankly, I'd always have swapped a win against Villa for wins in our next three League games. Surviving in the League is more important than winning a cup tie. If you'd offered me ten League points – or a win at Villa Park – I'd have taken the points.' City's share of the receipts from a near 40,000 crowd was expected to provide funds for new players and pay day-to-day bills for the rest of the season. One of the final pieces in Joyce's grand scheme to re-build his squad was Gary Brabin. A former nightclub bouncer, 'Brabs' was almost broader than he was tall. However, he fitted Joyce's brief perfectly. If City were to stave off relegation, they would effectively have to kick their way out of trouble. In the shape of player like Brabin, plus Perry, Whitney, Whittle, Swales – and Joyce himself to some extent – City had suddenly gone from being a soft touch to genuine hard cases.

The first League game of 1999 was at home to Rotherham, then one of the front runners for promotion. City won 1-0 with loan signing Mark Bonner scoring. The team (Whittle was banned after picking up five bookings) was:

Oakes, Greaves, Whitney, Perry, Edwards, Joyce, Bonner, D'Auria, Brown, Brabin, Williams.

The line-up – unrecognisable from the Hateley era – was a clear indication of the changing times at the club. Still, no one could predict events that followed on from that Rotherham victory. It proved to be the start of the club's legendary Great Escape. Bonner had set the ball rolling in his one and only game for City. Two days after that Rotherham game, he was injured in training and returned to Cardiff. By now, City's training base was at Brantingham Park, the home of Hull Ionians Rugby Union club. Joyce had been desperate for better facilities, preferably on the western approaches to the city. It meant he didn't have to go into the house on North Road too often. I was friendly with Ionians' chairman Roger Gosling. I mentioned to him that City were looking for a new training ground. A week later, City moved in. Joyce was more than happy, especially as he – and seemingly half his squad – travelled into Hull from Merseyside on a daily basis. He rarely went to Boothferry Park, except on match days. If the directors wanted to see him, it usually meant a summons to Mr Chu's Chinese restaurant overlooking the Humber. There, Buchanan and Hinchliffe held court surrounded by copious amounts of food and wine. Sometimes, I was 'invited' to meet them. The call usually came at very short notice. I didn't say no. It was an offer I couldn't refuse. Hinchliffe relished putting me in a head-lock. Then, he'd rub his knuckles over the top of my head. All good fun. When I did 'visit' Mr Chu's, Hinchliffe and Buchanan always asked if I wanted a drink or anything to eat. The various dishes had usually been well-picked over. More often than not, they would be joined by some or other mysterious figures. I learned not to ask their identity. Belton, though, kept his distance from these gatherings. Perhaps he didn't like sweet and sour chicken.

On the pitch, City went from strength-to-strength. Hartlepool were thrashed 4-0. David Brown, who was once on Manchester United's books, scored twice. 'Brownie' was usually moaning about something, or someone. He just about managed a smile after that Hartlepool game. Draws against Peterborough – thanks to the goal of the season from Whitney – and Shrewsbury meant City had completed January with an unbeaten record in the League. The Great Escape was under way. After several near misses, Joyce finally signed the big striker he desperately needed: Colin Alcide. Apparently, Alcide would cost around £80,000 but City had initially arranged the deal on a loan basis. Like most other things, the transfer did not go to plan. When

Alcide arrived at Boothferry Park for the first time, he went through the wrong entrance and ended up in Kwik Save. Then, when he did finally find City's reception, he was directed to Joyce's office on the other side of the ground. I was waiting with Joyce. We were on our fourth cup of tea. The phone rang to tell Joyce that Alcide was on his way. Thirty minutes later and Alcide had still not arrived. Joyce headed for reception. I waited in the office. No one knew where Alcide was. Eventually, I found him wondering in the dark corridor beneath the main West Stand. He was hopelessly lost and there was no reception on his mobile phone. Alcide didn't score as many goals as everyone had hoped, but he was still a key figure in the recovery.

The success story continued. Throughout February, City lost just once – in front of the Sky Sports cameras at Rochdale. Four other games that month produced three wins and a draw. The three wins all came away from home: Brentford, Darlington and Halifax. The football wasn't pretty and just about every single goal seemed to stem from an in swinging Joyce freak kick or corner. Still, the method didn't matter. The transformation was remarkable. Perhaps the best victory came at Brentford, then at the top-of-the-table. City's fans 'invaded' Brentford's ground in their thousands, packing out a double tier stand behind one of the goals. Those fans never stopped singing. 'Warren Joyce's black and amber army' was becoming more popular. That support was rewarded with a 2-0 win, Alcide and Brown scoring the all-important goals. Brentford claimed Alcide was yards off-side when he scored. The referee and his assistant thought otherwise. Everything seemed to be going City's way. The gap between them and the rest of the sides battling against relegation had been reduced. Joyce nonetheless refused to get carried away.

'I'll be happy when we know for certain that we can't go down.' Thanks to him, City had gone from the team everyone wanted to play against to the team everyone feared. If you kicked a City player, there were four or five of his team-mates waiting to kick you back twice as hard. In particular no one argued with Brabin except the occasional referee. At the back, Whittle held everything together. He was strong, quick and quiet, the silent assassin. City were beaten just once in March and by the end of the month, they'd hauled themselves off the foot of the table. No one could believe it.

When Scarborough visited Boothferry Park on April 3, 13,000 came through the turnstiles. Asked about the attendance, Belton – or 'Uncle Tom' as he was now known to City's admiring fans – just shrugged his shoulders, lit another cigarette and smiled. I'd got to know Belton pretty well by now. I used to sit with him on the team coach for the trips to the away games that involved an overnight stay. And we had a new coach for the last few games of that season. I say new. It was actually 12 years old; 'grey, green and rust' someone commented at the time. One of the players reckoned it had come from Belton's farm, where it had housed chickens. Actually, it belonged to D'Elegance Travel, one of Hinchliffe's companies. Records later showed City had paid £82,250 for the coach – on April Fools' Day. It was a rare moment of extravagance by City's owners. When Joyce wanted funds for a new player, he'd often been reduced to playing 'knuckles' with Buchanan and Hinchliffe. And, despite the out-lay on that coach, there were tell-tale signs of approaching financial problems. Lloyd began to complain that he hadn't received a single penny in rent for Boothferry Park. Gosling rang me regularly to say Ionians hadn't been paid for the use of their training ground. On one occasion, I went to Mr Chu's for a meal with a friend. The staff must have recognised me because I spent most of the evening listening to complaints that City owed the restaurant lots of money. There were other signs as well. In April, City faced an away game at Brighton, who were then playing at Gillingham's ground. We stayed at a fairly nice hotel in the Kent countryside. We were due to leave the hotel at lunchtime. Belton, however, called everyone together and said we were booking out earlier. The reason for the sudden departure? He knew the cheque would bounce and he wanted to be long gone before the hotel found out. So we all made a hasty exit. It was only when we'd travelled a few miles up the road that we realised we'd left Whittle behind. He hadn't got the message about the early departure and was fast asleep in his room. Fortunately, Mann had travelled down to the hotel in his car. He drove back to the hotel, picked Whittle up and took him to the ground. City drew that game 0-0 and, after the match, the coach called at a fish and chip shop close to the Gillingham's ground. The owner couldn't believe his luck as the order went in: fish-and chips 30 times. His stock of pies disappeared as well. Buchanan and Hinchliffe had travelled to the game independently, but came back on the coach. They were more interested in the shop two doors away. It was an off licence.

Now City were no longer in danger of relegation. April had featured some more excellent results, including a 1-1 draw at Cardiff who, along with Brentford and Cambridge, went on to secure promotion. I can remember being particularly impressed with one Cambridge midfielder that season: Ian Ashbee. He was one of the few players not intimidated by Brabin. City eventually finished 21st. Given their form in the second half of the campaign, it was something of an anti-climax. Still, they were safe. Joyce, McGovern – and the players – had performed that miracle. It was party time at the final home game of the season against Torquay. Joyce and McGovern strode onto the pitch to a hero's reception and signed new contracts. Rob Smith remembers that particularly ceremony. 'At one stage, there was no way Joycey wanted to do it. We persuaded him to sign . . . just for the photographers. They were proper Football League contracts but I remember getting them back. John had signed his but Warren had signed his as Mickey Mouse. I kept them for a while as souvenirs.'

Like most people, Joyce had a difficult relationship with City's owners. He had performed wonders to keep the club in the League, but felt he'd been let down by false promises – not least when it came to signing new players. That contract signing apart, Joyce was always totally professional. Privately, I knew about his growing frustration at off-the-field events. Publicly, he never had a bad word to say about anyone at the club. Of all the people I've ever met in professional sport, he is up there as the person I most respect. Even he struggled to explain the reasons behind the Great Escape. He said: 'We knew we had to change things. We brought new players in. We got one or two results and the confidence went from there. It was an amazing second half (of the season) but the players deserve a lot of the credit. They made it happen.' There was still one game left to play that season – at Swansea. Again, I travelled on the team coach only to find we'd been booked into a hotel in the middle of an industrial estate. There was a lake, but the colour of the water – somewhere between yellow and orange - said everything. We arrived at the hotel at tea-time. Everyone filed into the dining room. As ever,

Brabs was at the front of the queue. George, the coach driver, had just made a welcome return after what we understood was a lengthy illness. However, as we filled our plates, George lifted up his shirt to show everyone he'd had his stomach stapled. There was quite a bit of spare food that night. Even Brabs was put off his pork chops. Overnight it rained cats and dogs. When we arrived at Vetch Field, the pitch was waterlogged. The League suggested delaying the game until Sunday or Monday. There was just one problem. The entire City staff were booked on a plane from Liverpool that night to fly out to Spain for an end-of-season holiday. Swansea wanted the game played as well. After much debate, their ground staff swept most of the water off the pitch. The referee was happy to play – just – and City lost 2-0. The result hardly mattered.

Taking everything into account, the Great Escape was one of the most amazing achievements in City's history. Joyce deserved that holiday, and McGovern deserved his bottle or two of Rioja. Whittle will never forget that season: 'We were such a physical presence,' he said. 'We didn't play the best football but everyone gave 100 per cent and knew their jobs in the side. Others teams tried to play football against us and basically, we kicked them to death. Teams hated playing against us. We had ten kickers and one ball player – and he was the goalkeeper. If Brabs didn't get you, then someone else did. To be fair, we did have players who could play but we also had players who could do the other side of it. If we'd had ten footballers, I don't think we'd have got out of the mess we were in.'

Whittle's thoughts are echoed by D'Auria who was captain. 'To be honest with you,' he says 'Joycey knew what the club wanted. He didn't sign any fancy-dan players. He went out and signed real experienced battlers like Whitney, Perry, Brabin and Whittle. We could play a fair bit but we could also fight. We could battle and we dug in for each other. If Joycey hadn't changed it, we probably wouldn't have won another game that season. Just think, if we had have gone down, where would the club be now?' City had lost just four of their last 25 matches that season – a record not even champions Brentford could match. It did top one table – for the number of red and yellow cards. No one cared, though. It was onwards – and upwards.

Or so I thought.

Chapter Four:

An anti-climax

June, 1999 - May, 2000

After the drama of the Great Escape, anyone expecting a quiet time at Hull City during the summer of 1999 was disappointed. Only a month after Warren Joyce and his players pulled off their astonishing feat on the pitch, David Lloyd took centre stage off it – again. Still the owner of Boothferry Park, and some of the land surrounding it too, Lloyd threatened to block urgent repair work to the ground after claiming that he was owed thousands of pounds in unpaid rent. If the work didn't go ahead, the capacity would be cut from 13,000 to less than 5,000. The loss of so much gate revenue was potentially a crippling financial blow. The concerned club even discussed sharing with York.

Simmering boardroom tension came to the surface too. Tom Belton was dismissed as chairman and removed from the board along with fellow director David Bennett. Belton and Bennett promised High Court action, and accusations and counter-accusations darkened the air. Essentially Belton and Bennett were claiming this: Bennett's money had bought the club from

Lloyd. There were suggestions that Lloyd had paid as little as £100,000 for it. Belton and Bennett were also alarmed about Stephen Hinchliffe's role at City. Constrained by his seven-year ban as a director, imposed by the Department of Trade and Industry, Hinchliffe maintained he only acted in an advisory role as the major shareholder. His advice, he insisted, was purely confined to football matters, such as potential new signings. He claimed to have no direct input into the club's financial affairs and challenged his two accusers to put up or shut up. Belton was unrepentant. During the previous May, he'd written to his fellow directors alleging Hinchliffe had, indeed, become embroiled in the day-to-day running of the club and entered into financial transactions on its behalf, including negotiating new contracts for Joyce and McGovern. That involvement, said Belton, was in direct conflict to the DTI ban. Belton warned he and his fellow directors risked possible prosecution – and potential action from the Football League as a consequence. The letter – and the subsequent fall-out from it – led to the removal of Belton and Bennett.

For Belton, it was a massive fall from power. Just weeks earlier, his role in the Great Escape had earned him the club's Supporter of the Year award. The fans were behind Belton. There was mounting suspicion about Hinchliffe and Nick Buchanan. Hinchliffe made matters worse by inviting his own son to design a new club crest – a rather tame-looking Tiger – which was not universally approved. The boardroom shenanigans attracted the attention of the Football Association and their trouble-shooter, Graham Bean. Humberside Police Fraud Squad was eventually drawn into the affair too. I never met Bean face-to-face but spoke to him on the phone. Before joining the Football Association, he'd been a police officer. He was a burly figure with closely cropped grey hair. He'd only been working for the Football Association for a matter of months but was already known as The Sleazebuster.

Lloyd would not go away either. Apart from his battle to claim unpaid rent, he was still actively trying to secure planning permission for a wide-scale re-development of the Boothferry Park site. As he still owned Hull Sharks, he offered City the use of the Boulevard again as a temporary home. He also said he was in negotiations with the City Council regarding a potential new stadium. Crucially, there was little or no comment from City Hall. City had received a grant of more than £68,000 from the Football Trust to pay for the ground improvements at Boothferry Park. But City needed the permission of Lloyd as landlord before work could be carried out. His spokesman said: 'It would not make economic sense to spend thousands of pounds on Boothferry Park if the club is moving to a new stadium within three years.'

Buchanan, who had taken over the role of chairman from Belton, said he was seeking urgent talks with Lloyd. He maintained City were still keen to buy Boothferry Park from Lloyd 'lock, stock and barrel.' Apart from the Football Trust grant, City had topped up their coffers during the summer with a couple of sizeable outgoing transfers. Goalkeeper Andy Oakes was sold to Derby County for £470,000, a hefty profit on a player who had cost just £12,000 from non-League Winsford Town the previous season. As Adam Bolder had also been sold to Derby just before the end of the Great Escape, the popular perception was that City's bank account was now healthy, especially after adding in receipts from the FA Cup tie at Aston

Villa. So Joyce attempted to strengthen his squad. Expectations were sky-high. The talk was not just of promotion, but a title as well. City's form in the second half of the Great Escape certainly suggested it was feasible. Joyce duly bought goalkeeper Lee Bracey, defenders Jon Schofield and Steve Morgan and strikers Jason Harris, Jamie Wood and John Eyre. The majority of the players arrived on free transfers, though Harris cost in the region of £45,000. Others departed, including McGinty, Dewhurst, Rioch, Richard Peacock and French.

Joyce rang me to tell me about Bracey's signing. He said: 'He's big, strong and has played in the Premier League.' In fact, what he didn't mention is that one of Bracey's few top flight appearances came in Ipswich's 9-0 mauling at Liverpool. Morgan was a former team-mate of Joyce's. He was big and imposing and his deep voice suggested a previous career as a bassist in a Welsh male voice choir. Harris – the most expensive signing at around £40,000 – proudly boasted he'd come to Hull to 'score goals.' The most popular signing was Eyre. Although born in Hull, he'd spent the last few seasons banging in the goals for Scunthorpe – generally against City. During the Great Escape campaign, he scored in a 3-2 win for Scunthorpe at Boothferry Park, a result that helped seal Scunthorpe's promotion. Eyre looked as if he could be a 20-goal-a-season man. If not, there was always Harris to rely on along with Alcide and Brown. Joyce wasn't exactly short of options when it came to strikers, and his defence and midfield featured all the heroes of the previous campaign.

City's pre-season form was full of promise. Joyce appeared to have recruited sagely, and I can remember McGovern – by now a good friend – telling me: 'I think we'll do okay.' For

McGovern, who usually chose his words carefully, I thought he probably meant promotion. We headed off for the first game of the season at Exeter in good spirits. We booked into a decent hotel overlooking the cathedral. It was worryingly close to the city centre, but in all the time I travelled with Joyce's squad I cannot recall one incident of the players going AWOL. They were all tucked up in bed early. The non-playing staff did venture out. McGovern's favourite tipple was still Rioja and by eight o'clock, he'd had a few glasses of it. That's when we walked into a pub packed with youngsters. Fortunately, the DJ was playing 1970s music, and McGovern promptly jumped on the table but didn't impress everyone with his efforts on the air-guitar. We left swiftly, and it was well after midnight when we staggered back to the hotel. A couple of hours later and I had to help carry Andy Daykin to bed. His mobile phone, containing hundreds of numbers, dropped out of his pocket as we carried him up the stairs. The next morning, I'd gone for a walk when he surfaced a little worse for wear. His first reaction was: 'I've lost my phone.' It was panic stations. He spent the next three hours re-visiting every pub in Exeter trying to find it. Imagine his reaction when I walked back in and handed it straight to him.

The game was an anti-climax. City lost 1-0. Eyre didn't play, Harris didn't score and Bracey let in the only goal. The journey back to Hull was very quiet. There was, though, City's very own version of motorway madness. As I've mentioned before, Joyce – and seemingly half the side – travelled in his people carrier. For matches south of Birmingham, he would meet the team coach at a pre-designated spot, usually a service station. The slight snag was Joyce parked his car at the services on the southbound carriageway. On the return journey, we were heading north. So the team coach would pull up on the hard shoulder and – if there wasn't a bridge to cross – Joyce and half-a-dozen players used to sprint across the carriageway to reach his car. Then, he'd drive down to the next exit, re-enter the motorway and head north again. Often, he'd pass the team coach within the first ten miles. I say often because sometimes the speed restrictor on the coach didn't work. I wish you could have seen the smile on George's face when he realised he could go faster than 60 miles an hour.

Defeat at Exeter was disappointing, but there was little or no time to recover before City faced a midweek trip to Rotherham in the first round of the Worthington Cup. By now, the problems in the boardroom were common knowledge. Buchanan assured everyone that he'd got things under control – even though fans were asking where all the money had gone. The whispers suggested that City's financial problems were mounting – and not just because of Lloyd and the unpaid rent. A national newspaper reported the club had been involved in 'irregular dealings' over Oakes' transfer to Derby. As part of the deal that had brought him to Hull, Oakes' former club Winsford were scheduled to receive a 25 per cent share of any 'sell-on.' The newspaper report claimed City had contacted Winsford's chairman Terry Savage prior to that Derby deal and offered to pay him £40,000, and club itself £10,000, to 'forego' that clause. Savage refused, and shortly afterwards City sold Oakes to Derby for £470,000; Winsford's share was around £120,000. At the time, Savage said almost all his negotiations with City had been conducted with Hinchliffe, though letters and faxes had been signed by Richard Ibbotson, then a City director. Quite apart from the offer to Savage, Hinchliffe's role appeared to contradict the terms of his DTI ban – and the claims by his fellow directors that he was 'only advising' the club. There were other allegations, other rumours. But investigations by the FA and the Fraud Squad and the Crown Prosecution Service announced there was 'insufficient evidence' to level charges against any of City's directors or Hinchliffe.

For me, Hinchliffe was always plausible. He certainly relished the good life. Apart from his home in Sheffield, he owned at least one property in London. Whenever City played in the south of the country, Hinchliffe would usually travel to games or the team hotel in a chauffeur-driven Bentley. He drank expensive wine and smoked equally expensive cigars.

The Worthington Cup tie at Rotherham was nonetheless a watershed. The players hadn't been paid for the previous month (July) and there was a very real threat they wouldn't play. Joyce had told me what was going on. I was standing just outside the dressing room at the time and left shortly before Buchanan arrived for a crisis meeting. I made my way up to the Rotherham press box. 'Got any news regarding your team,' asked one veteran scribe. 'Err, no,' I replied. 'There are one or two doubts and one or two problems to sort out.' The players did play that night, and won 1-0 thanks to Eyre's first goal. However, City lost their next three League games and already dreams of promotion were fading.

To add to the growing air of despondency, City had been hit with a transfer embargo after borrowing £50,000 from the Football League to pay the players' wages. Still, the Worthington Cup offered some solace. City defeated Rotherham 2-0 in the second leg. When the draw for the next round was made, Joyce picked out a jewel: Liverpool. Sky Sports were televising the first leg at Boothferry Park, guaranteeing an estimated £80,000. Over the two legs, the club banked £200,000. In addition, Derby were due to pay the final instalment on the Oakes deal and the Football Trust had promised to stump up another £40,000 towards ground improvements. Buchanan announced Lloyd had relented in his threat to block the work. He also stressed City were close to reaching an agreement with Lloyd to buy Boothferry Park and said the council's proposals for a new stadium interested them. The council was awash with cash after selling its shares in Kingston Communications and, with some of the profits, had pledged to deliver a state-of-the-art stadium. It wasn't all good news, though. The Football League was angered after allegations that City had channelled money specifically meant for their youth set-up into other areas. Graham Bean stepped up his investigation. Daykin, now the club's commercial director, told fans there was no need to worry about money. He said: 'There is no drama and no crisis. We just needed a bit of help from the PFA to see us through a cash-flow problem. Most clubs at this level experience that from time to time.' City, apparently, had re-paid the loan.

As if to emphasise the point, they made a high-profile move to sign striker Graeme Jones. Joyce expected him to arrive at Boothferry Park for talks. He never showed. It emerged the transfer embargo was still in place. The Liverpool tie could not come quickly enough – if only to put the focus back on playing matters. Belton was effectively barred from watching the tie at Boothferry Park after being refused tickets. The former chairman decided to speak out and defend his actions against Hinchliffe's presence at the club. He said: 'I felt it was my duty to inform the club about his (DTI) ban. The position had been brought to my attention by solicitors and I was concerned that we might be accused of contravening company law by condoning the involvement of Stephen Hinchliffe as a shadow director.' Hinchliffe again hit back: 'All I do is advise,' he said. 'The Football League has done a full report and given me a clean bill of health.' He claimed that while Belton was still technically a director and a shareholder, he'd been too late in applying for his tickets for the Liverpool tie. I thought that would have been the end of the matter – for a while at any rate. But Hinchliffe chose to outline his exact role at City in the programme for that Liverpool game. The Football League and the FA were not impressed. Bean's investigation intensified.

By the time the first leg at Boothferry Park came around on September 14, City had won back-to-back League games against Chester and Torquay. The bandwagon was rolling at last. Probably predictably, it came off the rails when Liverpool romped to a 5-1 win with safety restrictions limiting the crowd to just over 10,000. David Brown scored for City, but Liverpool were in a different class. For Neil Mann, it was another night he'd rather forget. He attempted his comeback after that horrific injury at Scunthorpe almost ten months earlier. I'd followed Manny's progress through his rehabilitation closely. I knew how much suggestions that he wouldn't play again hurt him. He got his chance to prove everyone wrong against Liverpool. Again, things didn't go to plan. He said 'It was great to be picked against Liverpool. Growing up, the likes of Dalglish and Souness were heroes of mine. For the first 20 minutes against Liverpool, everything went okay. Then, a ball came over the top. Michael Owen was chasing me. I did him for pace – naturally. I managed to clear the ball. There was no contact with him, but I landed on my knee and rotated it around.' This time Mann was ruled out for a year-and-a-half.

City came back from the Liverpool defeat to beat Swansea 2-0. Joyce's men were climbing the table. The second leg at Anfield the following Wednesday was almost academic. Nevertheless, more than 6,000 City fans made the trek to Anfield and turned one end of the stadium into a sea of black and amber. It was an amazing sight. I'd managed to persuade Joyce to let me take charge of the skip containing the kit that night. I was able to stroll past the stewards – and shook hands with a few important-looking people inside the corridors of power at Anfield. I even got a guided tour of the dressing rooms and the rest of the inner sanctum. It was a marvellous experience. There was a chance to ask for a couple of autographs. One fresh-faced Liverpool player scrawled his signature on my programme. His name? Steven Gerrard. I walked down the players' tunnel. Unfortunately, I couldn't get back out of the players' tunnel to pick up my tickets for the press box. Because it was a midweek game, the deadline for the match report was right on the final whistle. I phoned everything back to the office from a seat next to the Liverpool dug-out. Liverpool's substitutes kindly corrected any mistake I made regarding their players. The game itself was over almost before it began. Danny Murphy scored early on to make it 6-1 on aggregate. Then Bracey was sent off for handling the ball a long way outside his area. That meant a rare first team appearance for rookie goalkeeper Matt Baker. He recalled: 'It was a wet, miserable night and the pitch was really slippery. I can still remember the reception I got from the Kop, running towards them at the start of the second half. That was great. In the end, we lost 4-2 and Karlheinz Reidle scored their last two goals. They'd just signed him for £18m. I wanted to swap my shirt at the end, but we'd been warned before the game not to do that because the club didn't have enough spares. Times were difficult. On the way back to Hull, I was dropped off by the team coach at a motorway service station. It was raining, blowing a gale and about one o'clock in the morning. There I was, trying to find enough money to buy a ham sandwich at a petrol station just a few hours after playing in front of almost 30,000 fans at Anfield.'

Attention quickly turned to City's League campaign. Unfortunately, the first four games in October brought three defeats, one draw and no goals. However, two other events dominated the month: City's signing of two Jamaican World Cup stars and news that a new £38m stadium project – funded entirely by the council – would finally go ahead. The arrival of the Jamaicans stunned the football establishment. No one knew how they'd come to be linked with City in the first place. Joyce did tip me off at a training session about the possibility of the double signing. But I'm not so sure he was certain it would go ahead. He swore me to secrecy and I would never have betrayed his trust. By now, our relationship went further than manager-reporter. We were good friends and his wife reckoned he spent more time on the phone to me than he did talking to her. She was probably right. The position of player-manager is particularly difficult. In the one sense, you have to distance yourself from your team-mates. In the other, though, you are one of the team. Joyce needed someone he could trust on the periphery of things, apart from McGovern. I guess I was in the right place at the right time.

The two Jamaicans City were midfielder Theodore Whitmore

and Ian Goodison. They'd both made more than 70 appearances for their country, and had appeared in the World Cup. City, though, wanted to keep things quiet. Whitmore and Goodison were scheduled to arrive on October 2 and link up with the City squad that was playing at Barnet on the same day. Rob Smith was handed the role of their minder. He remembers: 'I was in the directors' lounge before the game, and the actor Sean Bean was with us having pre-match dinner. He had strong Sheffield United connections and knew Andy Daykin, who used to work at Bramall Lane. I knew the Jamaicans were safe downstairs in another room, but it was Sean Bean who was attracting all the attention as we took our seats for the game. He put his sun-glasses on, so we all put our sun-glasses on. There we were about 15 of us, all in a row, wearing sun-glasses and trying to look like we were film stars. I'm not so sure it was even sunny. We must have looked like real dickheads. I went to check on the Jamaicans at half time. They looked like refugees. They all had big coats and huge kit bags with them.' There was another shock for City – and Smith. The club had only been expecting two Jamaicans. Instead, five had arrived. Smith explains: 'They'd come straight from the airport, and packed into a Mercedes that was driven by their agent. I tried my best to explain to them what we were doing at the end of the game and where they could find the team coach. At the end of the match, they were nowhere to be found. Apparently, they had all piled into the Mercedes again and their agent had tried to drive them back to Hull himself. I got all the way back to the Jarvis Hotel in Hull at about two o'clock in the morning when my phone rang. It was the Jamaicans. They were in Birmingham – hopelessly lost. I directed them to Hull the best way I could. Eventually, they arrived as daylight was breaking, tired and cold. It took them two weeks to thaw out.'

The Jamaicans played in a reserve team game and Joyce saw enough of Whitmore and Goodison to sign them straightaway. The other three players – a striker, a goalkeeper and a full back – stayed on trial for a little longer before being released. Whitmore and Goodison made their first team debuts in a League game at Rochdale on November 2. It was a Tuesday night and – as ever in Rochdale – it was cold, wet and windy. As the pair warmed up, they looked like a couple of mountaineers about to tackle Everest in countless layers of clothes. Whitmore took to the field wearing gloves. He was miffed after being told he had to take off his woolly hat. Goodison was a substitute. However, he came off the bench to help set up a goal for Whitmore that clinched a 2-0 win. Whitmore's skills were amazing. He almost looked out of place in the hurly-burly world of the League's bottom Division. But he settled much better than Goodison and it wasn't long before rival clubs were wondering how City had actually brought the pair to this country and signed them. There were allegations that an unlicensed agent had been used. The Football League looked into the deal, but took no action. Whitmore and Goodison both played in the second round of the FA Cup at non-League Hayes later in November. City scraped a 2-2 draw. That match marked the end of Dave D'Auira in City's side. 'I knew Chesterfield were interested,' he said. 'It was a good move for me. They were playing at a higher level but I didn't want to go. After that Hayes game, Joycey came up to me and said: "I don't want you to go but the club needs the money."'

The Hayes game brought City's mascot, Roary the Tiger, into the national limelight. He'd been thrown out of the ground for improper behaviour after winding up the home fans and also pretending to fall asleep against the foot of a goal-post. He managed to sneak back in and joined City's fans behind one of the goals. It later emerged that Roary had relied on a touch of Dutch courage before the game. He'd consumed half-a-bottle of Vodka and several cans of extra-strong lager on the coach journey from Hull to Hayes to steady his nerves. Rob Smith recalls: 'The lad who wore the Roary costume was a bit of a character. He was a painter and decorator and we once employed him to decorate a room next to the board-room at Boothferry Park. We left him there overnight and when we came back in the morning, he was sprawled out on the floor fast asleep. He hadn't even started painting – but he had found the key to the drinks cabinet.' As news of his behaviour at Hayes leaked out, City were forced to issue an apology. On the Monday after the game, I was dispatched to interview him. He was, he said, very sorry and promised it wouldn't happen again. It wasn't long before 'Roary' was signed by Exeter, where he dressed like an ancient Greek, short tunic and all.

The episode came at a time when it was impossible to keep City off the front and back pages. Even the arrival of the Jamaicans was overshadowed by the announcement that the city council was to fund a new £38m super-stadium on the back of that huge windfall from the flotation of Hull's telecommunications company. The site was revealed as the Circle, on Anlaby Road – ironically on the very land where City had played for almost 40 years before moving to Boothferry Park in 1946. The council wanted all three of the city's professional clubs to be involved. The stadium would have a capacity of 30,000, eventually rising to 40,000. The development would also feature a separate indoor sports arena, floodlit synthetic pitches for a variety of sports, classrooms, a sports injury clinic, lecture rooms, conference facilities and retail outlets. It would be ready for the start of the 2001-02 season. The council had banked £255m from the flotation of the telecommunications company and owned £800m of shares. Money was not an issue. There was talk of new roads to ease traffic congestion, a walkway to the city centre and even a railway halt.

Ian Blakey, a former City director, was appointed as chairman of the board overseeing the project. The planning process was due to be completed in six months' time with work starting a month later. The consultants were named as Drivers Jonas, a company with vast experience of similar developments. There was, though, just one snag. On the day the council announced their plans, Lloyd confirmed he was considering merging Hull Sharks with Gateshead Thunder. He still owned a controlling interest in the Sharks. At the time, the RFL was offering clubs a £1.25m sweetener to merge and the money would have cleared the Sharks' debts of around £1.6m. The merger went ahead only hours before the Sharks were due to go bust. There was a new management team in place at the rugby club, headed by former Gateshead supremo Shane Richardson; Lloyd severed his links with the rugby club. The new club – nicknamed Gateshull by some – retained its Super League status and would stay at the Boulevard until the new stadium was ready. The City Council announced it would eventually buy the Boulevard for £750,000 and turn it into a community-based stadium. There was no news, though, on Boothferry Park. Buchanan confirmed City wanted to play in the new stadium. 'We'd be fools not to,' he added. But with no-long-term future for professional football at Boothferry Park, the pressure was back on Lloyd.

With so much happening off-the-field, it was difficult to concentrate on events on it. City did reach the third round of the FA Cup after beating Hayes in a replay. Their reward was a money-spinning tie against Chelsea. Again, concerns about safety issues meant the capacity was fixed at just over 10,000, costing hard-up City thousands of pounds in lost revenue. It was money the club could not afford to lose. Chelsea cantered to a 6-1 victory. There was some consolation for City because various newspapers linked Whitmore with a £1m plus move to Stamford Bridge, and other clubs were reported to be tracking the Jamaican star too. The reports, as usual, came to nothing and the Jamaicans could not ignite a promotion challenge. City's campaign laboured through December and into January. With Eyre sold, the others strikers failed to deliver. In a six game spell between February 12 and March 10, City scored just two goals in six games. Attendances dipped, though the crowds were still among the best in the Division. The average home crowd was over 6,000. Easter brought some respite with a hat-trick of wins against Carlisle (4-0), Leyton Orient (2-0) and Mansfield (1-0). But Joyce and McGovern were promptly sacked. I'd met Joyce at training the morning he was dismissed. He told me he'd been summoned to Boothferry Park for a meeting. He said he knew what would happen. I told him he was talking rubbish. He and McGovern still had the backing of the fans who were venting their anger and frustration at the directors. Joyce walked off, shaking his head. He was resigned to his fate. Early in the afternoon, he rang me at home. 'That's it,' he said. 'I've gone. They've got their way.' Less than a year after leading the club to that amazing escape, Joyce was out of a job. As he cleared his desk, he didn't have to worry about slamming the door to his office. It had fallen off weeks before and hadn't been repaired. I was distraught. Perhaps I was too close to Joyce. Still, he deserved better. I rang Buchanan for a statement. He could sense my anger – and hurt. 'Your mate's gone,' he taunted me. Buchanan also told me to be careful about what I wrote. Daykin did exactly the same in a phone call later that day.

Joyce was the consummate professional. He could have caused City huge embarrassment with his inside knowledge. To this day, he's never said a detrimental word about the club – or the directors involved in his downfall. I know him. He never will. I put pressure on him that day to effectively dish the dirt. He didn't. Although Joyce had been sacked as manager, he was still under contract to City as a player. So, as the search for a new manager started, Joyce continued to train with his team-mates (though there was still the matter of compensation for the remainder of Joyce and McGovern's contracts). A never ending list of candidates was mentioned. In the meantime, youth team boss Billy Russell took charge on a caretaker capacity. He guided City to some impressive results, including a 1-0 win at Plymouth. I'd been booked in to stay with the team only to find we were billeted at three different hotels. Supposedly there were not enough rooms at any single hotel. I didn't believe it. This was another indication of the club's financial problems. City, though, were still able to appoint the vastly experienced Brian Little, who had once led Aston Villa into Europe. He resigned from Villa in 1998 and went on to manage Stoke and West Brom. Little had been sacked by West Brom a month before he arrived at City. He watched the last game of the season. City slumped 3-0 at home to Hartlepool.

Then the fun really started.

Chapter five:

Against all odds

June, 2000 - May, 2001

I have nothing but respect for Brian Little. He's as honest as the day is long. His knowledge of football would put anyone to shame. He also cares about people. When he took charge at Hull City our relationship was difficult. He obviously knew all about my connections with Warren Joyce. In fact, Joycey was still training with the club. Eventually, his compensation package was sorted out and Joyce headed to Leeds – without that people carrier. Little's vast experience meant he was used to dealing with the media and it wasn't long before we were working closely together. He's a rare breed of manager in that he was happy to invite you round to his house to discuss life – and tactics – over a cup of tea. For the life of me, though, I can't understand why he came to Hull. Yes, he wanted a challenge. Yes, he could 'feel' the potential. Yes, he wanted to re-build his own career. Yes, he wanted take City to a higher level. However, he must have known the odds were stacked against him. He also must have known all about the mounting off-the-field problems at the club. Quite how Nick Buchanan had 'sold' Hull City to Little, I'll never know. To be fair, Buchanan had played ball over the appointment. I knew Little was in the frame, but Buchanan didn't want anything in the paper until a contract had been signed and sealed. He headed off to meet Little for lunch and told me that if I didn't print any details, he'd let me speak to the new boss. Sure enough, Buchanan rang me and handed his phone to Little.

Little's job, of course, was to focus on football matters. However, as he moved into his new home in a west Hull village, he didn't need to look far for reminders of the turmoil City were in. A High Court action – brought by Belton and Bennett and centred around their acrimonious departure from the City board – was on-going. The Football Association and Humberside Police's fraud squad were investigating City's affairs. That team bus – allegedly bought for £82,000 from one of Hinchliffe's myriad of companies, was one small part of the various probes. There were also fresh allegations that money, supposedly meant for City's youth team, had been spent elsewhere. And City confirmed they had again borrowed funds from the Professional Footballers' Association to pay players' wages. The League responded by slapping another transfer embargo on the club. Welcome to Hull, Brian. Things, though, were going to get worse.

Lloyd locked City out of Boothferry Park in the dispute over unpaid rent. Lloyd claimed he was owed £100,000. Buchanan tried to make light of the various problems. Staff, though, weren't smiling when they turned up for work to find all the locks had been changed and some of their computers had been carted off by the Fraud Squad. As City attempted to get back into their ground, John Cooper was a central figure in the events that followed. He explained: 'The lock-out was obviously pre-arranged because all the media were there. It wasn't just something that had happened. I parked my car on Boothferry Road because I know if I'd used the car park, I'd have been under siege because the media were desperate for information. I met the staff and suggested we went into Kwik-Save for a cup of tea. Although we weren't playing any games at that stage of the year, it was an important time because the day after the lock-out we were due to start selling passes for the new season. It was a vital form of income. I think that's why Lloyd timed the lock-out for when he did. He knew he was hurting the club. In addition, we'd also just started work on improving the pitch. The company involved only had that week to do it because they were due to start another job at Fulham the following Monday. Unfortunately, all their equipment was locked in at Boothferry Park and they couldn't get at it.' Cooper rang Buchanan and was told not to worry. Cooper added: 'Nick said it was temporary. He told me they were in negotiations with Lloyd and we'd soon have the keys to get in.' Buchanan was true to his word. Within a couple of days, the staff were back at work.

Cooper explained: 'On the morning the lock-out ended, I got a call from Philip Webster (a City director) telling me everything had been sorted. He told me to get down to the ground. He'd arranged for all the paperwork to be delivered for me to present to the security company Lloyd was using. I arrived and again the media were out in force. I told them there would be no statements but said I'd show them round when we'd got back in again. At the time, Webster's partner was a serving officer with Humberside Police. I couldn't believe my eyes when a police car swept into the ground. She was obviously bringing the paperwork. I told the media that the car was just there to make sure everything was okay. I rushed over to her and she handed me all the documents. I shoved them down the front of my shirt and told her to get out of the place double quick before the media realised what was happening.' A few minutes later, the doors were unlocked.

City were able to open the ticket office. However, they were still barred from entering the ground itself. Cooper says: 'My understanding is that Lloyd had put the actual stadium on a separate lease agreement to the rest of the site, including the offices. So, while we could get back into the offices, we couldn't get into the ground. It was bizarre. I didn't dare tell the media that. Instead, I made a joke that we hadn't got the keys for the stadium. I actually tried to unlock the gates, but of course I knew the keys wouldn't fit. I assured them the right keys would be arriving the next day and they seemed happy with that.'

It was, said Buchanan, 'a storm in a teacup.' He was upset with Lloyd, but could not afford to fall out with someone who still owned Boothferry Park. Little began to make his own plans and had been promised there were 'limited' funds for new players. Little soon dispensed with Brantingham Park as a training base and moved to Hull University instead. Ionians were probably relieved. They always seemed to be chasing City for the rent and I was embarrassed fielding telephone calls from Roger Gosling. As for the University, at least the local traffic wardens were pleased. The car park at the complex was far too small for the number of vehicles. Anyone who left their car on the road outside paid a hefty price. Eventually, the Football League transfer embargo, imposed over that youth team money and the PFA loan, was lifted. Then, ten days later, it was put back in place again. It seriously restricted Little's attempts to strengthen his squad.

A dramatic twist in the Belton and Bennett saga followed. They suddenly announced they wanted to buy the club with the backing of a Jersey-based millionaire Alan Devy. I met them in at pub in the village of South Cave, just outside Hull. It was the first time I'd seen Belton in weeks. He still wearing the same overcoat and, of course, had a cigarette in his hand. Bennett, who I really didn't know, came across well. Devy was sandy haired. You could tell he was from Jersey because he was the only one of us with a sun tan. They outlined their plans and seemed upfront and honest. Devy didn't say too much, but there were assurances that finance would not be a problem. Apparently, Devy had made his money from tiles before selling up and moving to Jersey. I ran the story about their plans in the Hull Daily Mail the following day. Buchanan, though, was not interested. 'This club is not for sale' he said. He also expressed doubts about Devy's credibility. As Buchanan and Hinchliffe held more than 60 per cent of City's shares, there was nothing Belton and Bennett could do. What worried me is that Buchanan knew exactly where I'd met Belton, Bennett and Devy and even what we'd ordered for lunch. I spent the next few days looking over my shoulder. Paranoid? Perhaps. However, this is about the time the phone calls started about concrete coffins and the Humber. To be fair, I never had a problem with Buchanan – or Hinchliffe for that matter. They were good company on away trips. Of course, there were rumours about the club's finances, but with investigations by the Football League and the Fraud Squad, it was difficult, if not impossible, to write anything that even hinted at impropriety. Buchanan regularly met fans and usually managed to get his message across. He was always happy to be interviewed and Hinchliffe would usually return calls, despite mounting trouble in his business empire. The trio of Belton, Bennett and Devy slowly faded into the background and a new season kicked off with all the old concerns.

There were just two new faces in Little's squad for the opening game of the campaign at Blackpool: Phil Brumwell and Lee Philpott. Despite the many – and very obvious problems off the field – the talk of promotion was in the air again. Realistically, Little was forced to rely on the majority of players who had struggled for consistency the previous season under Joyce. City had eventually finished 14th, an improvement on previous seasons but clearly not sufficient progress. Little's appointment meant a series of rules and regulations were imposed on the media. Fair enough. Little liked to know who I planned to interview, and why. His rules were nothing out of the ordinary. Travelling with the team was now off the agenda. Again, I had no complaints about that. Instead, it was off to Blackpool by rail for me. On the outward journey, the train seemed to stop at every station between Leeds and Blackpool . . . and a few more besides. At least, though, the train ran pretty much to time, unlike the return journey. It was more than an hour late arriving at Blackpool. And the resort's North Shore Station is no place to be at nine o'clock on a Saturday night. There were plenty of City fans waiting for the same train. At least they had plenty of time to reflect on a 3-1 defeat. The general consensus was that Little would turn things around. I had my niggling doubts because of so much turmoil off the field. There were further additions to the squad over the next few weeks, including centre half David Brightwell and striker Clint Marcelle. However, Little had to wait until the middle of September for the first win: a 1-0 victory at home to Shrewsbury. He quickly decided what we all knew: Bracey was not the solution to the goalkeeping position. He brought in the experienced Paul Musselwhite. However, City's form was frustratingly inconsistent. They defeated much-fancied Cardiff 2-0 at Boothferry Park only to lose against the likes of Cheltenham and Chesterfield. The low point in the first half of the campaign came in the FA Cup at non-League Kettering. Somehow, City survived a battering at Kettering but lost the replay 1-0 at Boothferry Park. A vital chance for much needed revenue disappeared.

Buchanan was coming under increasing pressure. Lloyd again threatened action over unpaid rent. Shortly afterwards, Lloyd announced he was ready to sell Boothferry Park to a London-based consortium headed by developer Mel Griffin. It was Lloyd's last link with Hull. No one was sad to see him go and I was left with the feeling he thought the same way about Hull. Exactly how much money Lloyd pumped into professional sport in the city will always be open to question: £3m-£4m seems to be the best estimate. His PR was a disaster, and so were some of his key appointments. If Lloyd had got things right, then his dream of a new stadium could well have been delivered. Perhaps he was just two or three years early. Wrong place, wrong time. The stadium was ticking along, though the process was slow. And so was City's anticipated climb up the table. December brought just one win – at Scunthorpe. Christmas produced a 0-0 draw at home to Kidderminster and a 1-0 defeat at Rochdale on Boxing Day. It was hardly the stuff on which to build dreams of promotion. After that Rochdale game, I recall asking Little if he still thought City could go up. For the first and only time, he bit my head off. 'What kind of question is that?' he said. I thought it was a fair one. He obviously didn't. It was a clear sign of the mounting pressure he – and City – were under.

I continued to hear whispers about City's financial predicament. The Football League, the FA and the Fraud Squad were giving nothing away apart from the bog-standard line: 'Our investigations are continuing.' However, when City's scheduled game against Blackpool on New Year's Day was called off, it brought things to a head. It emerged the directors had been banking on revenue from that one game to pay outstanding wages. Rob Smith recalled: 'I went down to the ground on New Year's Eve with Andy Daykin and John Cooper. The pitch was rock-hard under a covering of snow and we brought in a local referee, who had no hesitation in calling the game off. The look on Dayks' face said it all. He knew the club desperately needed the money to pay wages. Really, the loss of that game to the weather was the catalyst.' By the end of the month, City had failed to pay outstanding wages totalling around £110,000. Worse followed. The club owed Her Majesty's Customs and Excise an estimated £500,000. City were due in the High Court on February 7 to face a winding up order sought by the tax-man. Buchanan and his fellow directors held a series of hastily arranged meetings. The outcome was not good. The club was around £2m in debt. Creditors – and not just the tax-man – wanted paying quickly. City were broke. Buchanan revealed he'd held talks with several 'interested parties' who had enquired about buying the club. Those talks, however, had come to nothing. Buchanan branded some of those interested parties as timewasters. He said: 'I am passionate about this club and I will do everything I can to make sure it survives – even if it means me walking out. But I will only go if I am sure the people I leave this club to have better means than me. But so far, I have seen nothing that has convinced me otherwise. Everyone who has said they want to buy the club are all bay windows and no curtains. I have a responsibility to Hull City and I am not going to just sell the club to anyone.' City faced oblivion.

Somehow Little kept the players as focussed as he could. But just 24 hours before City were due in the High Court to face that winding up order, Lloyd locked the club out of Boothferry Park for a second time. He'd still not been paid that outstanding rent. This time, it was serious. City had a home game against Leyton Orient scheduled at the end of the week. If the game couldn't go ahead, the Football League admitted they might have to take action. Deducting points was a possibility. Any action taken by the Football League could have proved to be punitive if the High Court granted that order. Rob Smith admitted: 'Everyone knew Lloyd was owed money for the rent but the decision to lock us out still came as a shock. It was the timing of it. We got to work on the Monday morning and thought: 'What's going on here?' All the locks had been changed and we couldn't get into the offices. There was the game against Orient to prepare for. So we worked from a pub just up the road. We worked in offices that some of our sponsors loaned us. We even worked in the backs of our cars. Basically we made the best of what we could because we had to get that game on.' John Cooper and his staff had other problems: getting the pitch ready. He explained: 'We'd got wind that something was imminent. I'd put a plan in place to claim squatters' rights. We'd even been sleeping inside the stadium on a few nights prior to previous matches. Fortunately, I knew the movements of the security company Lloyd used. So, when they weren't there, we were. We managed to get in and do the work.'

It was a Churchillian spirit. The club's staff, who hadn't been paid either, forged on with arrangements for that Orient game. But how long could City survive? They could become only the third Football League club to fold in the past 40 years, joining Accrington Stanley and Bradford Park Avenue. Others tried to be more optimistic and said even administration wasn't necessarily the end of the road. They pointed to former League club, Aldershot, who were playing again, albeit in the Premier Division of the Ryman League. City could do the same, but would probably have to start in Division One of the North Counties East League. If that happened, there would be local derby against Hall Road Rangers, who were then averaging gates of around 50. Potential opponents would include Bridlington Town, who had been a pub team six years earlier. Quite how City v Bridlington Town would pan out in a new £38m, 30,000 capacity super stadium was anyone's guess. Lloyd was on holiday in Australia. Buchanan was incandescent about his decision to lock the club out. He said: 'It has got personal and it's very sad Mr Lloyd has decided to take this course of action. I don't really understand what he is attempting to achieve because he has to realise he is not hurting Nick Buchanan, he is hurting Hull City Football Club and all its fans and they don't really deserve that. The overriding concern of both myself and my fellow directors is ensuring that Hull City continues in existence. We've faced all the other problems and not run away. We are not going to start now. If we have to play the Orient game at Scunthorpe, Grimsby, York, Mansfield – or anywhere else –

we will do. David Lloyd will not win because if he does, there will be no football club and I won't allow this football club to go under.'

As the High Court hearing approached, something had to give. All the indications suggested the tax-man would close the club down unless there were some assurances that payment would be handed over. Little summed up the growing apprehension and said: 'We have not been paid for five or six weeks now. Everyone wants to soldier on in the hope the club continues. But if it's liquidation, it's liquidation. That's what I have been told.' At the eleventh hour, Belton again tried to buy the club. He said: 'The offer is on the table but I can't wait forever. I want to do all I can to help Hull City and believe I could turn the club into a success again.' Buchanan again dismissed Belton's bid. As the tension mounted and the hearing approached, Lloyd warned he was standing firm. He said: 'It (the pitch) seems to be the only way to get all the parties around the table. They can't play football unless I allow them to. I'm led to believe the directors want to put the club into some form of administration, but I don't think that's best for Hull City. It can't work in administration. There are no assets because they don't own the only asset. They will have to get around the table.'

Supporters' organisations were desperately trying to raise funds to buy a stake in the club. Time, though, was running out. With all other avenues closed, Buchanan decided to apply to put the club into voluntary administration. If nothing else, it would keep the tax-man at arms' length. The High Court agreed to that stay of execution for just 14 days. The firm of Kroll, Bulcher and Phillips were appointed as administrators. On the day of the hearing, Buchanan resigned with the parting shot: 'I've fought and tried – and fought and tried again – to turn the club around, but decided it's better if someone else has a go.' To compound matters, a few days later, Hinchliffe was jailed for five years (later reduced to four on appeal) for corruption and bribery following the collapse of his company Facia.

Paul Holder, from Kroll, Bulcher, Phillips, was the new man in charge and he had two weeks to find a buyer. But he had an even more pressing concern: getting that Leyton Orient game played. Fortunately, Lloyd agreed to lift the lock-out. The hard work of staff such as Cooper and Smith had paid off. Smith revealed: 'We'd just gone ahead as though the game would be played. We had the programmes printed, all the hospitality packages were sold, sponsors were in place. But all the directors had gone, including Dayks. I remember lying in the bath on the night before the game rehearsing my lines for my 'debut' in the sponsors' lounge. It just seemed surreal but it was business as usual. I was getting married that June. Did I think of walking away? Oh God, no, never. No one considered it. I know two or three of the players left – and it was hard to blame them – but the staff stayed on. There was money being dripped through, but most of it went to the players. We didn't get a penny.' That Orient game went ahead and a Rodney Rowe goal earned an emotional win in front of almost 9,000 fans. In fact, City won all six of their games in February and Little won the Manager of the Month award. The club, however, was back in the High Court on February 22. Would the tax-man hold off again?

A judge ruled the administration order would continue until April 30. The court heard that an unnamed buyer had come forward and would pay £85,000 to keep the club trading until March 8. That money would pay players' wages and the outstanding rent to Lloyd. By March 8, the plan was this: creditors and shareholders would vote on a Creditors Voluntary Arrangement. If accepted, the court was told the club would be sold for £360,000. The court also heard another 'mystery party' had expressed an interest in buying City, but administrators refused to confirm that particular approach had come from two American-based millionaires. Interestingly, a couple of years later, Oldham were taken over. The buyers, three American-based businessmen – Simon Blitz, Simon Corney and Danny Gazal – admitted they had come close to purchasing City. At the time of the turmoil in and out of the courts, City were 10th in the table, just four points off a play-off place. Little said: 'It seems that because we are winning people think that things can't be too bad. But they are so wrong. It has been so difficult. Players have not been paid, we have had two (players) leave us for a new club and we have had to reduce training sessions during the week because some of the lads cannot afford to get to the ground.' As the calendar started to turn towards that March 8 deadline, everyone wanted to know the identity of the mystery buyer. In the meantime, there were games to be won.

City took maximum points from all but one game: a 2-0 defeat at Cardiff on a Friday night. Attention turned to City's AGM in the first week of March at the Jarvis Hotel in Willerby, the scene of Lloyd's dramatic walk-out 12 months previously. Creditors and shareholders were scheduled to vote on a rescue package, fronted by the as yet unnamed buyer. The individual involved had insisted his identity should be kept secret until the meeting had taken place. All kinds of names were floating around. By now I knew the name of the 'mystery man', which created a dilemma. If I named him, the deal could have been called off and City forced out of business. So I kept quiet. A list of creditors, published in the build up to that meeting, made interesting reading. Several local companies were owed money, including Mr Chu's which was seeking over £5,000. Kwik-Fit were owed just over £100. Humberside Police were owed more than £60,000, and John McGovern around £30,000. The key player, though, was the tax-man. All the indications were the tax-man would vote for the rescue package. However, there was – as always with City – a last minute drama. Buchanan, who had taken over the jailed Hinchliffe's shares, suggested he would vote against the deal. As he had over 60 per cent, he could have killed any rescue stone dead. Fortunately, Buchanan had a change of heart and the deal went through.

The day afterwards, City's new owner was unmasked: Adam Pearson, a true white knight, shining armour and all. Pearson, a former commercial director of Leeds United, was backed by Peter Wilkinson, a Harrogate-based internet entrepreneur. The deal effectively meant the formation of a new company. City's new owners had reached an agreement with the tax-man and the Football League before that AGM. The League sanctioned the takeover without imposing any punishment. From day one, Pearson was welcomed by fans, and the local business community. He was at the other end of the scale from Lloyd as well as Buchanan and company. Pearson had an impeccable background in business and in football. He'd attended Hull University. His first job was as a trainee manager at the city centre branch of Marks and Spencer. He'd done his homework and was ready to invest his own money into re-building the club. He said: 'The main thing is to stabilise the club and I think that's what we have done already. I am going to ensure that the players are paid every penny they are owed. I hope to put together a two-year business plan and break even within 12 months.' Pearson admitted proposals for the new stadium – now proceeding at pace – were a large part of the attraction to buy City. As Pearson moved in, there is no doubt that the City Council breathed a huge sigh of relief. Pearson added: 'I have been looking to take over a club for some-time now and Hull is one of only two or three places I would have been interested in. The potential here is tremendous. It's a very exciting time. I'm not saying we are going to be a Premier League club in five or six years, but we're going to give it a good try. It is a great city. The people are crying out for success. They are waiting for something to happen.' Those 'people' were soon hanging on Pearson's every word. He became a popular and charismatic figure.

Pearson confirmed he had struck a deal to keep City at Boothferry Park until the summer of 2002 when the new stadium was due to be completed. One of his first tasks was to move his own offices out of the Boothferry Park complex. Instead, he operated from a portable building on the car park. It was a far cry from what he'd been used to at Elland Road, particularly as he'd left Leeds when they were playing in the Champions' League. He once told me he could not stand the lingering stench of cigar smoke in City's old offices. Pearson needed the local paper on his side, and I don't think he ever failed to return a telephone call or refused a request for an interview. From a professional point of view, It seemed as though I'd been working with Pearson for years. The transition from Buchanan to the new owner was seamless. What I didn't know at the time was that Pearson had already checked me out. My first job in journalism was at the Wakefield Express. My duties included covering the local

Rugby Union club. Pearson was educated at Queen Elizabeth Grammar School in Wakefield. He was a talented rugby union player, a centre or fly half. Only injury prevented him from touring Australia with the England Schoolboys' side. However, he did play a few games for Wakefield before joining their Yorkshire rivals Harrogate. I knew several of Wakefield's players. So did Pearson. Apparently, one of his first tasks as City owner was to ask them what I was like. As I'd bought them all beer at some stage, they gave me a sound reference, and Pearson trusted me from the very start. The feeling was mutual. He always came across as calm and confident. He could, though, be ruthless. He had to get rid of many staff members who had worked for the previous regime. He did that with the minimum of fuss. Smith and Cooper were two of the few to stay on. He brought in John Holmes as commercial director and Mal Branagan as finance director. It was his team.

On the pitch, Pearson pledged to try to strengthen a team that was chasing a top six place. Andy Holt arrived from Oldham on loan. With City riding high in the table, Pearson assured Little his job was safe. 'I'm very happy leaving Brian in charge of on-the-field activities. I believe he is one of the best managers in the country. He has done an absolutely amazing job here, especially when you consider the background he has had to work under.' Pearson had taken a watching brief for the first time in City's clash at Plymouth on March 13. They drew 1-1. However, he was fully in charge the following week for the home game against Exeter. City won 2-1 and followed up with important victories against Rochdale and Scunthorpe. The Scunthorpe clash attracted an attendance of 10,000-plus – clear proof, if Pearson ever needed it, of the potential.

HERE'S LOOKING AT YOU: Colin Alcide (left) and John Eyre celebrate a City goal during the 1999-2000 campaign. Unfortunately, it was a rare moment of success in another frustrating season.

THE NEW MAN: Brian Little, Warren Joyce's successor, meets the media for the first time following his appointment, flanked by Stephen Hinchliffe (right).

THE FAMOUS FIVE: Hull City's directors at the start of the 2000-01 campaign (from left to right), David Capper, Philip Webster, Nick Buchanan, Richard Ibbotson and Andy R. Daykin. All five were part of the investigations by the Football League and the Fraud Squad and although they were eventually cleared, they had left the club by the end of the season.

SIDE BY SIDE: The Kwik Save supermarket and the main Hull City offices at Boothferry Park. The fact the supermarket's owners had a long and watertight lease prevented David Lloyd from selling Boothferry Park and proceeding with his American-style 'leisure city' elsewhere in Hull.

KEEP OUT: The padlock says it all. The Tigers are locked out of their own ground as part of the on-going dispute between the club's directors and David Lloyd over unpaid rent. Not even the local Fraud Squad could gain entry.

KEEPING THE FAITH: City's long-suffering fans turn out in force for one of several games billed as the 'last ever match' at Boothferry Park as financial problems mounted.

FROZEN OFF: The covers are off and there is some grass on view but the thaw had come too late to 'save' the home game against Blackpool at the turn of the year in 2000. The postponement and loss of revenue hastened the club's slide into administration and near closure.

THE MESSIAH: City's saviour Adam Pearson attends one of his first matches at Boothferry Park, wearing the overcoat that was never far from his side . . . even in the middle of summer.

AGAINST ALL ODDS: John Eyre races away in triumph after scoring City's goal in the first leg of the play-off victory against Leyton Orient at Boothferry Park at the end of the 2000-01 campaign. With Pearson now at the helm, Brian Little had somehow managed to overcome administration and guide the Tigers into the top six. Unfortunately, they were beaten by Orient, 2-1 on aggregate.

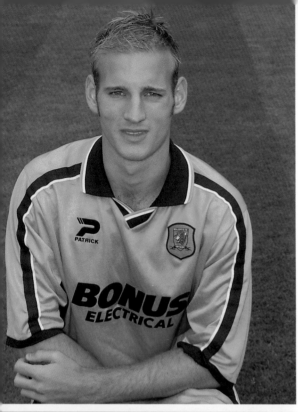

SIGNING SPREE: Lawrie Dudfield, Hull City's record buy at £245,000, who was one of more than a dozen new signings who arrived at the club during Adam Pearson's spend, spend, spend policy during the summer of 2001.

CASTING THE NET: Julian Johnsson, the Faroe Island international, who joined City as Brian Little scoured pretty much uncharted territory in his search for new players. Johnsson left the club after just one season, soon after Little was sacked.

GREAT DANE: Jan Molby, he might have been a legend at Liverpool, but he failed as manager at City and endured one of the shortest tenures in the club's history.

NEW RECRUITS: Jan Molby did make some shrewd signings before the start of the 2002-03 season, (from left to right) John Anderson, Stuart Green, Stuart Elliott, Greg Strong, Shaun Smith, Richie Appleby and Ian Ashbee. Some went on to achieve great things . . . others didn't.

Above:
FAREWELL
OLD FRIEND:
The crowd spill onto the pitch after the last match at Boothferry Park against Darlington on December 14, 2002. City lost 1-0.

Left:
FROM THIS:
The West Stand at Boothferry Park had clearly seen better times as Hull City prepared to move out.

Opposite:
TO THIS:
The magnificent Kingston Communications Stadium, built at a cost of £43m.

LOOKING GOOD: The KC Stadium in all its glory for the Yorkshire derby against Huddersfield Town in April 2004.

ANYONE FOR CRICKET?: This was the site of the KC Stadium, The Circle in West Park. It was previously the home of local Amateur Rugby League side West Hull while the ground was also on Yorkshire County Cricket Club's rota.

OLD PALS: Manager Peter Taylor (right) and assistant Colin Murphy who guided the club to back-to-back promotions and proved to be one of the most successful partnerships in City's history. They weren't always this happy though.

WHO ME?: Steve Melton celebrates after scoring the first-ever goal at the KC Stadium in a friendly against Sunderland.

WHAT A GOAL: Ian Ashbee (No 4) races off to congratulate Dean Keates after he scored the first league goal at the KC Stadium in the win against Hartlepool on Boxing Day 2002. A crowd of more than 22,000 watched City beat Hartlepool in Division Three.

YOU BEAUTY:
Stuart Elliott (centre) embraces Stuart Green (left) after his goal in the first league game at the KC Stadium against Hartlepool. Dean Keates (right) prepares to join the fun.

THE LUCK OF THE IRISH: Stuart Elliott (front centre) is bobbed by delighted team-mates after scoring City's winning goal against Swansea at the KC Stadium in the 2003-04 campaign. Elliott scored 14 goals that season to help City to promotion - and 27 the following season to clinch a place in the Championship.

IN - AND OUT: Portuguese goalkeeper Sergio Leite who was living proof that not everything Peter Taylor touched at City turned to gold.

Opposite:
THE WINNER:
Captain Ian Ashbee celebrates his goal in the win at Yeovil at the end of the 2003-04 season . . . .a result that clinched the first of Hull City's promotions under Taylor.

GETTING SHIRTY: Jason Price might not win any Mr Universe contest but he looks happy as he celebrates his hat-trick goal in a 3-1 win against Doncaster at the KC. Doncaster, though, had the last laugh and won the Division Three title ahead of City.

WETTING THEIR APPETITE: Taylor cracks open the champagne as he stands on the balcony at the City Hall amid the celebrations surrounding that first promotion. It was, said Taylor, the best day of his life . . . a statement that he was to often repeat in his time in charge.

Little went through April unbeaten and clinched the point that sealed a play-off place in a 1-1 draw at Southend on May 1. Fittingly, the goal came from Mike Edwards, a Hull-born defender who was a survivor of the Great Escape. Edwards had made his debut at the age of 18. Now, like his team-mates, he'd come of age. Little had worked wonders putting together a winning side. Musselwhite was in goal, the defence featured Edwards, Whitney, Whittle and Goodison. These were players who had all stuck with the club through the difficult times. Brabin was still a key figure in midfield, but Whitmore – troubled by injury and personal problems at home in Jamaica – was only a bit-part player. Up front, City possessed the 'little and large' pairing of Kevin Francis and Rodney Rowe with support from Eyre. None of the players were household names on a national scale. It didn't matter. City had shown tremendous spirit. Considering the events of the previous few months, it was staggering that the club had finished the season at all, never mind in sixth place and the play-offs. Their opponents were Orient. The two sides had to play each other on a home and away basis. The first leg, at Boothferry Park on May 13, saw Eyre give City a precious lead with the only goal of the game in front of 13,000. Afterwards, Little was the calmest man in the entire ground. Everyone else was talking about a possible appearance in a play-off final, but Little said: 'We're only at half time.' It was typical of him. A total of 3,000 City fans made the trek to Brisbane Road for the second leg in midweek. The team, however, looked jaded and lost 2-0, despite some heroics from Musselwhite.

Still, City had come through one of the most traumatic seasons in their history. Fans nonetheless wanted answers about what had happened during the previous regime. The FA confirmed it had handed all the details of their investigation over to the Fraud Squad. There was no action until May 2002, Buchanan and Hinchliffe were arrested along with former directors Ibbotson, Daykin, David Capper and Webster. Charges of corruption and fraudulent trading were considered. In March, 2004, the Crown Prosecution Service announced there was 'insufficient evidence' to charge anyone. Buchanan said he and his fellow directors felt vindicated. He said: 'I have been gutted by the whole affair and said from the beginning that we had done nothing wrong. Far from taking money out, as alleged, I lent £55,000 and more to the club. The whole thing cost me £150,000. This all came from an aggressive investigation by the FA and their compliance officer, Graham Bean. I can only assume because Stephen Hinchliffe was involved.' Buchanan defended his role and again insisted Hinchliffe had never acted as a shadow director. He also said the infamous grey-and-green coach had been independently valued by a finance company. He said: 'There was never any need to bring an investigation and we are all absolutely delighted our names have been cleared. It's unfortunate how it turned out. We bought Hull City as a hobby and toy.' The FA confirmed it would review all its files while Bean, who had left the FA, declined to comment. Buchanan has never returned to a football boardroom. Hinchliffe's business empire continued to attract investigation. However, that CPS decision meant the final link with City's past had been well and truly severed. Not, I thought, before time.

Chapter six:

A new beginning

June, 2001 - May, 2002

A new owner and new hope. That was the feeling among Hull City supporters during the summer of 2001. No one wanted a repeat of the trials and tribulations of the previous campaign. By City's standards, the off-season passed relatively quietly. Adam Pearson worked tirelessly, restoring the credibility of a club that had been damaged by a succession of previous regimes. It was a difficult task, but he quickly made progress. Soon, sponsors were flooding back. Confidence from the City Council – and the local business community – followed. As for supporters, there was a genuine feeling that City had the chairman – and the manager – to finally deliver a promotion-winning season. As for the team . . . well, that was a different matter.

Pearson and Brian Little knew changes had to be made. Finally, though, Pearson had the resources to make a major difference. For the first time since the days of Harold Neelder, City actually had a chairman who delivered what he promised. Little had worked remarkably well during the previous campaign, guiding City into the play-offs against considerable odds. He admitted: 'What the players achieved was outstanding and all credit to them. However, I think they accept that changes must be made if the club wants to continue to progress. We now have a very ambitious chairman and I share that ambition. I want to take this club forward.' It wasn't all football for Little. He got married that summer and headed off to the Caribbean on a honeymoon. Rumour has it that before he left, he handed a piece of paper to Adam Pearson. It was a list of the players he was interested in signing. By the time he returned, every single one of those players had arrived at Boothferry Park. That, in many ways, was typical Pearson: totally professional, totally thorough. He was determined to provide a team the fans deserved. My telephone hardly stopped ringing as Pearson revealed details of all those signings: all 13 of them. Twelve players left the club including former Great Escape heroes Brabin, Brown, Perry, Swales and Whitney. Other casualties included Bracey, Eyre, Francis, Harris, Marcelle and Jamie Wood.

Wood was certainly an interesting character. While with City, he'd joined the club's small but illustrious band of international players after being called up for the Cayman Islands. I recall arriving at training one day and 'Woody' – footballers are nothing but original when it comes to nicknames – asked me: 'Where are the Cayman Islands?' 'Why,' I replied. 'Are you going there on holiday.' 'No,' he said. 'I'm playing for them next Saturday.' He duly made two appearances for the Cayman Islands, including a game against Jamaica whose line-up included Goodison and Whitmore. Three City players on the same pitch in an international. Was that a record? When Wood returned from his first game for the Caymans, everyone wanted to know where he'd been. So, it seems, did Woody. 'So where were the Cayman Islands?' I asked. 'Err, somewhere near America,' came the reply. Wood was one of several players who had struggled to make an impact at Boothferry Park. He had a decent pedigree, having come through the youth system at Manchester United. However, he wasn't the first player to struggle to progress.

Goodison and Whitmore at least survived that end of season clear-out, but their days at Boothferry Park were rumoured to be numbered too. The pair of them had not really lived up to their reputation, or early claims that they would net at least £1m on the open transfer market. Rob Smith recalled: 'I don't think I've ever met two such laid back characters in my life as Ian and Theo. I can remember being a designated driver for away games when the club couldn't afford to pay for the team coach. To save on petrol, I'd pick up several of the local players, including Justin Whittle and Steve Harper, in my car. There was barely room to swing a cat and we literally had to shoe-horn everyone in and out, especially with all the kit bags and footballs and the like. We'd then meet up with the two Jamaicans en-route and they would follow us in their hire car. One minute, you'd be looking in your mirror and they were about two miles behind. The next, they were sitting on your rear bumper two inches away. I think Theo was driving but when I looked in my mirror, I'd swear to this day that they both had their feet on the dashboard.' The two Reggae Boyz were still regular members of the Jamaican squad and spent a good deal of time flying back and forth to the Caribbean. The exact date of their return always seemed to be shrouded in doubt. Smith added: 'When they got called up for international duty, they'd drive down to London and just abandon their car somewhere near Heathrow. There were all kinds of security alerts. The car was registered to the club so we'd get the call from Scotland Yard.' Goodison and Whitmore were away on international duty most of that summer and so missed the many comings and goings. There weren't too many shocks surrounding the players who had been allowed to leave.

Perhaps the one surprise was the decision to release Brabin. He'd become a cult figure with the fans and had hardly missed a game the previous season. He was a character – on and off-the-pitch. Some said he'd never be as influential after Joyce had departed, but he showed tremendous loyalty to the club. Brabin, more than anyone, epitomised the spirit that had dragged City through the dark days of the previous two seasons. His commitment never faltered. He was a better player – and a better trainer – than a lot of people gave him credit for. However, he didn't fit into Little's plans for the new campaign. There was a feeling in some quarters that, because Brabin was still a big friend of Joyce's, he was a link with the past; a past Pearson wanted to bury. Brabin made almost 100 appearances for City and never gave less than 100 per cent. Today, he's survived a heart scare that ended his playing career and he is now managing Blue Square Premier League side Cambridge United with some success. He said: 'It was a genuinely sad day when I left Hull. I thought I still had another season in me. I'll always look back on my time there as the highlight of my career. When I signed for Hull all my mates told me I was mad. The first time I walked into the dressing room, I agreed with them. The attitude was all wrong. Too many players seemed resigned to relegation. That's why Joycey changed things. That's why he brought the new players in. We went from losers to winners. No one wanted to play against us. It's a shame we didn't really build on that, but everyone can look back on that season with a lot of pride.' When Brabin left City, he signed for Torquay and was promptly sent off on his first return to Boothferry Park with his new club. That, in many ways, was Gary Brabin – nightclub bouncer, Hull City legend.

His departure left something of a void in Little's squad, but City quickly brought in those dozen or so replacements. The list of new signings featured Gary Alexander, David Beresford, Rob Matthews, Lawrie Dudfield, Matt Glennon, Julian Johnsson, David Lee, Nicky Mohan, Ben Petty, Michael Price, Ryan Williams and Scott Kerr. Holt turned his loan move from Oldham, into a longer-term deal. Most of the players cost sizeable fees and Dudfield – £225,000 from Leicester – represented a new club record. Dudfield and Alexander formed an attacking spearhead. Wingers Beresford and Williams would supply the ammunition. Johnsson, Lee and Kerr would add to the competition in midfield. The experienced Mohan and Petty would stiffen the defence. Glennon was reported to be one of the most promising goalkeepers in the country. Pearson had been true to his word. He'd promised funds would be available for new signings. In all, he spent more than £1m. It was all too easy to get carried away on the tidal wave of expectation. In hindsight, were there too many new signings? Pearson admitted so later.

Little faced a difficult task helping the various recruits settle in. The first pre-season training session took place in a public park, a few hundred yards along the road from Boothferry Park. Little insisted the players had their names on the back of their training kit so he could recognise everyone. The atmosphere was certainly different. All the talk among the players back then had been whether their next pay cheque would bounce. Pearson's considerable backing meant City had become the big spenders of the bottom Division. Some rivals were not happy that a club which had gone into administration – with debts of at least £2m – could recover and flourish so quickly, and without punishment. There is little doubt that events at City before the Pearson takeover led to the football authorities re-thinking the rules and regulations regarding clubs entering administration. It is also worth remembering that some of the local businesses owed money by the previous City regime did not receive a penny. Some of them never recovered. Pearson was determined to look to the future. He made attempts for more fan involvement; something that had always undermined Lloyd's efforts. One of his first decisions was to scrap the logo designed by Hinchliffe's son. It was a masterstroke, an example of successful PR that Lloyd could – and should – have done.

When Little's new-look side won their opening fixture, 3-1 at Exeter, the bookmakers were deluged with bets on the City going up. Little was always a relaxed figure. He was always helpful too, always willing to talk. He would give a one-on-one interview after a game – win, lose or draw. At one training session early on in the season, he was suffering from a cold. He could have opted not to be interviewed. Instead, he invited me into his car and we talked for ages. He didn't mind criticism of his side or himself provided it was fair and balanced. He never ranted and raved. That didn't mean he couldn't deliver the odd verbal ear-bashing to his players. However, what was said was always kept behind closed doors. That's exactly how it should be. He could be protective about some things: For example, he never gave me his home telephone number. I secured it from other sources, but never used it. By mid-September, City were at the top-of-the-table following wins against Rochdale and Swansea.

That new attacking spearhead of Alexander and Dudfield – they'd cost over £500,000 between them – were scoring goals. Not every game went to the master-plan. For example, City lost 4-2 at Mansfield after being out-played and out-fought. But, when there was a set-back, it usually meant another new signing would arrive: Richard Sneekes, Michael Ready, Caleb Folan and, later in the season, Adrian Caceres and Jason Van Blerk. Johnsson was perhaps the most unusual of all the new signings. He was certainly City's first player from that renowned hot-bed of football – the Faroe Islands. 'We have more sheep than people,' he once told me, 'but we love our football more than the sheep. Everyone in the country is a big fan of Manchester United but they know a bit about Hull City now.' Unlike some of those summer signings, Johnsson was a regular. Kerr never got to kick a ball. Lee scored one superb goal – a stunning free kick in a 4-0 thrashing of York – and was rarely seen again. City lost in the early stages of the FA Cup to Oldham and were knocked out of the Worthington Cup by Derby, who were then in the top flight. A feature of the visit to Derby was their impressive new stadium Pride Park. It had earned high praise, but would – we were told – be bettered by the City's new home.

Off-the-field, it was all quiet after the drama of the previous few years. With Pearson in control, all eyes were on the new stadium – and football instead of the High Court. City went through October with an unbeaten record and Alexander scored in four of the five games during that month. November started with a 5-1 win against Cheltenham in front of more than 9,000 fans at Boothferry Park. The following week City lost 4-0 at Hartlepool and 2-1 at Lincoln. For all the resources at his disposal, Little was still striving for consistency. It was a similar story in December. City whipped Exeter 3-0 at home, but lost 2-1 at Scunthorpe, drew 0-0 at home to Southend and were then thumped 3-0 at Kidderminster Harriers, who appeared to be inspired by manager Jan Molby. By Christmas, City were struggling to stay with the promotion pack. After a 1-0 defeat at Plymouth on January 12, there was a rare show of anger from Little when he was asked about City's chances of promotion. You could sense his feeling of despair. The look on Pearson's face after that game also said it all. He was becoming increasingly concerned. City needed attendances of around 8,000 to break even. He needed the prospect of promotion to stay on the agenda.

In many ways, that Plymouth game summed up City's season. They might have salvaged a point. Whitmore produced a sublime piece of skill to dance through virtually the entire Plymouth side, only to fall flat on his backside as he attempted to tap the ball into an empty net. Pearson reacted to those fears about promotion. More new signings had arrived – including centre half Matthew Wicks. As the goals from Dudfield and Alexander dried up, striker Neil Roberts was drafted in on-loan. Still, City still lacked consistency. Pearson increasingly sought out the opinion of people outside the dressing room in a bid to solve what had gone wrong. Relationships between chairman and manager became fraught. There were rumours of a fall out, and Little was annoyed when Pearson started to criticise the team in public. These were worrying times. However, reports that the pair fell out after Little went shopping, instead of meeting his chairman to sign a new player, were wide of the mark.

A top six finish was still a possibility until, after a 1-0 defeat at Swansea at the start of March, Pearson lost patience. I knew he wasn't happy with the performances of the team. He called me at lunch-time to tell me he was meeting Little that afternoon. He 'advised' me not to stray far from the phone later that afternoon. I guessed what was going to happen. At tea-time, he rang and said. 'Brian has gone.' Pearson outlined the reasons behind his decision. It was almost as though he needed reassurance that he'd got things right. My next call was to Little. Although genuinely disappointed, he refused to criticise either the chairman or the club. Indeed, with typical professionalism, he wished City all the best for the future. Deep down, I could sense the hurt in his voice and the frustration that he could not deliver promotion. He wouldn't be leading City into life at their new £38m home either.

The big move was set for the middle of the following season. I genuinely thought Pearson had acted hastily, a fact he admitted himself a few months on. Pearson, though, was totally driven by success. He could, at times, be dictatorial. There again, we'd all seen what could happen when more than one person took charge of the club. It was clear Pearson's first full season in charge was heading for a frustrating climax, despite that substantial outlay on new players. Would Little have turned things around if he'd stayed on? Would he have secured a play-off place? Would he have led City to promotion the following season? We'll never know. As ever, Billy Russell took charge on a caretaker basis, assisted by Rod Arnold. City won their first match after Little's departure, 4-1 against Mansfield with Bradshaw on target.

Later to be assisted by the now retired Neil Mann, Russell had worked tirelessly re-building City's battered and bruised youth system. Yet, for all their efforts, Bradshaw was one of the few young players to have progressed through the ranks. At one stage, Bradshaw looked to be a cracking prospect. Like many before him, he failed to make the grade. Despite that win against Mansfield, the dream of an automatic promotion place had long since disappeared. The play-offs, though, were still a possibility, which made the Little decision even more baffling to me. Unfortunately, City only won one of their last ten games. They finished 11th - 12 points off the last play-off place, claimed by Rushden and Diamonds. Before the end of the campaign, Pearson had appointed a new manager – former Liverpool star Jan Molby. The Dane signed a three-year deal after resigning from Kidderminster the week before he was appointed by City. Kidderminster were furious. There were allegations Molby had been approached illegally. Kidderminster demanded compensation. A figure of £100,000 was mooted. Eventually, an agreement was reached. Molby settled into the manager's chair along with his assistant Gary Barnett. Pearson said 'We've got the ideal man to take this club forward. Jan shares my ambition and passion. In fact, his determination to succeed made him the ideal candidate. He understands football and he has a hunger to manage at the top level.' Molby kept a pretty low profile immediately following his appointment. There were only a couple of games left to play. As for Pearson, his five-year master-plan for Premier League football had suffered a set back.

It was, he promised, only a temporary delay.

Chapter seven:

Home, sweet home

July 2002 - May 2003

The sky-line of Hull was changing massively in the summer of
2002. As the steelwork for the new stadium rose above West
Park, it could be seen from miles around. It was all change at
City as well. Jan Molby began his own building work. Just
before the end of the previous season, football had been rocked
by the collapse of a multi-million pound deal with ITV, which
had negotiated a deal for exclusive coverage of all games below
the Premier League. Clubs were set for a bonanza. Many
chairmen spent the money before it came through. Then ITV
pulled the plug. It was widely thought many lower Division
clubs, who were relying on their share-out from the TV contract,
would go bust. Not all those clubs were as fortunate as City, who
had a wealthy owner in Adam Pearson backed by an even
wealthier benefactor, Peter Wilkinson. While other clubs
panicked, Pearson assured fans that City's finances were in good
order He said the collapse of the ITV deal would not affect his
plans. Again, true to his word, he backed his manager with a

number of new signings that summer.

The first player to arrive was Stuart Green, a talented young midfielder snapped up on loan from Newcastle. City splashed out £175,000 to sign Northern Ireland international Stuart Elliott from Motherwell. Elliott was largely unknown and a few fans were stunned by the price City had paid. Molby promised the player 'would score goals.' He also brought in two new centre halves from the Premier League in Scotland: Greg Strong and John Anderson. His search for a left back finally ended when he persuaded Shaun Smith to leave Crewe and head across the Pennines. The arrivals continued. Molby raided his former club Kidderminster to sign Richie Appleby who, according to the City manager, was one of the best play-makers outside the top flight. Last, but not least, Molby snapped up Ian Ashbee from Cambridge United. Ashbee had been a tremendous servant to Cambridge, helping them to promotion. However, he decided to move on and his name was duly circulated to other clubs. He recalled: 'A few clubs were sniffing around. I went to Oxford and Northampton. In fact, the morning I was going to Oxford to think about signing, Jan Molby rang. The call came out of the blue. He said he wanted to sign me, told me what was happening at Hull, and so I thought: Why not go up there and have a look around.' He headed to Hull, met Adam Pearson and Molby and also looked at the new stadium. 'We met at Boothferry Park and let's face it, the old ground didn't exactly win me over,' he said. 'Hull was a club with a great tradition and generally, Boothferry Park was regarded in the game as a horrible place to go to. Away teams didn't like playing there. But I met the chairman and he had tremendous ambition. I got to look at the new stadium being built and just thought: There's only one way this club is going.'

All the new arrivals settled in well as Molby guided his team through a busy pre-season programme. Elliott made one of his first appearances on a wet and windy night at Whitby Town, whose ground overlooks the North Sea. He was so frail looking, he looked to be in danger of being blown into the nearby harbour. However, Elliott scored two goals, and appeared to have 'springs' in both his boots. He gave his first interview after the match that night and surprised everyone when he revealed God had told him to come to Hull. He was – and still is – a deeply religious man. Strong and Anderson were solid, no-nonsense characters at the back, as you'd expect from two players who had regularly appeared in top flight Scottish football. Appleby missed much of the build-up through injury, earning the nick-name 'sick note' from fans. When he played, he looked promising; the ideal partner for the more competitive Ashbee. Molby, though, just couldn't get Appleby on the pitch often enough. Generally, the mix of old and new pointed towards a promising season. Once again, talk of promotion filled the air. Molby was keen to play down the expectations.

I found him a difficult man to work out. One minute he was my best friend. The next, he'd cut me short or even refuse to speak. I remember a pre-season game at Selby. He kept me waiting a good 30 minutes after the game, and then walked straight past. He was a legend on Merseyside; the red part of it at any rate. To me, he seemed aloof and almost arrogant – not in the same League as either Joyce or Little. A week after that Selby game, City visited Goole, and Molby became embroiled in a row with a fan that almost ended in fisticuffs. It was not a good sign. There is no doubt Molby arrived in Hull with a good reputation as a manager and a coach. You could not argue with his record as a player. The guy was a magician. He'd worked wonders at Kidderminster – and on a shoe-string too. One of his first moves at City was to establish a new training base. Again, I found myself as the go-between, tipping Pearson and Molby off about some spare land next to Cottingham Golf Club. The site was on a slope, but City moved in. There was no changing accommodation. The players would get stripped at Boothfery Park and drive to Cottingham in their cars. Then, after training, they'd drive back to Boothferry Park for a shower. I could never understand why they didn't use the facilities at the golf club. They'd probably have saved themselves in fortune in car valleting bills.

More than 10,000 fans attended the first match of the season at home to Southend. City were expected to stroll to victory. They drew 2-2, and Ashbee was sent off. Three days later, City drew 1-1 at Bristol Rovers. This time, Strong was sent off in the closing stages. In the post-match interview, Molby laid into Strong – his captain – and basically said he was unprofessional and had cost City the game. I couldn't believe what Molby had said. I even checked if he wanted his quotes to appear in the paper. He replied: 'You're supposed to be a journalist. I've said it. It's up to you whether you write it.' When the story duly appeared Molby, rang to complain. He never actually accused me of missquoting him, but he didn't like the tone of the story. What was I supposed to have done? He'd said pretty much the same thing on the radio straight after the game.

City duly lost two of their next three matches: 3-1 at Exeter and 2-0 at Hartlepool. By now, I thought I'd got to know Exeter pretty well. Wrong. Sure enough, I took a wrong turning after leaving the ground and it took another hour to reach the M5. City were also losing their way. After the defeat at Hartlepool, Molby ripped into his players again. I could see now why a colleague, who had covered Kidderminster during the Molby era, had told me that I'd never be short of quotes. City's players were stung by the public criticism from their new manager. Rumours began to circulate that all was not well in the dressing room. However, wins at Cambridge and at home to Carlisle lifted some of the pressure and silenced the cynics. Whittle – back in the side because of an injury to Strong – scored the winning goal at Cambridge. Alexander scored a superb hat-trick in the 4-0 drubbing of Carlisle. The rot set in nonetheless. City failed to win any of their next three games. A 3-1 defeat at home to Macclesfield was particularly embarrassing. City were booed off at half time and at the final whistle. Molby was not happy. Neither was Pearson. Neither was Alexander, who was reduced to training with the youth team.

When City lost again – ironically at Kidderminster – on October 5, Molby was sacked. His reign of 16 games was one of the shortest by any manager in City's history. To be honest, I felt he'd got what he deserved. Ashbee explained: 'It just didn't work out as well as we thought it would. Jan definitely lost the dressing room. It is always hard when a manager comes in and is working with a lot of players he hadn't signed. He'd inherited players from two previous managers. Personally, I don't think his management skills were very clever. Some of the things he said in the press were spot on, but he shouldn't have said it in public. He should have kept it 'in house.' He was maybe being too honest. The players got touchy. Some players can take that sort of criticism. Some can't. To be fair, I think Jan lost it pretty early on. Maybe some of the lads didn't like running around for him.' City had been tipped by many experts as promotion certainties. Just two months into the new season and they were looking for a new manager – again.

Russell took over as caretaker – for just one game at home to Rochdale. By then, Pearson had appointed Molby's successor Peter Taylor, who had managed Leicester in the top flight. What attracted Pearson was Taylor's experience in gaining promotion in the lower Divisions with Brighton and Gillingham. He'd also managed England at senior level, albeit for one game in which (he often reminded me) he'd handed David Beckham the captaincy for the first time. He was also a successful and respected coach of the national Under 21 side, working with some of the country's top young players. When his name was first linked with the City job, many people suggested it was too far north for him. He and his family were settled in the south-east. But Taylor was duly introduced to the crowd before the Rochdale game. City won 3-0 with on-loan strikers Phil Jevons and Michael Branch getting the goals. Ironically, Russell revealed after the match that Molby had actually picked the winning team before clearing his desk. I met Taylor straight after the game. The interview took place in the car park, just behind the main stand. We were backed up against a fence, and Taylor was almost wiped out before he'd taken the job. The driver of the Rochdale team coach reversed and came within inches of squashing Taylor – and me – against the fence. It would have been carnage, but I shoved Taylor out of the way in the nick of time. I thought he'd have been grateful. At his press conference on the Monday afternoon, Taylor still kept me waiting until last in line. Then, he took me into the corridor which led to the home dressing room. He stood there and drew an imaginary line across the corridor with his foot.

'You,' he said, 'will never cross that line.' I never did. Early on, he was deeply suspicious of the media, not surprising given the bad press he'd received after being hounded out of the job at Leicester. There again, he had signed Ade Akinbiyi. It wasn't the best of starts for me and there was certainly no place on the team coach for Taylor's first official game in charge at Torquay. City won 4-1 and Ashbee scored a real corker. Pearson – as ever – backed his new manager with cash for new signings. Taylor raided Leicester to sign Damien Delaney, a promising young Irish defender. Another of his ex-players – Danny Webb – soon followed. We were told Webb had been brought in to score goals. City were unbeaten in their next six games under Taylor. A whirlwind start. Slowly, his icy attitude started to melt. The promotion bandwagon was rolling again. By now, all attention was turning to the new stadium.

Work had finally been completed. I'd visited the stadium on a regular basis over the previous 18 months. After all the politics of the Lloyd era, I couldn't actually believe it when work had started. Now, it was amazing to see the final, finishing touches being put in place. It looked magnificent, almost out of place in Hull. My only doubt was the location of the press box – at the back of the very top tier of the West Stand and miles away from the dressing room and the players' tunnel. You'd need binoculars to see anything. Perhaps that was Taylor's influence. It was confirmed Premier League Sunderland would provide the opposition for the first game – a friendly for the Raich Carter Trophy. It was a nice touch as Carter had given such tremendous service to both clubs. The first League game would be against Hartlepool on Boxing Day. Before then, Taylor tried to focus his players on the League, and not their pending move to a new ground. When Delaney scored a fluke goal in a 1-0 win against Boston on November 23, no one thought it would be the last goal ever scored by a City player at Boothferry Park. Why? Well, Darlington still had to visit the famous old ground for the last game. They gate-crashed the farewell party, winning 1-0 in front of almost 15,000 fans. It was sad to see the old place go. A lot of fans had tears in their eyes. Boothferry Park was much loved, even though it had hardly been a lucky ground over the years. Personally, I was glad to see the back of it and the rickety steps of the Main Stand that led to the press box. If it was raining, you took your life in your hands. I recall Buchanan telling me – with a smile on his face – that City's insurance did not cover me for an accidental fall. I could understand the tradition of the old ground and the hold it held over many of the fans, who had been watching City through thick – but mainly thin – for many years. But, given the fact it was falling down, I couldn't comprehend why some wanted to stay at the place. The new facilities at the KC were state of the art. I wondered what Lloyd must have thought on that opening night. When the floodlights were switched on for the first time, it was the culmination of almost six years of hard work.

It was a long and drawn out process. At many stages, it looked like the whole scheme would collapse. There were arguments about the colour of the seats; football fans didn't want black-and-white (the colours of the rugby league club); rugby fans didn't want black and amber. Now, on opening night, there it was: a spectacular vision of brilliant white from the outside, equally as impressive on the inside. It is impossible to under-estimate the importance of the stadium in City's resurrection. If the club had stayed at Boothferry Park, it could well have been the end of the line. Certainly, Pearson's arrival on the Hull sporting scene was timely. There was a school of thought that the City Council never wanted to do business with Lloyd – or Buchanan and Hinchliffe for that matter. However, John Cooper dismisses that out of hand. 'Right back at the start of the scheme, I can remember going to Sheffield with a representative of Hull City Council (John Topliss) to meet Buchanan and Hinchliffe in Sheffield,' he says. 'I was told to drive to Sheffield railway station and then wait for instructions. There was nothing sinister or secret about that. It's just there wasn't any satellite navigation and we knew where the station was. We were directed to a palatial mansion house in Dore, a suburb on the other side of Sheffield to the motorway and the station. When we drove in (to the mansion house) the gate opened and the first thing you saw were peacocks and a row of vintage cars. This was the base of Hinchliffe's business empire. John Topliss was beside me in the car. It was the first meeting between City's directors at the time and Drivers Jonas about the new stadium. It all went back to that time. There were definitely meetings. I should know. I was there. It was a very interesting meeting. Certainly, the plans were exciting but I came away knowing the key to it all was keeping Hull City at Boothferry Park in the short term. I still say that if we'd moved to the Boulevard, the club wouldn't have been here now and there would have been no need for a stadium. Professional sport in this city would have gone.'

Initially, there had been opposition to the stadium, not least because it was built in a popular public park. Campaigners also hit out at the cost – an estimated £34m – claiming the council's money could have been spent on better things, such as hospitals and new schools. As the opening of the new stadium approached, there was a major PR exercise, aimed at promoting the complex's benefits for the entire community. Pearson had been appointed chairman of the Stadium Management Board. (SMB). He was joined by representatives from Hull Sharks and the City Council. Effectively, though, he was in charge. He promised an exciting future and was already looking at the possibility of further development in the immediate area. Pearson said: 'I certainly think the business potential of developing around the stadium is something that interests me in the long-term. With conference facilities, banqueting and exhibitions likely to be staged here, there will be a need for some beds so I can see the need for a hotel – and maybe a casino – to offer a completely inclusive package.' City and the Sharks had to pay for the pleasure of actually playing at the new stadium, and Pearson warned about the increase in rental charges for the football club. He said: 'It is an absolutely massive increase - about 15 to 20 times what we were paying at Boothferry Park. The utility company charges are going up ten-fold. Operating costs will be high but we believe they can be controlled.' He also said he was talking to Boothferry Park's owners about the possibility of using the club's old ground for training and reserve team matches. No agreement was ever reached.

That opening game against Sunderland took place on December 18. A crowd of 22,407 saw City beat their top flight opponents 1-0. The scorer of the first ever goal at the KC was Steve Melton. The new facility was declared a major success. Even Sunderland, who had recently moved into The Stadium of Light, were impressed. So were a long list of dignitaries who had been invited to the opening match. The first ball on the new pitch

– plastic inserts and all – was kicked by life-long Tigers' fan Frank Barratt. He could remember watching the first-ever game at Boothferry Park, in 1946. He said: 'Of course, I'll miss the old place. I've got some great memories . . . although not too many from the last two or three years. I certainly won't miss the cramped seats, the poor views, the smelly toilets and the bucketful of rust that fell on your head every time the ball hit the main stand roof.' There was another 20,000-plus crowd on Boxing Day for that inaugural League match against top-of-the-table Hartlepool. Goals from one of Molby's last signing as City's manager, Dean Keates, and Green clinched a 2-0 victory. Keates admitted the new surroundings had brought the best out of City's players, saying: 'It was great scoring the first League goal there. I wonder how many people will remember that in years to come?' For Ashbee, the game was a major part of City's progress. He said: 'You can't help but be impressed by the place. It's a bit different to Boothferry Park. It almost looks out of place at this level of the game.' As for Taylor, he was more concerned with the three points. He said: 'I told the players to forget the pomp and ceremony and make sure we made a winning start and we did. Everything about the stadium is first class. The challenge is to go on from here and to make sure the fans keep coming back.'

A new stadium, a new team and a new-ish manager. City were the envy of all the rivals in the Division, and many other higher-ranked clubs. Everyone thought Taylor's Tigers would go on and clinch promotion that season. It didn't happen. City were frustratingly inconsistent. A top heavy squad was carrying too many players; players who weren't good enough for a promotion challenge. Taylor was a good and a shrewd manager. He wasn't though, a miracle worker. He could only pick 11 players. Those not in the side on a regular basis became disillusioned with life at the club. At the start of February, City were stuffed 3-0 at Taylor's former club Southend United. It was a shocking display and Southend manager Rob Newman certainly stuck the boot in with his post-match comments, which were along the lines of money not guaranteeing anything.

Taylor was already brassed off before that game. Things weren't going his way and if fans weren't complaining about tactics and selections, they were moaning about the amount of time Taylor spent at home in Kent. After the Southend game, he resigned but was persuaded to carry on in a frantic telephone conversation with Pearson. I wasn't privy to exactly what had been said. At that time, I was banned because of the fiasco concerning the Hull Daily Mail's decision to door-step Stuart Elliott. Elliott's family allegedly had links with a terrorist organisation in Northern Ireland. The paper knew about the rumours and decided to interview Elliott – without the club's or Taylor's permission. To compound the problem, the paper sent a reporter to carry out the interview on a Friday, the day before a game. I knew there would be trouble. I rang Taylor – even though I knew my job could be on the line – to tell him what the paper was doing. He went ballistic. He drove to Elliott's home and stopped the interview. In the event, the Hull Daily Mail did publish an article based around Elliott's religious beliefs. Taylor – backed by Pearson – banned the paper. He told me: 'We're going to have to ban you as well, otherwise there's not much point.' As a result, I couldn't speak to the players but Taylor kept me supplied with a steady stream of information. When relationships were restored, the Hull Daily Mail agreed not to approach players without the club's permission, especially on the day before a match.

City were marooned in mid-table. There was time to mount a challenge for the top six, but their form rarely suggested that would happen. Taylor was already looking to the following season. He brought in Jon Walters on loan and he promptly scored two goals on his debut in a 5-1 win at Carlisle. That Carlisle victory showed what might have been. Two weeks later, though, and City lost 4-2 at title-chasing Rushden. Those two results highlighted the problems Taylor had faced all season – a struggle for goals. Taylor did not think Alexander and Dudfield were the answer. Towards the end of the campaign, he signed a new striker, Ben Burgess. Another forward, Danny Allsopp, was to follow in the summer. City, though, lost three of their final four games of the season, including a humbling 4-2 defeat at Swansea on the last day. They finished 13th, behind the likes of Cambridge, Kidderminster, York, Torquay and Oxford – five clubs who today aren't even in the Football League. Rushden topped the table – 28 points clear of City.

Pearson's master-plan was on hold. And the jury was definitely still out on Taylor. Was he really the right person to take the club forward?

Chapter eight:

Up, up and away

June, 2003 - May, 2004

Another summer, another half million pounds spent, another batch of new players, another promotion-winning campaign to anticipate. The revolving door was in constant use again. That was the story behind the off-season of 2003. This time, though, the various events unfolded in a majestic new stadium, and not in a clapped out ground where what was left of the illuminated sign outside read:

Oothfery ark

When the inevitable inquests had started into the failings of the previous season, Peter Taylor said one of the major reasons was the fact that it wasn't his team. He'd already started the re-building progress in the closing weeks, spending more than £125,000 to sign Ben Burgess, a gangling striker. 'He'll score goals,' said Taylor. Somehow, I'd heard it all before. To partner Burgess, Taylor brought in Danny Allsopp – an Australian-born player with Premier League experience, albeit very limited, at Manchester City. Guess what? The manager promised he'd score goals as well. Jason Price was added to the squad to provide width, and crosses for the predatory Burgess to feed off. The defence was strengthened with the addition of Richard Hinds, Alton Thelwell and Andy Dawson. Thelwell arrived from Spurs while Dawson joined the select band of players who had crossed the Humber. He signed from Scunthorpe. Alan Fettis, a former City player under Terry Dolan, was brought back into the fold in a bid to solve the goalkeeping position. Just weeks after taking the supporters' player-of-the-season award, John Anderson was released. So was Melton, scorer of that first-ever goal at the KC. His next club was Boston United.

Taylor's international connections – and the fact he job-shared the City position with managing the England Under 21 side – had started to pay off. In June, the KC Stadium staged its first England game: an Under-21 friendly against Serbia and Montenegro. England secured a thrilling 3-2 victory and the FA hierarchy promised they would return. The following month, there was an even bigger star in town. Elton John performed the first concert to be staged at the KC. He performed to a packed-house, belted out hit-after-hit and the evening was a runaway success. The fact Elton John had visited Hull was proof of the impact the KC Stadium was having on the local feel-good factor. Somehow, it was hard to imagine him ever playing his piano at Boothferry Park. As one fan commented: 'If he'd tried, someone would have nicked it before he'd had time to sit down.'

Taylor stepped up his preparations. He took the City on a pre-season tour of Essex, playing friendlies against Canvey Island and Bishop's Stortford. That latter game was certainly interesting as the pitch was located about 500 yards from the end of the main runway at Stanstead Airport. I could almost pick out the faces of the passengers as the giant jets took off. City launched their campaign at home to Darlington. The cynics were still sniping, claiming Taylor was not committed to Hull and couldn't manage club and country. His new look side won their opening game, 4-1, in front of almost 15,000 fans. Four of his new signings – Burgess, Price, Thelwell and Allsopp – scored. The local bookies reported record business after that game. City's promotion odds were slashed. Surely nothing could stop them.

One of City's main rivals that season were Oxford. The two sides clashed at Oxford's new Kassam Stadium (it wasn't a patch on the KC) in the second game of the campaign. City lost 2-1 and Taylor was criticised for leaving out Whittle, the only (and much loved) survivor of the Great Escape, and playing summer signing Marc Joseph instead. Taylor positively bristled and lambasted me for suggesting Whittle deserved a place in the side. 'You can't pick a team on sentiment,' he said. 'Justin is a marvellous competitor. I know the fans love him but we're looking to take this club forward and we need defenders who can do more than run, tackle and head. They need to be able to pass the ball.' A 3-3 draw at home to Cheltenham the following week did not settle too many frayed nerves. Ironically, Joseph then suffered an injury, allowing Whittle to come back into the side. Fettis was also an early season casualty. Taylor raided his former club to sign Michael Kuipers on loan. Kuipers was certainly the first former Dutch SAS solider to pull on a City jersey. He was not someone you upset in a hurry. It was still early days and the manager's penchant for chopping and changing his side led to the nickname 'tinker Taylor.' City, though, impressed in the opening weeks of September, thrashing Kidderminster 6-1 with

Burgess bagging a hat-trick. The acid test was a top-of-the-table clash against Swansea on September 30. It was a Tuesday night. Amazingly, more than 20,000 fans packed into the stadium. At kick-off, an estimated 3,000-4,000 more were locked outside. Elliot scored the only goal of the game with a header that was fast becoming a trademark of his game. City were leading the promotion pack. Taylor attempted to calm the growing optimism. 'We've done well, but there's still a long, long way to go.' The fans were lapping up every minute of this new-found success. It was a long time since they had seen City at the top of any table.

Taylor's team appeared to be taking everything in their stride and a stunning 5-1 win at Northampton featured one of the best away performances I'd seen from them. They played fast, fluent, attacking football. They took their chances, and Northampton were blown away. Musselwhite was now in goal because Kuipers had returned to Brighton. City tried to sign Kuipers on a long-term basis but he was injured – and Brighton weren't particularly interested. Taylor turned his attentions elsewhere and confirmed he was trailing a young American-born goalkeeper called Boaz Myhill. Although on Aston Villa's books, Myhill was on loan at Macclesfield. He subsequently impressed in Macclesfield's 2-2 draw at the KC at the start of November. That Macclesfield clash had marked the start of a wobbly spell for City, and for Taylor. Myhill arrived and Taylor assured everyone the £50,000 fee would be a bargain. 'The lad has got potential,' he said. 'He could go all the way to the top.' I was on a night out with the family when Taylor rang me to tell me about Myhill's signing. He said: 'This is Bo's phone number and he's waiting for your call now. I've told him not to talk to anyone else so ring him.' I pulled off the M62, parked in a lay-by and half-an-hour later, the exclusive was in the bag. It was good of Taylor to ring me and tip me off, but he wasn't always that helpful. He could be frustratingly inconsistent with his various rules and regulations. One minute, he was my best friend. The next, my worst enemy. For instance, he would sometimes insist I had to ask him for permission to talk to an individual player. Fair enough. He rarely refused permission anyway. The next day, I'd ask permission again and Taylor would go off on one, telling me I should know by now that I could talk to who I wanted and basically not to waste his time. So, the following day, I'd button-hole a player only to find Taylor screaming in my ear: 'Hey, you know the rules. You ask for permission first.' Life was never dull.

City were still unbeaten at home going into December, but that proud record came to an end when Mansfield grabbed a surprise 1-0 victory. Neil Mackenzie – one of Ian Ashbee's best friends – scored the goal. City bounced back to beat local rivals York 2-0 with Myhill climbing off his sick bed to record a clean-sheet at Bootham Crescent. City's goal-scorers were Burgess and Jamie Forrester, who had been brought in to add some cover for the striking positions. Taylor also signed another of his former players, Junior Lewis, to bolster midfield. Lewis was a throwback to the days of Goodison and Whitmore. He was so laid-back, he was in danger of falling over. Sometimes, he played like that too. Taylor, though, was a big fan. Lewis, he pointed out, had twice helped him win promotions at other clubs. Three days after Christmas and City faced another top-of-the-table clash at the KC against Doncaster. The game attracted a record crowd of over 23,000 and Price relished the big-mach atmosphere. He bagged a hat-trick in a 3-1 win. Promotion fever was rampant. City reeled off four wins out of four in January, but just when fans began to dream of League One, the wheels came off. Taylor's side lost three games in a row against Torquay, Lincoln and Mansfield. They didn't score a goal during that sequence and Doncaster took full advantage to open up a sizeable lead at the top. That game at Lincoln almost proved to be my last covering City.

As we drove out of Sincil Bank, with Mick Matthews directing as usual, another car over-took a line of stationary traffic and ploughed straight into the back of us. I was travelling with a girl photographer, Susi Bateman. The force of the impact saw the lethal looking 'spiked' end of her tripod drive into the back of my seat. It stopped about an inch from my back. As the police stood and watched, the occupants of the car, who looked about 12 years old, ran off. When I saw how close the spike had come to perhaps killing me, I was sick on the side of the road. The police promptly breathalysed me. I never saw the mangled company car again.

After those three defeats, City needed a win and fortunately normal service was restored against Scunthorpe, Burgess scoring twice in a 2-1 victory. The points continued to roll in. Doncaster still led the title race, though City closed the gap with a nail-biting 2-1 success at play-off hopefuls Boston at the end of March. Into April, the penultimate month of the season, and with the tension mounting City could only draw 1-1 at Kidderminster in their next game – a clash which marked the end of loan signing Lee Marshall's career. He suffered a broken leg in a horrific tackle right in front of the main stand. I can still hear that 'snap' of bone. City were desperately close to promotion, but could only inch towards the final finishing line. A rare goal from Joseph secured a 1-1 draw at Macclesfield, while Lewis and Ashbee scored to earn a 2-2 draw at Southend.

The champagne was still on ice four days later when Huddersfield left the KC Stadium following a 0-0 draw. City suffered a blow in that Huddersfield clash when Burgess was injured in a challenge with visiting goalkeeper Paul Rachubka. The fans were incensed. City weren't even awarded a free kick. Burgess missed virtually the whole of the next season. So, it was on to Yeovil, hardly the venue you'd pick for a promotion party. The title was beyond City's reach, but a win would take them up. The game took place on a Bank Holiday weekend. I was travelling with City's press officer Brendon Smurthwaite and we'd driven down on the Friday, the day before the game. We were booked into the team hotel. The traffic was horrendous, particularly on the M5 around Bristol. It was stop-start for virtually two hours. Eventually, we got through the various jams. Clear road ahead. Then, Smurthwaite's phone rang. It was Pearson, asking if we'd wait at the next junction to pick up director Mal Branagan. Apparently, he was travelling to the South West with his the family. His wife wanted to drop him off before continuing to Cornwall. We were assured the Branagan clan were just minutes behind us. Two hours later, he finally arrived, after the team coach and Pearson's own car had raced by us while we waited at the side of the road. We got to the hotel at about ten o'clock. The kitchens had closed. The smile on Pearson's face said it all. 'I think they've left a sandwich for you,' he said.

On the morning of the game, we all went for a walk around the local town. It was one of the most important games in City's history but the players were amazingly relaxed. Taylor and his staff had done a tremendous job. The game was a tense affair. City scored early from a Stuart Green penalty. Yeovil equalised and the result could have gone either way. Then, deep in the second half, the ball broke to Ashbee 25 yards out and he curled an unstoppable shot into the top corner. Around 1,500 City fans, packed onto a tiny terrace behind one of the goals, went mad. City won 2-1. The scenes at the final whistle were amazing. It was City's first promotion since 1985. Nineteen years of agony and hurt were over. Taylor invited me into the dressing room to join in the celebrations. I was soon drenched in champagne. The players kept racing back outside to celebrate with the fans, who chanted for Pearson, surely the most popular chairman in the country at that moment. He, though, stayed in the corridor beneath the stand. He was clearly emotional. Those last few, nerve-wracking weeks had taken their toll. 'This is a time for Peter and for his players,' he said. 'Not me.' He did, though, shake my hand with the words: 'We've done it.' My mobile phone never stopped ringing on the return journey. At one stage, there were so many calls I had to tell people I'd ring them back. In my excitement, I thought I was ringing Smurthwaite, now on the team coach. Inadvertently, I'd scrolled down to the name below his (Brendon) on my list of saved numbers. The phone rang. A gruff voice growled: 'Nick Buchanan. Can I help you?' I hung up – quickly. As for Pearson, he headed back to Hull in double-quick time by helicopter. He had to attend a pop concert, featuring Blue and Girls' Aloud, at the KC Stadium that same night. The helicopter landed at Boothferry Park on the old pitch. Pearson was joined on the flight by Branagan and commercial director John Holmes. Guess what? I was never offered a lift.

There was just one game left to play – at home to Bristol Rovers. It threatened to be an anti-climax, but wasn't. City won 3-1 and there were more celebrations at the end of that game. No one wanted to go home. No one seemed to care City hadn't won the title. Someone even produced a trophy. A relieved Taylor admitted: 'It's a fantastic feeling. We've worked so hard for this. Winning promotion for the first time was superb. I think I even planted a bloody great kiss on Colin Murphy (his assistant). I just hope the cameras didn't pick that one up. Seriously, the players have done brilliantly. It's the first promotion but we've got to look to push on.'

Damien Delaney, the only ever present that season, added: 'I'm so proud – and so happy. Ever since I came to this club, I knew the potential. I can remember the first day I drove into the old ground. Half the letters were missing from the sign outside. I thought I was making a huge mistake. Now, look at this. It's been a long, hard slog, but we can look forward to League One next season and you know what? I don't think we've anything to fear.' As the celebrations finally died down – and the fans made their way home – Ashbee sat in a quiet corner of the home dressing room. 'It's one of the best days of my career but hopefully there are a lot more highs to come,' he said. 'This club has long way to go yet.' There was an open-top bus tour and a civic reception. The players who had secured promotion took centre stage. The staff, though, who had survived the previous few years, must have struggled to take everything in. I know I did. It was a very emotional day.

But the Premier League still looked miles away.

Chapter nine:

At the double

July, 2004 - May, 2005

There was no sign of Elton John at the KC Stadium in the summer of 2004. Instead, music fans had to make do with Canadian-born rocker Brian Adams, dubbed in some quarters as 'The Groover From Vancouver.' As far as Hull City fans were concerned, the star attraction was Nick Barmby. The Hull-born former England star had come home. Barmby's career had started at a local junior side, Springhead United. He was once a mascot at a City game at Boothferry Park, but that's as close as he got to playing for his hometown club. He wasn't the only potential star from the East Riding to slip through the recruiting net. Barmby's first club was Spurs. To be fair, City could hardly compete with the North London giants. He'd shone in the Premier League, first at White Hart Lane and then Everton, Liverpool and Middlesbrough. He then moved to Leeds. His 34 England caps included an appearance in the famous 5-1 thrashing of Germany in Munich. Now he'd decided to join City. He was arguably the biggest signing in the club's history; if not in terms of money then certainly in terms of profile. The cynics said his best days were over. Nevertheless, the fact City could attract a player of Barmby's calibre – and his willingness to come to the KC – highlighted their improving credibility. Barmby admitted: 'I'd always said I wanted to move back to Hull towards the end of my career. I'd watched the progress the club had made since Adam Pearson had taken over. The team had won promotion the previous season – for the first time in years. I looked at the KC Stadium and spoke to Pearson and Peter Taylor, and I realised it was only the start of things. They were really ambitious – and so was I. I wanted to put something back into my hometown club. People said I was mad, but I knew it was the right decision.'

Barmby wasn't the only new face. With Burgess sidelined by a career-threatening knee injury, Taylor needed a new centre forward. Several names were linked with City. Many fans hoped Taylor would make a move for another Hull-born player with top flight experience: Dean Windass. He was playing for League One rivals Bradford, but there were strong rumours that he wanted a move back to Hull. He'd first signed for City as a trainee in 1987 only to be told by the then manager Brian Horton that he would never be good enough to make it as a pro. Windass had a variety of jobs, from bricklayer to fish filleter, and played for local amateur side North Ferriby United. He was given a second chance by Terry Dolan and made the most of it before being sold to Aberdeen in 1995. The money from the transfer stopped City from going bust. Like Barmby, Windass went on to play in the Premier League. He should have played for England. He'd been asked to play for the Republic or Ireland, but couldn't find a suitable relative to help him qualify. Deano, though, wanted to come home. He told me as much in a number of telephone conversations that summer. 'Me and Nicky Barmby together,' he drooled. 'The dream team.'

I know Pearson would have sanctioned the move. Deano would certainly have put bums on seats at the KC. But Taylor wasn't interested, and I believe it was because he didn't want a larger-that-life character in his dressing room. Barmby was quiet and unassuming. Windass . . . well, Windass wasn't either of those. In the end, Taylor went for two forwards with slightly less of a profile: Aaron Wilbraham and Delroy Facey. Wilbraham was signed from Stockport County for £100,000. And, yes, Taylor promised: 'He'll score goals.' Leon Cort was brought in to strengthen the defence. Roland Edge, a left back from Gillingham – another player with an ex-Taylor connection – arrived in the opening weeks of the campaign to add competition. Michael Keane was the major addition in midfield and the Republic of Ireland born player was tipped to make a big impact. I remember meeting Keane just after he'd signed. He could talk for Britain and appeared to be particularly knowledgeable about horses and greyhounds. They said he had Romany blood in him too.

Taylor's rebuilding wasn't just confined to new arrivals. Among the departures was that Great Escape hero Justin Whittle. He'd been a bit-part player the previous season, making 18 appearances, the last of them in a 2-1 win at home to York. I always sensed Whittle was something of a thorn in Taylor's side. Yes, there was respect there but the manager preferred Joseph. The fans wanted Whittle. It was easy to see why Whittle was a favourite. He always took time out for the supporters, even if he was out shopping with his wife and kids. And those supporters hadn't forgotten his role in saving the club from relegation to the Conference. However, Cort's arrival, plus the presence of Delaney and Joseph, meant Taylor could not guarantee Whittle a place. So Sarge packed his bags for the final time and headed off to Grimsby. Whittle had always plied his trade in the lower Divisions. Nevertheless, Grimsby's Blundell Park ground must have come as something as a culture shock. Whittle admits: 'He (Taylor) knew what I could do and what I couldn't do. I always trained 100 per cent and gave 100 per cent when I played. But I needed to play so it was time to move on. Grimsby was the ideal move for me. My family was happily settled in the Hull area. The kids were at school. It was a 45-minute drive away. If I'd stayed at Hull, I might have got another chance. Who knows? But I made the decision to go. It was a sad day but all good things come to an end. I still regularly drive into Hull, past Boothferry Park. I always have a little look. In fact, they're still picking a few of my passes off the train line at the back of the East Stand. I was tempted to have a look at the old ground because I've got so many fantastic memories of the place. But I probably wouldn't have liked it. I know it overgrown and falling down. It's sad. At least, you'll never take away the memories – the times we had, the stories I could tell you. What happened, though, stays behind the dressing room door.' There are some who believe Whittle was treated unfairly. I'll always hold him in high regard as a player and a person. Popular and likeable, the fact is Whittle would have struggled to play at a higher level. As Taylor often reminded me, there's no room in football for sentiment. Then, he'd go out and sign another of his ex-players.

Thanks to his role in the Great Escape, Whittle will always have a special place in the hearts of City fans. And, as he waved farewell to the KC Stadium for the last time (at least as a player) he revealed the spirit of that epic season still lived on. 'I still bump into a few lads, including Joycey. He's the same as he always was although he's not driving a people carrier to matches now with half the team in it. I also saw 'Whits' (Jon Whitney). He's a physio now. He's actually mending players when he spent most of his career kicking lumps out of them.' Whittle was one of the last links with City's infamous past featuring those colourful characters Messrs Buchanan and Hinchliffe. I bet they never played knuckles with Sarge.

All eyes, though, were on Barmby. I remember the press conference called to announce his signing. The national media turned out in force. I'd never seen that before. It always used to be me, Radio Humberside and the local commercial station, if they could be bothered to send anyone. If they did, it was usually a dizzy blonde who tottered over the training pitch in skin-tight jeans, high heels and knew little or nothing about football. Taylor always used to seem to prefer talking to them than me. I can't understand why. The fact Barmby's conference attracted the 'big boys' was a sign of the changing times. Barmby incongruously made his City debut in a pre-season friendly at Canvey Island. I know people have a go about Hull . . . but Canvey Island? I ask you. It's like one big Butlins' camp. Walk down the main street and you almost expect to bump into Ted Bovis shouting: 'Hi-di-hi!' There were rumours City would head abroad in that pre-season. Taylor tried to tempt me with talk of a week or so in Spain, or Portugal. In years gone by, City had gone to America. Scandinavia was another possible destination. The club's all-time record win was 16-1 against Swedish side Trondhjem. Stan Alexander scored 11 goals. Mind you, that was before the First World War. Any foreign shore would have done. Unfortunately, Taylor decided to stay at home – very near to his home in fact. He took the players away to a training camp at a plush hotel in Essex. A couple of games were played in that area. On the Friday, City played at Dagenham and Redbridge. Driving through London on a Friday night is always a pleasure. While the team returned to their five-star hotel for the weekend, I had to drive back to Hull to work on the Hull Daily Mail's pre-season supplement. Then, it was back to Essex on Monday for that Canvey Island game. I got to know the M11 pretty well. At least, though, there was no congestion charge involved. Barmby's appearance attracted a good sized crowd, including the local fire brigade. They had arranged a couple of practice drills, which conveniently took place on a flat roofed building overlooking the ground. I stood a few yards away with City's football secretary Phil Hough. As usual, Houghie was wearing his club tie. As City's players ran out, one of the firemen looked in our direction, spotted the tie, and asked: 'Which one is he then?' I replied: 'The number eight.' The fireman came straight back: 'Not very big, is he?' 'No,' I said, 'but he can play. He won 30-odd caps for England.' The reply was predictable. 'So what's he doing playing for a crap team like Hull then?' 'He was born in Hull,' I said. 'I was born in Ramsgate,' added the fireman 'but I don't bloody want to go there too often.'

A few City fans had travelled to witness Barmby's debut. When he set up a goal with a typically incisive pass, even the local fire brigade were impressed. From day one, Barmby stressed he was proud to play for City. There was a bonus for him after his move to the KC Stadium. It meant he could get in free to watch his beloved Hull FC. There are some who think

Barmby only came back to Hull for one final pay day. Rubbish. It was never about money. He wanted to help Hull achieve their Premier League dream. The first time I met him, I could sense the passion, the determination. He'd been born in Hull. He'd moved back to Hull. He certainly hadn't come to finish his career in League One.

After the sterling efforts of the previous season, there was a whiff of promotion in the air at the KC. However, having taken so long to get out of the bottom Division, no one mentioned another promotion too loudly. It was probably tempting fate. But Taylor and the players did not lack confidence. When the season kicked off, City were installed as one of the title favourites. Once again, their spending power – based on Pearson's sound investment and regular 16,000-plus attendances – gave them an edge over many of their rivals. As far as the fans were concerned, Pearson could do no wrong. Not everything was going to plan for the chairman, though. His attempts to re-develop land surrounding the KC Stadium appeared to have stalled. Pearson had a vision of a hotel, a casino; perhaps even a sporting museum. As ever, there was also talk of various retail outlets. In this aspect – and only this aspect – he was no different to David Lloyd. Pearson, though, knew how to play the PR game. He and his top level of management staff all presented the right image and said the right things – again, unlike Lloyd. Pearson's success at driving through the development of the KC Stadium meant he certainly had the ear of the council and the respect of the business community. No one had a bad word to say about him. For some reason, though, all-important planning and funding for development projects always seemed to be channelled into schemes in other areas of the city. Visit the immediate approaches to the KC Stadium today and they are still wide-open spaces. There's a bowling green and a kids' paddling pool that always seems to be shut. There is no casino or hotel, though. The nearest shop has been boarded up for months. Looking at developments at other new stadiums up and down the country – Coventry, for example – and you can't help but feel everyone in Hull has missed a trick. Certainly, the Walton Street car park, which is used on match-days, would have benefited from some form of re-development – or at least having the pot-holes filled in.

City's season started with a home game against Bournemouth. There were 17,500 fans to give Barmby a rousing welcome. A Green penalty secured the points. It was a solid rather than spectacular start. Four days later, City headed off to Torquay, not always a happy hunting ground. I can remember driving to the game. It seemed a million years since that visit to the Pantomime with Joyce and his squad. Back then, City had been something of a laughing stock. Now, a few years on, they were a respected – and envied – club in League One. Elliott scored two goals in a 3-0 win. Elliott had been one of the stars of that first promotion, a tally of 14 goals only bettered by twin strikers Burgess and Allsopp. His performance at Torquay was to be the springboard for a memorable season. Barmby duly scored his first goal for the club at Port Vale, but it was not enough to stave off a 3-2 defeat. Thankfully it was a rare setback.

Bradford – with Windass – grabbed a 1-0 win at the KC. The game was televised live and Pearson hoped it would be a perfect occasion to show-off the club's new strip. At the last minute, though, the referee was worried the stripes on City's and Bradford's shirts were too similar. He ordered a change.

Bradford hadn't brought an alternative kit. City were forced to play in their away kit. In the first week of September, City headed to Huddersfield for another Yorkshire derby – minus their manager. Taylor was away with the England Under-21 side for a European Championship qualifier in Germany. City produced a woeful performance and lost 4-0. They were lucky it was only four. It was bitterly disappointing for around 5,000 travelling fans. To add to the feeling of frustration, it took the majority of those fans at least an hour to travel the short distance from the M62 to the Huddersfield's ground. The delay was caused by a temporary set of traffic lights at a railway bridge. There wasn't a workman in sight and a tiny hole in the road hardly merited the lights anyway. On the way to ground, the lights seemed to be stuck on red. On the way back to the motorway, they seemed to be stuck on red.

Taylor's assistant, the experienced Murphy, faced the press after the game. Murphy admitted City were poor, but was soon fending off questions that Taylor's absence was the sole reason for the defeat rather than the countless and very obvious individual errors. I'd spent plenty of time in Murphy's company. He could have entertained a packed house at the Palladium with his life story. It featured a very interesting spell in charge of the Vietnamese national side. After listening to some of Murph's memories, I always fancied visiting Saigon. I felt sorry for Murphy that afternoon. He was in an impossible position. He couldn't get away from the press conference quickly enough. On my return journey from Huddersfield, my phone rang. It was Taylor. 'What the bloody hell is going on?' he ranted. 'I hear you're blaming me for the defeat.' I'd actually tried to help Murphy in the press conference and warned him about the line of the questions he could expect. I was about the only journalist present who hadn't asked about Taylor's absence. I tried to explain that fact to Taylor. Listening was never one of his strong points. He wasn't convinced. 'You're out of line,' he said. 'You're talking bull. You're trying to stir things up for me. We didn't lose because I wasn't there. We lost because we were crap. I happen to know Alex Ferguson wasn't at a Manchester United match last season. Did everyone say they lost because he wasn't there? It's complete bollocks. People don't know what they are talking about.' With that, the phone went dead.

The pressure was clearly getting to Taylor. There was the constant sniping that he was unsettled in Hull because his wife didn't like it 'up north'. It was always suggested – and not always subtly – that he couldn't manage City and England at the same time. Critics said he was more interested in hob-knobbing with England's young stars and the FA's top brass. I know that was never the case. Taylor gave Hull City 110 per cent. He was totally committed, totally passionate. I'd been on the wrong end of enough of his rollickings to know how much he cared. That night, though, I genuinely thought Taylor might quit. He didn't. Pearson was worried about the dual role, but did not take any further action. Taylor carried on with both jobs. It was the sensible course to take. Had Pearson pushed Taylor, he would probably have walked away. However, he'd built his team at City. They were his players. The last thing Pearson wanted was another new manager, another Molby scenario. It can't have been easy for Taylor. I knew how much the England job meant to him. I also knew how much he wanted to bring success to Hull. He was always stressing City could only benefit from his association with the England squad. Fair enough. The Under-21 internationals did bring in some extra revenue and prestige. The KC certainly looked impressive on Sky Sports. As yet, though, there was no sign of the potential top flight loan signings that had been hinted at. Immediately after that Huddersfield game, fans were clamouring for Taylor's head. Or at least for him to resign from the England job. As ever, the row was quickly forgotten, largely because City started winning again. Elliott could hardly stop scoring and it was probably just as well because summer signings, Wilbraham and Facey, were hardly bursting the back of the net. Wilbraham was one of the nicest people you could wish to meet; almost too nice in fact, especially in a Division dominated by granite-like defenders who kicked anything and anyone that moved.

City did beat Blackpool and Peterborough, but were then held to a 0-0 at home by Stockport. A 2-0 defeat at Hartlepool followed. They were struggling to stay in the top six. Taylor was not happy after that Hartlepool game and stormed off after my second question at the post match interview. An hour later, he rang me and said: 'Right, what do you want to know?' Typical. The pressure became greater. One of the key games in the first half of the season was always going to be the visit of leaders Luton Town in mid-October. By now, Taylor had wisely abandoned his early season experiment of playing Junior Lewis as a centre forward. Facey grabbed his second goal of the season, Elliott banged in two more and Luton were sent packing on the back of a 3-0 defeat. 'You've just been mauled by the Tigers,' chanted the fans. They were spot on. That Luton clash sparked a 16-game run that featured just one defeat: a surprising 4-2 loss at Swindon on a snowy Saturday afternoon. One of Swindon's stars was striker Sam Parkin, who was being linked with a move to City in what would have been a record transfer. Some reports suggested the price could have been £600,000. Taylor certainly needed a reliable goal-scorer to boost his promotion aspirations and take some of the pressure of Elliott. He'd signed a number of strikers – from Webb to Walters – without finding the solution, though Burgess had been desperately unlucky with that injury. Parkin, Taylor assured us, was the answer. First, the deal was on, and then off. Finally, it never happened. With no alternatives, Taylor persevered with Facey who was never going to be a prolific scorer along the lines of Luton's Steve Howard. Wilbraham spent most of his time either injured or on the subs' bench.

Perhaps the defining moment of that season came in December during another Yorkshire derby against Sheffield Wednesday at Hillsborough. The crowd of 28,701 highlighted the importance of the occasion, although I'd swear there were at least 10,000 more supporters inside the stadium that night. There were at least 6,000 travelling fans from Hull. Unfortunately, Wednesday were totally unprepared and had seriously under-estimated the likely strength of City's following. There weren't enough turnstiles open and City fans were still trying to get into the ground at half time. It was totally unprofessional of the host club. City opened up a 3-1 lead after arguably their best performance under Taylor. Keane scored early on, and Barmby, who had been criticised because of his lack of goals, added two more, including a contender for goal of the season. He chested a through ball down and swept it into the back of the net in one glorious moment. Barmby reckoned that volleyed goal was the best of his career. Wednesday threatened a fight-back in the second half. But City defended superbly and Allsopp settled the contest when he came off the bench to score: 4-2. Even Taylor seemed taken aback by the level of the performance. For some reason, his interview with me took place in a broom cupboard. His message was: 'If we build on this, we've got every chance of going up.' City then won at Colchester with Elliott again on target alongside Ryan France, a Murphy discovery and a bargain buy from non-League football the previous season. France has one of the broadest Yorkshire accents I'd ever heard ('eeh-by-gum lad') and it always used to be a source of amusement as to how his team-mates – and Taylor – ever understood him. A week later, City faced another six pointer against Tranmere – and Brian Little, Whitmore and Goodison – at the KC. Under Little's astute management, Tranmere were one of City's main rivals for one of the two promotion places, along with Luton. In the build up to the game, Little dismissed any suggestions that he was bitter about his exit from City. I'd spent most of the week before the game trying to track-down Whitmore and Goodison. I was given a mobile phone number and a woman answered. 'Hi, is Theo there?' I asked. 'Who's asking?' came the reply. 'It's John Fieldhouse,' I said. 'Hold on a minute,' she said and then added: 'Sorry, he's out.' I had another number for Goodison. I rang it. The same woman (or at least it sounded like the same woman) answered. Again the same routine ending with 'Sorry, he's out.' I did bump into Whitmore before the game. He smiled and shook my hand. I told him about the calls. 'Why worry man?' he said. 'You should have made it up just like you always did.' City won 6-1. Tranmere lost two goalkeepers through injury. Whitmore was forced to go between the posts and spent most of the afternoon picking the ball out of the back of the net. Almost inevitably, Elliott scored a hat-trick. Needless to say,

Whitmore turned down a request for an interview after the game. I made some quotes up anyway. I spent Christmas Day that year on my own. Divorce can be a lonely experience. It's at times like that when you discover who your friends are. Taylor was among them. He gave me more advice – and more support – than people I'd known for years. He also gave me the telephone number of what he said was a 'bloody good solicitor.' I rang. When I was quoted a fee, I assumed it was for the whole divorce only to be told: 'That is our weekly charge, of course.'

City were playing at Blackpool on Boxing Day. They won 2-0, Elliott scoring both goals. 'God was with me today,' he said afterwards, a huge smile on his face, as ever. The big clubs were reportedly tracking Elliott. Aston Villa were preparing a £1m-plus offer. City stressed their goal-scoring star was not for sale at any price. Elliott could not understand what all the fuss was about, adding: 'Why would I ever want to leave Hull? This club is heading for the Premier League and I just want to be part of that. God told me when to come to Hull and he'll tell when it's time to move on.' The important games were coming thick and fast. There was a record attendance of 24,117 at the KC for the clash against Doncaster on December 28, which City won 2-1. On New Year's Day, City defeated Huddersfield by the same margin, again at the KC. Wilbraham grabbed his first goal for the club. Taylor couldn't resist telling me after the game: 'I told you Albi would score.' 'Yeah,' I replied, 'but I didn't think you meant it would take six months.' The game was overshadowed by an injury to Elliott, who suffered a depressed fracture of his cheekbone in a clash with Huddersfield's Efe Sodje. The verdict was Elliott would be out for several weeks. Taylor shrugged off the loss of his leading scorer and backed his players to plug the considerable gap. However, reports suggested City were back in the hunt for Parkin – and several other strikers. But there were no new arrivals. Taylor's trust paid off with a 3-1 win at Stockport on January 3. Wilbraham bagged another goal, a cross that somehow ended up in the net. Then the goals dried up – and not just for Wilbraham either. City were beaten 1-0 at Doncaster and to add to Taylor's problems, Ashbee was sent off for a tackle that wouldn't have looked out of place on a rugby league pitch. It wasn't the first time City's captain had fallen foul of a match official. Taylor warned his captain that he would have to clean up his act. A few people interpreted that as a sign that Ashbee's days were numbered.

City spluttered into February, losing 1-0 at Luton, a result that was a hammer blow to their fast-emerging hopes of the title. Taylor needed to strengthen and set his sights on yet another striker: Craig Fagan, who had played and scored when Colchester knocked City out of the FA Cup at the KC in January. City made their move, but the transfer kept collapsing. It sounded depressingly like the Parkin scenario all over again. Colchester visited the KC Stadium again in February; this time for a League game. Fagan had been left out of their squad. Two days later, he was a City player. He arrived with a reputation for not talking to the press. Taylor told him I could be trusted and Fagan duly responded with his life story, told in a rich Birmingham accent. The new signing scored on his debut in a 3-1 win at Tranmere the following Saturday. It was a vital victory. Tranmere were a major threat to City's promotion chances and had games in hand. Taylor had done the 'double' over Little, and City's performance at Tranmere was certainly impressive. By now, Elliott was back in the side. City, though, had waved farewell to Keane after a short – and controversial – stay at the club. He really was an enigma. At his best – and who could forget a stunning winning goal at Barnsley? – Keane was as good as anything around in the Division. But there were always rumours of off-the-field problems. Keane was never the best of trainers and Taylor just seemed to run out of patience. Keane headed for Rotherham, but had thrown away the chance of a lifetime. He was last heard of playing in Ireland where he'd been suspended by his club for being overweight. Such talent. Such a waste.

After Tranmere, City settled into a winning groove again. Taylor warned his players they could not afford to ease off – and they didn't. The pick of some impressive results was a 4-0 win at Bournemouth, Elliott scoring twice. Given his amazing record that season – he also shone for Northern Ireland – it was amazing a top flight club did not take a punt on him. Perhaps they knew something we didn't. I stayed in the same sea-front hotel as the team for that Bournemouth game and it was two o'clock in the morning before I got to bed after listening to yet more of Murphy's memories. Taylor also contributed to a great evening and Pearson bought most of the drinks. The atmosphere was really relaxed and I'm convinced that rubbed off on the players. As well as City had done, April was always going to prove the crucial month and, in particular, two derbies against Barnsley and Bradford. City won both games. The performance against Bradford at Valley Parade was particularly impressive. City were virtually home and dry. For the second year in succession, the City Council was ordering an open top bus for the celebrations. A point at home to Swindon the following week was enough to clinch back-to-back promotions for the first time in the club's history. You could have cut the tension with a knife for that Swindon game. For 90 minutes, City hammered away at their opponents but could not score. Then, in the first minute of injury time, City were awarded a penalty. Fagan took charge and promptly saw his spot kick saved by Rhys Evans. Seconds later, the final whistle went: 0-0. Fagan buried his head in his hands. More than 23,000 fans thought City's celebrations would have to wait for another week and another away game, just like Yeovil. But news leaked through that third-placed Tranmere had also drawn. City were ten points clear of Tranmere . . . with three games to go. Like the previous years, the KC erupted in a cacophony of noise and a sea of black and amber. Fagan recalled: 'I'd like to say I knew we were already up when I missed the penalty – but it's not true. I thought I'd blown it but it all came right, and it was a great day for the club. We were in the Championship. That's all that mattered.' A relieved Taylor admitted: 'One minute I wanted to strangle Fages, the next I wanted to bloody hug him.'

City lost those final three games and no one really cared. Taylor's side finished seven points behind champions Luton and seven clear of third placed Tranmere. Just four seasons previously, the club was in real danger of going bust. Now it was heading for the Championship. Elliott was the star of the show with an incredible 27 goals from the left wing. If it hadn't been for that sickening injury, he might have scored 40. His haul left him level at the top of the Football League's scoring charts with – believe it or not – Dean Windass. Taylor deserved immense credit. It was his team and his players. Myhill was outstanding in goal. There was a welcome solidity about the defence with Cort and Delaney outstanding at centre back, and Dawson a reliable left back. Right back was the only headache for Taylor. He never really solved it. Ashbee proved to be a superb leader; a giant in midfield. Several players chipped in with important goals, but amazingly for a promoted side, no one managed to join Elliott in double figures. For Elliott, it was a dream season. With typical modesty, he added: 'I guess I was just in the right place at the right time. My team-mates made it easy for me.'

He – and City – had come a long way since that wet and windy Wednesday night in Whitby. With back-to-back promotions, Ashbee had become one of the most successful captains in City's history. He said: 'It honestly didn't surprise me. As soon as we started that second season, I thought we'd got a massive chance. The first promotion was probably harder, even though it was from a lower Division. It probably meant more to some people. There was a lot more pressure – and a lot more relief – when we sealed that first one. Still, the second promotion was another tremendous effort. We didn't always play brilliantly. Sometimes, we cut teams open but we were strong, resilient and we worked hard for each other. The important thing is that when things weren't going for us, we had players who could turn a game. Stu (Elliott) did brilliantly but he wouldn't have got all those goals if certain other people hadn't given him the licence to go and do what he did. But, back-to-back promotions? Yeah, it feels great.'

Barmby, as ever, took everything in his stride, but there was a rare show of emotion when he took his two young sons on a lap of honour around the KC pitch after the final home game against Sheffield Wednesday. He said: 'When I signed for the club, I thought we'd go up. It's an amazing feeling. I'm delighted for everyone – and especially for the fans. Look where this club has come from. It was on the seat of its pants not so long ago, a laughing stock. Now it's really going places. This promotion really does mean as much as anything in my career.' Taylor was rightly installed as the most successful manager in the City's history. He admitted: 'I always thought this bunch of players were special. The first promotion meant a lot but this means even more. After Yeovil last year, I'm just glad we did it in front of our own fans.'

Taylor went on to praise the importance of the KC Stadium in City's success story. 'I can remember coming up to Hull to discuss the manager's job with Adam and he showed me pictures of what the new stadium would be like. He didn't have to sell the club to me because I knew the potential but those pictures told me everything. At the time, the club was still at the old ground but I always knew the stadium was going to be special and I wasn't disappointed. It looked out of place in the bottom Division. Well, we've done something positive about that. It's an honour and a privilege to have been the first Hull City manager at the KC and the fact we've been successful is the icing on the cake.'

Taylor had succeeded where many people thought he would fail. Remember, he almost walked away after that humiliating defeat at Southend the previous season. Would anyone else have guided City to two promotions in two seasons? Amazingly, some people still criticised Taylor. They said he couldn't fail because of Pearson's financial backing. Really? Had they forgotten Little and Molby? Taylor had succeeded where so many before him had failed. He'd be the first to admit he didn't get every decision right. However, he stuck to his beliefs. He could be prickly. He could be unpredictable. He was, though, a winner. Taylor reflected: 'I think the first promotion was the key and we managed to build on that. I wouldn't say that everything always went to plan but there were a lot of high points. On a personal level, winning the promotions bettered anything I've done in my career. In fact, I'll always look back on this time with great fondness. We've come a long, long way, but I truly believe Hull City can go from strength to strength. Don't be surprised that if one day, the KC hosts Premier League football. I know that sounds daft, but it could happen.'

Daft? Not now.

Chapter ten:

Time to move on

July, 2005 - May, 2006

After the drama of those record-breaking back-to-back promotions, the 2005-06 campaign was always going to be a more sombre affair for Hull City. Two years earlier, they had trailed in behind Cambridge United, Kidderminster Harriers, York City, Torquay and Bury in the 'old' Division Three table. A quick glimpse at the fixture list showed the outstanding progress they had made during that Adam Pearson/Peter Taylor axis. Forget Plainmoor and Gigg Lane. City would now be playing against Wolves, Norwich, Derby, Coventry, Southampton, Leeds United – all club's with a recent Premier League pedigree. The Championship, though, presented a much tougher challenge. In previous seasons, City had been the proverbial big fish in a little pond. Their attendances at the KC, and Pearson's continued financial backing, meant they always had a significant advantage over their rivals, especially after the collapse of that ITV Digital deal. Many clubs had to tighten their belts. City – and Taylor – were able to carry on spending. Now it was a different story. Take the figure for average home attendances in the Championship; City came below mid-table. Their wage bill occupied a similar position compared to their fellow Championship sides. It was a factor not lost on Taylor as he prepared for the new campaign. 'We know we've come a long, long way,' he admitted, 'but in many ways, now the really hard work starts.'

Instead of the usual predictions about promotion, City fans were warned to prepare for a season of consolidation. Taylor said it could be another three campaigns at least before promotion was a possibility. That scenario would have fitted within Pearson's initial five-year plan to bring Premier League football to Hull. Some sceptics – and some of them were long-time fans – feared City might struggle to stay in the Championship. 'There is definitely pressure,' added Taylor, 'but it's a different kind of pressure this season. Since I came to the club, the pressure was all about producing promotions. Now, it's about making sure we are not relegated.' Slipping back a Division was certainly not on Pearson's agenda. He was ready to back his manager. The chairman could never be accused of a lack of ambition. He was aware some fans wanted him to spend, spend and spend again in a bid to go for instant promotion. Instead, he took a more sensible approach. However, Pearson denied survival was the only priority and declared he wanted City to be 'competitive.'

I had struggled to tell the difference between League Two and One. But the Championship was a big step up. The higher standard meant, of course, a better squad and Pearson agreed to almost double City's annual wage bill for players to £3.75m. Some people still thought Pearson was being too cautious.

However, they didn't have to look too far back in the history books for a reminder of the dangers of over-spending. In 1990-91 – the last time City had played in the then equivalent of the Championship – the club's directors had announced they were ready to 'break the bank' to finance an all out bid for the top flight. The club invested heavily in new players and improved results failed to materialise. That policy was the catalyst that had taken City to the verge of oblivion, first under Fish and then Lloyd and Buchanan and Hinchliffe. Pearson said: 'Mistakes were made in the past and I am not going to make the same mistakes again.' The most expensive season ticket, for example, was £425. Leeds' fans would be asked to spend over £640, and QPR supporters over £700. Pearson said: 'I think we can aim for a top ten finish. We will look to strengthen but we are not going to pay silly money. We're not looking to bring in too many older Premier League players at the end of their careers. That is not the way forward.' Many of City's rivals had built their squads on the back of money borrowed against the value of their grounds. That was not an option for City. They were tenants at the council owned KC Stadium.

During the summer, it emerged Pearson still had high hopes of developing land around the stadium. The Government announced it was planning to grant licences for a series of Super Casinos at various sites around the country. Pearson, backed by the council, staged a strong campaign to bring one of them to the KC. He said the casino would lead to additional leisure and retails development, creating thousands of jobs and boosting Hull's chances of becoming a top ten city. In addition, the income from the various developments could, perhaps, pay for an increase in capacity at the KC. The figure was restricted to around 25,000, but the stadium had been built with the potential to add a second tier to the East Stand. That would add almost 10,000 more seats. The cost, though, was almost as much as the complete stadium had taken to build in the first place. Anyway, could City fill a 35,000-capacity stadium on a regular basis, particularly in a season of consolidation? There was also the thorny issue of when any major re-building work could take place. City's co-tenants Hull FC played their Super League games during the summer. They would not look kindly on being asked to move elsewhere, albeit on a temporary basis. Perhaps they could share with Hull KR. When it came to progressing any plans for redevelopment, Pearson must have felt like he was banging his head against a brick-wall. Although he seemed to be loved by everyone in Hull, the all-important backing for his various proposals only ever seemed to get a lukewarm response. Perhaps the all-important decision-makers had their eyes fixed on similar developments elsewhere within the city boundary.

In hindsight, perhaps that lack of progress planted the first seeds of doubt in Pearson's own mind about his long-term involvement. Publicly, Pearson said nothing. Privately, he was frustrated at the situation. During the summer of 2005, the stadium continued to be a popular attraction for some of the world's top musicians. In May, Neil Diamond pulled in more than 22,000 fans. Two months later, REM attracted over 20,000. There was talk of a concert by Madonna, and Bon Jovi were rumoured to be appearing the following summer. City fans may have been expecting a few big name signings themselves. These didn't materialise. Taylor set his sights on more modest transfer targets and Pearson was forced to defend the policy at a fans' forum. He said: 'We have spent as much money this summer as this club can possibly afford and we have a wage bill that is in the top ten of the championship and yet I am still hearing comments from fans like: 'Why are we not signing big name players? Some of the rumours that have gone about in recent weeks have been ridiculous. I've heard we are supposed to be interested in Nicky Butt. He would be on at least £30,000-a-week. You can't afford to pay wages of more than £4-5,000 per week – not until you get the £20m of Sky Sports money that comes from being in the Premiership. But what is a big name player anyway? The way this club has been successful has been by bringing in younger players and developing them. That is one of the manager's skills. People say they have never heard of some of our signings. Well, they hadn't heard of Stuart Elliott, Boaz Myhill and Damien Delaney – and look at them now. The fans have got to be realistic.' City's recruits that summer were headed by striker Stephen McPhee, signed from Portuguese side Beira Mar for a club record fee of £400,000. McPhee was keen to return to England. Unfortunately, he was dogged by injury problems. He wasn't quite another Richie Appleby, but he was close. Keith Andrews arrived from Wolves while there was a modest outlay on Driffield-born Curtis Woodhouse. A former England Under-21 international, Woodhouse's career had stalled. Taylor believed he could get the best out of him. The signings continued: Sunderland's Mark Lynch, who had come through the ranks; Danny Coles for £200,000 after one of the most protracted transfers in the club's history. Perhaps the most interesting recruit, though, was Sergio Leite, a goalkeeper who, we were told, had played more than 80 times for his country at Under-21 level. He was, Taylor said, among the top three goalkeepers in his native country. Leite arrived on a free transfer.

Given his Portuguese background, it was decided to stage his 'welcome' photograph under the Humber Bridge on a tiny piece of so-called sand, Hessle Foreshore. Even on a good day, it is hardly the Algarve. On this particular day, it was grey, miserable and very cold. Someone had forgotten to bring the plastic palm tree. The 'beach' was filthy, washed by the suspiciously brown-coloured River Humber. Leite took one step onto the beach, trod in some dog-dirt and made straight for his car. He didn't even want the free fish-and-chips a kindly photographer had brought as another prop. Despite that tricky start, Leite said he was happy in Hull. His pedigree – he'd been on stand-by for Portugal's last World Cup squad – suggested he would be a bargain buy. Then he played a couple of pre-season matches against local amateur sides North Ferriby United and Winterton Rangers. Against Ferriby, he struggled on crosses. Fans dubbed him 'Dracula'; not because of his jet-black hair. City's management obviously had a word after that game because a couple of days later against Winterton, he came for every single cross. The trouble was he missed every single cross. To add to the problem, he kept cleaning out his own defenders, leaving opposition players with a simple tap-in. It didn't get any better for Leite. Eventually, one of Portugal's finest headed for home and was last heard of playing in Romania. Or was it Division Four of the Greek League? At least the sun probably shone there.

It emerged Leite had almost signed for City during the previous summer. The deal fell through after one of his relatives died and he missed the deadline to start pre-season training. Taylor, though, was persistent. Sometimes he was like a dog with a bone. He wouldn't let go. As I often discovered to my cost, he also had an amazing memory. Just when you thought you were getting on top in a discussion with him, he'd dredge up something I'd written a couple of years ago and chirp: 'You were wrong then – and you're wrong now.' Still, I loved the bloke; sometimes.

City's opening League game was against QPR at the KC. The match ended in a 0-0 draw and was dominated by the behaviour of a minority of so-called City fans. The game took place just after the tragic London bombings. During the second half, those fans chanted 'You are a town full of bombers' at QPR's followers. It was crass and cruel. City were hung, drawn and quartered. The vast majority of true supporters could only hang their heads in shame. Pearson apologised. The FA staged an enquiry and there were threats that the KC – or parts of it – could be closed down for a period, as punishment. In the event, City got off lightly. By mid-September, City had won just twice in the League and had also crashed out of the League Cup at Blackpool. That Blackpool clash marked the debut of John Welsh, the England Under-21 captain, who arrived on loan from Liverpool. Welsh was well-known to Taylor, who attracted the Liverpool player with his presence. Other re-enforcements were to follow at various stages, including winger Kevin Ellison and yet more strikers: Jon Parkin, Billy Paynter and Darryl Duffy. The list of players who left included Allsopp, who returned to Australia, and Lewis, Wilbraham, Facey, Joseph and Price. Pricey was a real character and I always got the impression that he was one of the few players who Taylor didn't know how to handle. He was always good value when it came to interviews, although to this day, he's probably moaning about how many marks out of ten I used to award him in the Hull Daily Mail. I was once on a night out with a friend at an expensive restaurant in Beverley. It cost me a fortune. Half-way through the meal, there was a slap on my back. The glass and the wine went flying. It was Pricey. 'Hey,' he said, 'any chance of more than a five this Saturday?' He duly had a blinder, and I gave him a four!

The new arrivals were certainly welcome because City suffered a series of injury setbacks in the opening weeks of the campaign. By far the worst was to Ashbee. Somehow, he had played in the opening six or seven games before having a check on a niggling knee injury. Apparently, he needed his cartilage trimming. It turned out Ashbee was suffering from a degenerative bone condition in the upper part of his leg. It was a career-threatening problem. I sat down with him in a quiet corner of the training ground. I'd been through a lot with Ash and, though he could be difficult, I always had total respect for him. Ash didn't 'do' worried, but his face that day said everything. He agreed to an interview, provided I stressed at the very start of the story that he would play again. I duly wrote the article as agreed and it made the front page. But Ashbee stressing he would play again was not the main emphasis. Ash wasn't happy and neither was I. He knew the editorial decision hadn't been mine. But he was still disappointed. He knew he'd be out for months – if, indeed, he did ever play again. The first stage of treatment involved drilling holes in what was effectively dead bone in a bid to stimulate new growth. Ashbee recalled: 'As a footballer, you get the knocks, the bumps and the bruises but this injury knocked me for six. In the very early stages, there were really dark days when you were lonely and when you just wanted to give up. No one can understand what you go through. Then, you'd sit back and tell yourself it isn't that big an issue. There are a lot worse things in the world than having a piece of dead bone in your leg. I had a lot of support from family and friends and from people at the club. Deep down, I knew I'd play again and that's what drove me on. There was no point crawling into a corner and feeling sorry for yourself. If you are strong mentally then that's a big part of the healing.' Although he missed the rest of that season, Ashbee did play again. That he made a comeback says everything about him.

Without Ashbee, City struggled. Andrews should have been the ideal replacement, but he was crocked in an early season game at his former club Wolves. Two goals from Welsh did earn three precious points at Coventry, and a sequence of three draws was followed by an important 2-1 win against Derby at the KC in October. Taylor was nonetheless under growing pressure. To add to his problems there were reports that Barmby had stormed away from the KC before the Derby game after being told he was not starting the match. Taylor played down the reports, but Pearson was rather more forthcoming in interviews. He said: 'Nick was one of three players dropped and was the most disappointed of the three. However, I'd be disappointed if Nick hadn't reacted like he did because it shows he cares. He's a Hull lad and it wasn't a case of him throwing his toy out of the pram.' Some interpreted Pearson's comments as proof that Barmby actually had stormed out. Taylor wasn't pleased. He felt his position had been undermined. Perhaps that episode was the first crack in the previous watertight relationship between manager and chairman. It must be said that Taylor never liked Pearson commenting on what he saw as 'team matters' in the press. And Pearson almost relished seeing his name in the papers. I was often guilty of ringing the chairman when Taylor refused to comment on something. Was that undermining Taylor? Not on my part. I was doing my job. Dealing with Taylor was always a delicate balancing act and he was well aware of my lengthy association with Pearson. In particular, Taylor liked to keep details of any signings out of the newspapers until the contract was signed, sealed and delivered. There had been previous instances when City had been caught cold after deals for Alan Thompson and Luke Beckett had collapsed at the last minute. Usually Taylor would ring me, mention the proposed deal and ask that I didn't print anything until everything had been agreed. Often the clubs from whom City were signing players released details before Taylor wanted to comment publicly. Hold on to the story, and I'd risk being last in the queue. Print it first, though, and I'd risk upsetting Taylor. More often than not Pearson would comment. 'Yes, we are interested' or 'yes, we are close to a deal.' When, in the case of Thompson and Beckett, the deals fell through, City were left in an embarrassing situation. I'm sure Taylor, like most managers, would prefer to have total control on all football matters. Sometimes, though, that is not always possible. Looking back and there were tell-tale signs of a split between chairman and manager. For the time being, however, everyone was focussed on football and the battle to stay in the Championship.

The Derby victory was followed by four defeats and, even though Taylor guided his side to wins against Cardiff and Sheffield Wednesday at the start of December, he was increasingly a target for criticism from fans. By now, it looked like Welsh would become a full-time City player with young winger Paul Anderson heading in the opposite direction in a 'dream' move to Anfield. Anderson hadn't played a first team game, but was very highly thought of by Liverpool's coaching

IRISH EYES: Cork-born defender Damien Delaney (centre) leads the promotion celebrations. Delaney was later sold to QPR who, he believed, stood a better chance of reaching the Premier League.

HERE'S LOOKING AT YOU: Ian Ashbee (left) and Peter Taylor celebrate the second of their back-to-back promotions.

Opposite: HOMETOWN HERO: Nick Barmby at the centre of the celebrations after a 0-0 draw against Swindon clinched Hull City's place in the Championship. It was a remarkable first season at the KC for the former England international.

Page 255: SAME AGAIN: The champagne is flowing again, this time as Hull City celebrate promotion from League One to the Championship.

I'M IN CHARGE: Phil Parkinson, who was appointed as Taylor's successor, but never settled at the club and was sacked with City worryingly close to the Championship relegation battle.

THE BOSS: Phil Brown, the man who took City into the Premier League for the first time in their history. First, though, he had to keep them in the Championship at the end of his first season in charge. He succeeded - just.

WELSH WIZARD: Boaz Myhill, City's American born goalkeeper, who came through all four divisions of the Football League with the club. His form earned him a call-up to the Welsh squad. Two years on and he's nearly learned the national anthem!

NICE SUIT: Smiles all around as Paul Duffen (right) and Adam Pearson at the press conference called to unveil City's new owners. For Pearson, it marked the end of the road in Hull.

OUT OF AFRICA: Jay-Jay Okocha, so good they named him twice. He doesn't look too happy after being sent off for the first - and only time - in his glittering career during the Championship clash against Burnley at the KC Stadium.

WEMBLEY HERE WE COME: The smile on Nick Barmby's face says it all as he races away after scoring in the second leg of the Championship play-off semi final against Watford at the KC Stadium.

A SEA OF FACES: The PA announcer's plea to 'please keep off the pitch' clearly didn't work as City fans celebrate the win against Watford at KC Stadium. Hours later and most of fans were queuing for Wembley tickets.
(1N6Q6863)

ONE OF THE CROWD: Paul Duffen is engulfed by happy Hull City fans as he joins in the celebrations after the play-off semi final victory against Watford.

SO PROUD: Andy Dawson (left) and hometown hero Nick Barmby walk out into the Wembley sun-shine.

WHAT A DAY: From Boothferry to Wembley . . . City skipper Ian Ashbee in action at that play-off final.

WHAT A STRIKE: The face might be hidden but there's no mistaking the figure of Dean Windass as he celebrates his stunning goal at Wembley. Some of his team-mates reckoned the last time Windass had moved as quickly, there was a McDonald's pitch-side.

YOUNG AND OLD: A youthful Fraizer Campbell jumps on the back of veteran Windass as the fans go mad after that Wembley winner.

PREMIER LEAGUE HERE WE COME: Ian Ashbee holds aloft the Championship play-off trophy at Wembley. Bo Myhill (right) shows what the win meant to him.

Opposite: WOULD THE LAST ONE TURN THE LIGHT OUT: A section of the black-and-amber army that travelled to Wembley . . . flags and all.

GOING UP: Hull City's players salute their travelling army of fans as the celebrations start at Wembley. No-one wanted to go home.

BUBBLE DOUBLE: Nathan Doyle (left) and Fraizer Campbell show off their winners' medals - and a couple of bottles of champagne.

WE'VE DONE IT: Nick Barmby (left), Craig Fagan (centre) and Henrik Pedersen can't hide their delight after beating Bristol City at Wembley. Pedersen, like Okocha, was left out of the starting line-up.

THE MANAGEMENT: The 'team' behind Hull City's successful campaign celebrate at Wembley (from left to right), Simon Maltby (physio), Sean Rush (conditioner), Steve Parkin (coach), Phil Brown (manager), Paul Duffen (chairman), Brian Horton (assistant manager).

ARMS ALOFT:
Dean Windass, bottle in one hand, trophy in the other, doesn't want to leave the Wembley pitch.

Opposite:
LET THE PARTY START:
The champagne corks have been popped as City's players toast their Wembley success.

Ian Ashbee (centre) holds aloft the play-off trophy at the start of the open-top bus tour of Hull.

THE HIGH LIFE: Wembley winner Dean Windass on the balcony at the City Hall celebrations.

THE FANS: Thousands of Tigers fans pack into City Square to join in the celebrations.

staff. At first, City tried to keep Anderson. The player understandably wanted to join Liverpool. Eventually the deal went ahead with Taylor admitting: 'How could I stand in his way? He's a young kid and at that age whose head wouldn't be turned by the chance to join a club like Liverpool?' It is doubtful whether Anderson would have figured in the first team that season; Taylor opted for experience ahead of youth. Anyway, Pearson had negotiated a decent fee – and a subsequent sell-on payment. The player hadn't cost City a fee. He joined them after being released from West Brom's youth system.

Ever since the fixture list had been published, Leeds had been the most talked about game. Now it was looming. Of all the Yorkshire derbies, it was *the* derby – at least as far as City supporters were concerned. For years, they'd had to endure the taunts of their Leeds counterparts who had been brought up on a cash-rich diet of top flight football and regular excursions into Europe. The once mighty United might have been on the wane, but there was always a fascination about facing them. The added presence of Pearson as a former Leeds' director added to the appeal. The build-up to the game was dominated by the police. At one stage, they insisted City fans could only attend the Elland Road game if they travelled on official coaches. Those coaches would be met on the motorway, escorted to the game and then escorted back to the motorway afterwards. Quite how the police planned to stop travel by private car – especially by City fans living close to Leeds – was beyond everyone's comprehension. It was Big Brother gone mad. Pearson went on the attack. He branded the police's proposals as a 'direct infringement of human rights.' At one stage, it seemed City would refuse to accept any tickets for the game. Finally, the row was settled.

Less than 2,000 City fans were allowed into Elland Road. The game, on New Year's Eve, kicked off at noon. The atmosphere was totally flat. The fact Leeds won 2-0 made the whole day seem even more unremarkable. City lost their next three matches – a run including a 1-0 defeat at home to Aston Villa in the FA Cup. It was a strangely passionless performance. Gareth Barry scored Villa's winner and played down suggestions his form would earn him an England recall.

By March, City had slipped into the relegation positions. Their major headache was a lack of goals. Elliott – the star of those back-to-back promotions – found Championship defences harder to penetrate than those in Leagues One and Two. Opposition sides had got wise to Elliott's uncanny ability to ghost into the box unnoticed at the far post before planting a header into the back of the net. In defence of Elliott, it must be said the supply line from midfield was hardly prolific. City were struggling. They did restore some confidence with a rousing 3-0 win at Stoke on January 21. An own goal – plus efforts from Parkin and Duffy – swept Taylor's side to a stunning win and reinforced the manager's opinion that his players were happier and less pressurised in away games. City's next match was at home to Coventry. I'll never forget the date: January 31. It was my last game covering the Tigers for the Hull Daily Mail. I won't bore you with the details, but I'd become increasingly disillusioned and frustrated with the newspaper. To say I didn't see eye-to-eye with the people who made editorial decisions is an understatement. A lot of the damage had been done a few months earlier when the Hull Daily Mail accused a new radio station KCFM of plagiarism. Pearson was one of KCFM's major backers. While the row was nothing to do with me, I was still banned from talking to City's players. There was talk of a ban from the KC Stadium until the council intervened. After a lot of mud-slinging, the issue was resolved. But I believe the Hull Daily Mail's relationship with Pearson was never the same again. City offered me a way out: a role within their media and publications department. I accepted. A week after the Coventry game, I turned up at the KC Stadium wearing a club tie. It might have been an old-style design – but it was still a club tie. My first job was to interview my new boss Pearson for the club's recently launched monthly magazine. 'This is interesting,' he said. 'I don't have to answer all your questions now, do I?' Working for the club was an eye-opening experience. I was seeing things from the inside. I tried to keep a low profile, but Taylor told everyone what I was doing at a fans' forum on Radio Humberside. My phone didn't stop ringing for days.

City were still toying with the relegation positions. However, wins at Plymouth and Crewe and a draw at Ipswich eased the way. The decisive result was a 1-0 win at home to Leeds on April 1. The formidable Parkin – known as 'The Beast' – scored the only goal with a 76th minute header. That win was the highlight of the entire campaign. The season was rounded off with four draws, finishing in 18th place. The inquests started almost immediately, along with rumours that Taylor could be leaving the club. Initially Pearson and Taylor had presented a united front as they reflected on a campaign in which major signings like McPhee and Coles had mustered just over a dozen starts between them. Pearson commented: 'It is a fantastic achievement to stay up. We knew it would be a difficult season but Peter and I feel we can go on from here. We can actually sit down and start planning for the new season.' City had lost just one of their final seven games and Pearson stressed both he and Taylor regarded it as a clear indication of coming to terms with the Championship. He promised funds were available for new players – with or without the success of those development plans. He had already budgeted for another increase in the club's wage bill – this time to almost £5m. Pearson again played down hopes of big-name signings: 'We don't want the club to get into trouble and the manager does not want a massively imbalanced squad in terms of wages. If we can be mid-table next season, between 10th and 14th, I think that would be considerable progress and it would mean we are above a lot of big clubs. You can always flirt with the play-offs then and keep that promotion dream alive as long as possible. Realistically, though, we don't see that as part of the development for Hull City next season. We see it as establishing Hull in the middle of the Division.' News promptly broke surrounding Taylor's future.

At the start of May, he had been strongly linked with the managerial vacancy at Charlton. After much deliberation, and a frank exchange of words between them, Pearson gave Taylor permission to speak to the London club. At one stage, Taylor looked certain to leave. Amid reports Charlton wanted him to give up the England Under-21 post, he decided to stay at City. 'Every day, I've thought about it but my heart is not really in it. My heart is saying stay with Hull City. When you get a gut feeling like that, I think you should stay put. I'm very proud of what has been achieved at Hull City. I still think there is more we can do. I know the chairman and I had a few rows at the start of the week (about Charlton's interest) but we've got a great relationship so I don't want to leave.' The damage had already been done, however. When Charlton appointed Iain Dowie, it left his old job at Crystal Palace open. Taylor took it because his relationship with Pearson had broken down. It wasn't just one thing which swayed him. It was a culmination of several factors. But there is little doubt Taylor's decision to ask to speak to Charlton was a major turning point. Taylor was quick to praise City and Pearson. 'It was sad to leave,' he said: 'It is a great club and I would like to thank Hull City and Adam Pearson for the three or four years I had there. I thoroughly enjoyed my time and it had to be something special for me to leave, but when I got the call from Simon Jordan (Crystal Palace chairman) there is no doubt in my mind that I wanted to come here.'

The most successful manager in City's history had severed his links with the club. Despite his back-to-back promotions, some fans were not sorry to see Taylor move on. From day one, his commitment and his tactics were often called into question. To my mind, it was totally unfair. While City weren't always the most entertaining of sides, Taylor's results spoke volumes. People ask where City would be without Adam Pearson? I ask: Where would they be without Peter Taylor? He was the one manager in the last few decades to actually deliver. And it wasn't just one promotion. Of course, Taylor had money to spend and some of his buys were unsuccessful. However, his record proved he got most things right. He showed tremendous courage in that difficult first season. Twelve months later, he rejected an approach from Reading. They opted for Steve Coppell instead. In the final analysis, I felt Taylor had taken City as far he could. As they say: All good things must come to an end. Taylor needed a fresh challenge. Had he stayed at City for the remaining 12 months of his contract, I honestly think he would have struggled. The search for a new manager began. The club had survived in the second tier of English football, but were now at the cross-roads. They desperately needed someone to take them on to the next stage.

Chapter eleven:

Hello and goodbye

June, 2006 - May, 2007

While Peter Taylor settled into his new job at Crystal Palace, the question was: Who would replace him? At one stage, Mick McCarthy was the nailed on front runner. He'd been spotted at every half-decent hotel and restaurant within a 20-mile radius of Hull. Someone even rang a local radio phone-in to say McCarthy and Adam Pearson had been seen sharing a burger at McDonald's off the main A63 leading into the city centre. McCarthy, though, joined Wolves. City supposedly turned their attention to Gary Megson, and then to Tony Mowbray. Other names linked with the club included Joe Royle, Dave Penny, Martin Allen and Steve Tilson – along with just about every out-of-work manager between John O'Groats and Gillingham. One of the few names not mentioned was Phil Parkinson, who had developed a solid reputation at Colchester, hardly the most fashionable club in the country. As other candidates fell by the wayside, it emerged that Parkinson had been Pearson's first choice from the very start. Just as an insurance policy, Pearson had spoken to several alternatives.

Colchester were determined to hang onto their manager, who had just guided them into the Championship. Parkinson indicated he was interested in the job. Colchester demanded compensation. At first, it was stalemate. In early June, Pearson increased his offer of compensation to £250,000. Colchester were not impressed and took out an injunction to prevent Parkinson from leaving. Pearson would not back down. And neither would Colchester. The matter looked destined to end in the courts. City, though, were scheduled to start pre-season training. Taylor's back-room staff had also left the club. In the event, Pearson appointed the vastly experienced Frank Barlow as caretaker manager. The idea was that once Parkinson joined City, Barlow would slot in alongside him as his assistant. Pearson explained: 'Frank will be in charge for as long as it takes to secure Phil Parkinson's services. It could take one day. It could take one year.' The City chairman was clearly prepared to tough it out and at least Barlow was able to take charge of planning – and training – for the new campaign. When fans thought City should have looked beyond Parkinson, the chairman was adamant: 'I believe that when we have the new first team manager in place, we will have a structure that is exceptionally strong and well-equipped to continue the progress and development of Hull City Football Club.' End of story.

It took another two weeks of intense negotiations before, at the end of June, Parkinson finally arrived. City agreed to pay Colchester around £400,000. Pearson admitted: 'It has been a long two weeks. However, we have finally secured one of the brightest young managers in the game and one who has been coveted by many, many clubs in the Championship over the past year. The approach of specifically only wanting Phil Parkinson as the new manager has brought its ultimate reward. We have paid a significant sum of compensation and the fee is in excess of the £300,000 we received from Crystal Palace for Peter Taylor. However, it is an investment that will pay for itself very quickly.' Pearson revealed he'd been a long-time admirer of Parkinson. In fact, when Taylor looked set to quit City to join the England set-up a couple of years earlier, Parkinson would have been the chairman's choice as a replacement. Parkinson faced the media for the first time. The look of relief on his face said it all. He looked nervous, anxious almost. Parkinson said: 'I'm just pleased it's been sorted out. It's a shame it came to this. It could have been done better. If you look at all the jobs that were available during the summer, I can honestly say that Hull City is the one that excited me the most, because of the sheer potential of the club. The structure of the club and the drive and ambition of Adam makes me think it really is ready to be moved forward. When the opportunity came up, I had to take it. It was an easy decision.' Colchester's loss was City's gain. Or so we thought.

Parkinson brought fitness expert Stuart Ayles with him from his former club. As part of the deal, City agreed not to approach Colchester for any other players or staff members for the next 12 months. People have often asked me what Parkinson was like. To be honest, he was totally different to Taylor. He was younger for a start. He was also quieter, certainly less emotional. He was difficult to get to know. At times, it was as though he'd erected a screen in front of himself. Of course, he hadn't come to Hull to win a Mr Personality contest. He'd been appointed because he'd proved at Colchester that he was an exceptional coach. He said: 'It's hard for people to know what we had to go through at

Colchester. Our wage structure was probably the lowest in all four Divisions, but when we got the players in we worked hard with them. Hull is a higher standard, but players are human beings and need to be spoken to in an adult manner and encouraged. It is my job – along with the rest of the staff – to get the best out of them. There are more resources available here to go out and buy players and in that respect it is different to Colchester. The potential here is frightening and that's why I'm delighted to be the manager. I intend to make the most of the opportunity that has been given to me.' Parkinson wasted no time in fine tuning City's training methods. He introduced more speed work and power weights. The new ideas were introduced straightaway. Suddenly, plastic bins full of icy water appeared at the training ground. There were also new signings. The most expensive was Dean Marney, a young midfielder who had come through the ranks at Spurs. He cost a record £500,000. The fee would double if promotion followed. Parkinson spent £350,000 on centre half Michael Turner from Brentford and a reported £225,000 on Welsh international full back Sam Ricketts from Swansea. He also snapped up David Livermore in one of the more bizarre transfers even by the standards of City's tangled history. Livermore had originally joined Leeds from Millwall only to be told he could leave without playing a game. City stepped in smartly. Yet another new striker, Nicky Forster, followed. Parkinson also recruited winger Mark Yates who, as a loan signing, had helped Colchester secure promotion to the Championship. Those who left included the unfortunate Burgess, never the same player after his knee injury. I recall travelling to Rotherham on a miserable night to watch his umpteenth long-awaited comeback. After the game, he walked up to me, shook my hand and said: 'Thanks for coming.' Robbie Stockdale and Kevin Ellison, both of whom had failed to impress, were released along with Andrews and Thelwell, who had spent more time on the treatment table than the pitch. Signings under Parkinson cost City around £2m.

At least Taylor contributed towards balancing books. He handed over a record fee of £1.25m for Leon Cort, a healthy profit on a player who had arrived at the KC from Southend for £50,000. He took Green to Crystal Palace for a more modest £75,000. Green's time at City was eventful to say the least. At one stage, he appeared to have played his last game for the club after being dropped. He promptly announced he wanted to join his hometown club Carlisle. After a loan spell there, he returned to the KC and scored some important goals in the two promotion-winning campaigns. The move to Palace suited him perfectly. Apparently, he was living with one of Taylor's daughters. Turner had been signed as a direct replacement for Cort. Parkinson also had Coles and Delaney as centre back options. City's squad looked a good deal stronger than the previous campaign. And, when it came to scoring goals, big things were expected of Parkin.

The Beast was a legend. Reports said he'd been put on a diet after returning to pre-season training overweight. He never wore socks. When you'd ask why, the reply was: 'Eee, I'm from Baaaarnsley lad. Dun't tha' know, we don't wear socks there.' Despite the new signings, there was a sense of apprehension as the new season approached. Ian Reid, a long-time fan, said: 'I think everyone wondered how the team would react to a new manager. There was a lot of optimism coming out of the club but the general feeling was we'd do well to finish mid-table.' The tension at City's training ground was obvious as Parkinson attempted to impose his innovative ideas. Barlow was a football man through and through and would happily talk for ages about his experiences in the game. Like Parkinson, though, he was a pretty dour character. In my experience, players often respond best to the 'good guy, bad guy' management approach, such as Joyce and McGovern. In Parkinson and Barlow, the mix was never right. There was never the sense of fun that had often existed under Taylor, who was an excellent man-manager. Perhaps Parkinson tried to change too much. Once again, he'd also fallen into the trap of inheriting too many players who were used to another regime; players who in different circumstances he would never have signed. There were rumours he'd upset some of the more influential players in City's dressing room, such as Ashbee and Barmby. Pearson had more moles than your average crown green bowling club. He must have been aware of what was going on. Like all good chairman, he didn't need to visit the training ground too often. There were always plenty of people willing to pass on information.

The opening game of the campaign delivered a tough test for the new regime at promotion favourites West Bromwich Albion. Parkinson's new-look line-up competed well and were trailing 1-0 when Welsh was brought down in the area. The stone wall penalty was turned down. West Brom broke to the other end of the pitch and John Hartson scored: 2-0. City's next game was at home to Barnsley, in front of the Sky Sports cameras. Parkin appeared to relish the fact he was facing his former club and grabbed two goals in the first ten minutes to put City ahead. Barnsley scored on the stroke of half time and added two more goals in the second half to register a 3-2 victory. City had still not won in a live TV appearance and Parkinson cut a forlorn figure in the dug-out. Pearson looked none too happy in the directors' seats either. City lost their next game – 2-1 at home to Derby. When Parkinson criticised the referee after the game, admittedly after awarding a controversial penalty, the alarm bells started to ring. City did pick up a creditable draw at Ipswich, but defeats against Coventry and Birmingham quickly followed. That Birmingham game did mark Ashbee's first appearance for more than a year. It was tremendous to see the City skipper back in action. Fans, though, had to wait until September 12 for the first League win. Michael Bridges, brought in to strengthen the squad along with ex-England defender Danny Mills, scored a superb goal in a 1-0 win at Leicester. Pearson must have endured sleepless nights while totting up the total amount he'd spent on centre forwards. Almost none of them could score. City added to that Leicester win with a victory against Sheffield Wednesday, Parkin claiming another double. Crowds were on the decline, and Parkinson's safety-first attitude did not win him many new friends. The visit of Crystal Palace – Taylor, Cort and Green – on September 30 was always going to be a vital game. In the build up, Pearson gave Parkinson what amounted to a vote of confidence and said he was convinced City would pull well clear of the relegation battle by Christmas. He basically said Parkinson just needed time to turn things around and added: 'You go into a club that has been moulded by another manager and it's a very difficult job. The new person coming in needs to be given a lot of time. If you don't give that manager time, everything goes back to the drawing board. That is not going to happen at this football club, and if it takes until the summer, he will be given all the time he needs.' Pearson confessed he was aware fans were turning against Parkinson and insisted nonetheless he would keep faith because 'of the manager's integrity, commitment, hard work and ability.' High praise. Taylor got a decent reception and City drew 1-1, courtesy of a last minute goal from Turner.

The side spluttered and stuttered into October and a sequence of two draws and three defeats plunged them into the relegation battle. By the end of the month, Pearson had taken decisive action. Barlow and Ayles were axed, and Phil Brown was appointed first team coach. Ayles was never popular with the players. In fact, soon after he left, City's squad were stunned to see him on TV working for LA Galaxy on the day David Beckham signed. Many expected Parkinson to leave at the same time as Barlow and Ayles. The manager stressed he was staying on. 'I've never walked away from anything in my life and I'm not about to start now.' Brown's appointment was an interesting choice. He'd made his name as an assistant to Sam Allardyce at Bolton. Then, he moved into his first management position at Derby. It was hardly a success and he was sacked. He'd then spent a long time out of football, applying for a variety of jobs without success. He didn't even get an interview at Carlisle or Bournemouth. Pearson, though, had done his homework and Brown came highly recommended. He had an excellent reputation for working with players on the training ground. Ironically, Brown's first game as City's coach was against Sunderland, the club he'd supported from his childhood. City lost 1-0 but did recover to beat relegation rivals Southend 3-2. A draw at Southampton and a 2-0 win at home to Wolves suggested things were on the up under the new-look management/coaching team. Brown certainly made a big impression. At training, his hands on role – and his ability to get on with the players – lifted morale. By now Parkinson, though still in charge, was becoming a more isolated figure. Brown said and did all the right things. 'The potential here is tremendous,' said Brown. That dreaded 'p' word had raised its head again. Just when a recovery was on the cards, City slumped to an embarrassing 5-1 defeat at, of all places, Colchester. Pearson was fuming and labelled the performance as 'totally unacceptable.' Again, everyone expected Parkinson to leave. He was still in the post for the next game, at home to Southampton. City lost 4-2. Pearson had seen enough and Parkinson departed on December 4 after a Monday morning meeting with the chairman. Pearson's statement said: 'It is with great regret I wish to announce the departure of Phil Parkinson. Unfortunately, results have not gone the way either Phil or the club would wish. On behalf of everyone connected with Hull City, I would like to wish Phil all the very best for his future managerial career where he is sure to go on and achieve significant success.' Pearson always admitted he'd been hasty in axing Brian Little. In the case of Parkinson, his timing was much better. The manager had lost the confidence of his players – if, indeed, he'd ever had it in the first place. Pearson now faced a dilemma. Should he bring in a new managerial team (again) or go for Brown? He had seen the potential pit-falls of appointment a new manager in mid-season. So Brown was elevated to the role of caretaker boss with Taylor's former number two, Colin Murphy, returning as assistant. The pair knew the players. The players knew them. It still appeared to be a stop-gap measure and the list of applicants for the manager's job was soon long, including one from Dowie, who had been sacked by Charlton. Among others linked with the post was Warren Joyce, who was now managing Belgian side Royal Antwerp as part of their link-up with Manchester United.

Brown had a chance to stake his claim first. He was certainly popular with the club's players. He also wanted the job. He said: 'I do want a return to management, but unfortunately I would not have chosen circumstances like this. Of course, I remain open minded. It would be an opportunity for any man in or out of football to be able to come to a great football club. You have to create a winning environment and get a team on the field of play that believes they can keep Hull City in the Championship. If we can transform the position we are currently in then hopefully the belief will start to come with winning games and then . . . who knows?' Brown's first game in charge brought an improved performance but the same end product: a 1-0 defeat at Plymouth. His chances of landing the job improved dramatically when City walloped Cardiff 4-1 in front of a packed house at the KC with many fans taking the opportunity to snap up cut price tickets at £5 each. Brown's standing was elevated even more after a 0-0 draw at Leeds on December 23. City lost 2-1 at home to Leicester on Boxing Day, despite a goal from Fagan who was attracting interest from several clubs, including promotion chasing Derby. But a Fagan penalty contributed to a win against Burnley before Barmby highlighted his liking for Hillsborough with a double in a 2-1 victory over Sheffield Wednesday. City were out of the relegation zone and Pearson told Brown the job belonged to him until the end of the season at least. There was a strong hint that, if Brown kept City up, he would secure a long-term contract. Pearson added: 'Phil has done very well in his time in charge. He's handled himself in a very professional manner. He's got the hunger and the attitude for it. He's made a real difference on the training ground and that has come across into games.' Brown lost the services of Fagan, who joined Derby for a fee of £750,000 with an additional payment of £500,000 due – if Fagan pushed his new club into the Premier League. Pearson stressed that the deal went though purely for financial reasons. It was the first indication his own supply of funds was running low.

The FA Cup briefly interrupted City's fight for Championship survival. A third round home tie against Middlesbrough ended 1-1. City were desperately unlucky to lose the replay 4-3. Pearson and Brown knew Fagan had to be replaced. The answer was a PR coup: Dean Windass arrived at the KC on loan from hard-up Bradford. Brown was prepared to take the gamble that at least three of his predecessors had shied away from. But City's League form was worrying. Draws against Crystal Palace and Derby were countered by defeats against Leeds, West Brom and Barnsley. The 3-0 defeat at Barnsley followed a particularly poor performance and the radio phone-ins were dominated by people suggesting Brown was not the man for the job. 'We should have gone with Dowie or Megson,' was the popular call. Pearson and Brown held firm. Former Arsenal and England midfielder Ray Parlour arrived on loan to add some much needed experience. Brown also paid Derby £100,000 for young utility player Nathan Doyle and then hardly picked him. Parlour was definitely at the tail end of his career and some people thought he seemed more interested in horse racing and poker. There again, he needed to supplement his income to pay his ex-wife in a divorce settlement that had previously hit the national headlines. Windass had announced his arrival in typical style, two goals securing a home win against Birmingham. He added two more against Ipswich at the KC but, unfortunately, the visitors found the back of the net five times. Coles was recalled for that Ipswich clash, but hardly covered himself in glory. The pressure was piling up, and City responded superbly. Goals from Foster and Livermore secured an important win against Preston and, three days later, Livermore and Turner were on target in a priceless victory at Luton. Livermore will hardly go down as the most successful signing in City's history, but without those two goals, securing back-to-back wins, the question has to be asked: What would have happened to the team? A 4-0 drubbing of Southend, featuring a hat trick from Windass (who else?) took City to the verge of safety. Going into the Easter programme, they were five points clear of the drop zone. Worryingly, the next four games produced just two points. Anxiety increased after defeats against Norwich and Wolves. Brown pleaded for patience; fans started to fear the worst. Even with Luton and Southend certain to occupy two of the three relegation positions, City were battling it out with Barnsley, Leicester, QPR, Coventry and Leeds to avoid the drop. Brown predictably attempted to deflect the attention from his players. He said: 'No one is even mentioning the r-word. We've just got to focus on our own games and not worry about what the sides in and around us are doing.' As ever, Windass was typically more ebullient. 'We won't go down,' he said. 'I'd stick my mortgage on that – but just don't tell the missus.'

A rare Forster goal earned a draw at home to Colchester who, ironically, were chasing a play-off place under Parkinson's successor, Geraint Williams. City played well but the result was still seen as two points lost rather than one gained. The fight for survival was going down to the wire. City desperately needed some positive return from a visit to Stoke. Parkin had linked up with Stoke on loan. Brown whipped up the atmosphere ahead of the game by recalling him. City grabbed a point because of a superbly taken effort from Barmby in the very last minute of normal time. It was his first goal since a brace against Sheffield Wednesday back on New Year's Day. Barmby admitted: 'I've been lucky enough to score some important goals in my time, but this is the most important.'

There were two games to go: Cardiff away and Plymouth at home. City needed three points to seal Leeds' fate. On the same day City travelled to Cardiff, Leeds were at home to Ipswich. Every City fan at Cardiff seemed to have their ear glued to a radio or a mobile phone. There were suggestions that Cardiff had nothing to play for, which was nonsense. Any player will tell you that Ninian Park is one of the toughest grounds outside the Premier League to get a result, whatever the circumstances. The atmosphere is always noisy and intimidating. City stayed calm and a second half goal from Windass clinched the three points. Back in Yorkshire, Leeds were winning, but their game had been delayed by a pitch invasion at Elland Road after Alan Lee had equalised for Ipswich. Ironically, Lee had come desperately close to joining City earlier in the season. A Leeds victory would have taken the relegation issue to the final game. As the clock ticked past five o'clock, Pearson prowled the touchline with the phone to his ear. In the dressing room, Brown and the players were asking anyone what was happening at Leeds. The news finally came through. Leeds had drawn and City were safe. The fact arch rivals Leeds were relegated and shunted into administration made safety seem that much sweeter. As far as Windass was concerned, it was Boys' Own stuff. 'I suppose it was a script just written for me. It's been an incredible experience. Full credit to the players, we got ourselves out of the mess we were in. We could have done it a lot earlier but then that's this club for you. Good or bad, it never does anything the easy way.' Windass was dubbed a hero for his Cardiff goal and yet he handed the praise to his team-mates – and Barmby in particular. 'If we'd lost at Stoke, after playing so well, we might not have come back from it. Thanks to Nick's goal, we went to Cardiff knowing a win would do it. We didn't want it to go down until the last game of the season and after what happened, it's just as well.' Windass scored eight goals in the closing weeks of the campaign, making him City's leading scorer. He knew the importance of avoiding relegation. 'This club has come so far in the last four years. I can remember standing on the terraces when we played Cardiff at Boothferry Park. David Lloyd owned the ground and everybody was saying that was our last ever game. I never lost hope. I was always confident I'd come back to the club. Now, look at the situation. A Championship club, a chairman who really cares, a fantastic stadium and 20,000 fans pouring through the turnstiles every game. The club is too big to go down. Everyone deserves a pat on the back. Now, we can look to the future and I'd love to get in the Premier League with Hull. I know that sounds daft after just avoiding relegation but in this business, you never say never.'

Pearson promised City would learn lessons from the season. A week or so after the Plymouth game, I sat with him in his office beneath the East Stand at the KC Stadium. As usual, there was a half-eaten plate of food on his table. He'd ripped off his tie and unfastened the top button of his bright pink shirt. That look of relief was still etched on his face. He defended his appointment of Parkinson, but admitted the former Colchester boss had probably tried to change too much too quickly. He also confirmed Brown would be offered the manager's job after steering City to safety. 'If Phil hadn't kept us up, then it would have been a much tougher decision. If he'd been in charge for the whole season, then he was on target for 60 points. That would have meant 15th place which would have been a pretty good return. There is no doubt we were having a shambolic season when he came in at the start of December. It needed major surgery. Phil achieved that and although it was a close run thing, he kept us in the Championship and for that, he deserves due credit – and he deserves the job.' Pearson was baffled by poor season ticket sales for the following campaign. He confirmed the figure was around 7,500 – down almost 6,500 on two years earlier. His application for the casino-led redevelopment at the KC had stalled. Rumour had it that his backer, Peter Wilkinson, had ended his financial support. Pearson admitted he was looking to attract fresh investment. Ideally, he said, he wanted to stay on as chairman and major shareholder. But, for the first time, he confessed that might not be possible. We'd been through a lot together. Keeping City in the Championship had drained him: physically, emotionally and financially. Pearson had always been a pleasure work with – and work for. I'd nothing but total respect for him, even though I'd been on the wrong end of a fair few of his legendary bollockings in my time. I could sense the hurt and emotion in his voice. Hull City was his club; the club he'd saved from going bust and then dragged screaming and kicking into the Championship.

Could he face another struggling season? All the signs were he didn't have the funds to strengthen the team. I knew he was holding something back. It was as though he wanted to tell me something – if only to take the weight off his shoulders. I pushed him. 'Will you still be here next season?' I asked. He shook his head. 'I honestly don't know,' he said. 'We'll have to wait and see.' A few minutes later, I left his office convinced he was selling Hull City lock, stock and barrel.

But I kept my thoughts to myself.

Chapter twelve:

All change

July, 2007 - May, 2008

It is impossible to keep a secret in football. However, as the tension of the 2007-08 campaign started to intensify, it became clear Pearson had been 'guilty' of a subterfuge that would have delighted MI5. If you'd watched Pearson closely in the second half of the season, you would have spotted that at many matches he was regularly accompanied by the same person. To be fair, no one paid too much attention. There were more pressing concerns, such as keeping Hull City in the Championship. The person in question was obviously a successful businessman and a snappy dresser. The pin-stripe suits and expensive coats were dead give-aways. At that all-important game at Cardiff, the 'mystery man' had sat beside Pearson and seemed to head every ball and make every tackle. To anyone who asked, he was 'just a good friend of Pearson's family'; even a relative of his wife Debbie. Another school of thought claimed he was one of the leading figures in the on-going bid to re-develop the KC Stadium site. Others even suggested he was Windass' agent.

However, midway through June of 2008, his identity was finally revealed. He was Paul Duffen – the club's new Chairman. My initial suspicion that Pearson had agreed to sell City was right.

Ever since Pearson admitted he lacked the finances to drive the club forward, people had suspected City were heading for a major change. Perhaps it would have been different if Pearson had received backing in his re-development plans. Or if the appointment of Phil Parkinson had worked out better. Or if he hadn't been obliged to spend almost £2m on new players to save the club from relegation. Then, of course, there was a 50 per cent reduction in revenue from season tickets sales. On top of it all, the last major concert at the stadium, featuring The Who, had reportedly made a loss of £100,000. Pearson had reached the end of the line. He'd wanted to stay on as chairman and major shareholder. However, it wouldn't be possible; The club was sold for a reported £10m and Duffen took over as chairman. It emerged that Duffen hadn't missed a game in the second half of the previous season. The thought of City without Pearson at the helm was still a frightening scenario. He stressed he was handing over control to the right people – football people. It had been a difficult and emotional decision for him. When the press conference announcing the news was over, he ushered me onto the walkway just outside the main reception area. It was our final interview. He said: 'The plan was to take this club into the Championship in five years and I've done that. However, I think people accept now that I don't have the financial resources to kick the whole thing on. To have a one-man band at this level of the game is just not possible any more.' Once the 'serious' stuff was out of the way, our discussion inevitably focussed on those previous five years; the good times, the difficult times. 'You know what?' added Pearson. 'My last game with Leeds United before coming to Hull was against Real Madrid at the Bernabeu. A couple of days later, I went to Boothferry Park for the first time. It was pretty frightening. It was a Monday night. It was raining; half the letters from the sign on the outside wall were missing. There were rats scurrying down the players' tunnel. Water was dripping down the inside of the walls. I did wonder what I'd done. In fact, friends told me I was mad, but I knew there were a lot of good people at this football club. People who made me feel very, very welcome.' Pearson went on to reel off his first game as chairman: 'Exeter at home and we won 2-1 . . . Rodney Rowe scored, a penalty. I look back now and they were great days. They were fun and sometimes I preferred being down there (League Two) to up here (the Championship).' I'd swear there were a few tears in his eyes. 'It's not been easy saying good-bye,' he added, 'but financially, the responsibility needed sharing out. Listen, you know I just couldn't go on. If I had, there was a very real danger of the club going backwards. After everything we've been though, that's the last thing I wanted.' As Pearson talked, the giant glass-fronted reception area soared above him. That showed the progress City had made under his leadership. Just behind him, the impressive West Stand rose high into the sky. At the start of the morning, it was raining. Now, even the sun came out to say farewell. However – as Pearson had often reminded me – there is no room for sentiment in football. What of the new man, the new regime? Pearson and I walked back through the main reception doors to meet Duffen. I knew the new chairman was based in the south-east, the same neck of the woods as David Lloyd. I couldn't help but think about it as I was introduced. Duffen was different to Lloyd. He didn't have a pigeon-toed walk. He knew his football. He knew Hull. He knew Hull City. Unlike Lloyd, he also looked you straight in the eye when he spoke. But what about that subterfuge of the previous season? Even Duffen seemed taken aback that the media had not uncovered his identity. He admitted: 'I met a lot of people, the senior management team, the key stakeholders in the club and in the city in general. I honestly thought someone would have leaked something. Now I know I'm very fortunate to be the custodian of this great club. It will be a privilege to play a part in the next chapter of a story that has already been 100 years in the writing.' Duffen's background was in the media business so his PR was gold standard. Yes, there was money for new players. No, he did not want to buy Hull Sharks. Yes, he wanted to take City into the Premier League.

It became clear Duffen had played a key role in several major decisions already taken that summer, including the appointment of Brown as manager. Duffen added: 'It's very important that people know I made the appointment. Since the legal papers were signed some weeks ago, Adam has been happy to involve me in every major decision. I negotiated the contract with Phil. I appointed him as manager. However, it was done before we announced we'd exchanged the contract of sale so Adam had to be the spokesperson.' From the very start, I was impressed with Duffen. Certainly, I didn't share the view, expressed in some quarters, that he was more interested in off-the-field developments than events on it. Still, looking back to those first hours in charge, I suppose it was only natural people were a little wary. After all, a Surrey-based millionaire in control of Hull City? He even admitted he liked tennis. Now who did that remind us of? Duffen summed things up in a typically honest and candid style: He said: 'As a southerner coming into a Yorkshire club, I have a few hearts and minds to win over, especially as the last southerner to run the club didn't exactly endear himself to them.' There was no doubting Duffen's business acumen. He was a founder of Catalyst Media and had built a considerable fortune. Also behind the takeover was Russell Bartlett, a highly successful Essex-based property investor. Duffen, though, would be the hands on chairman, the person in charge; the 'new Pearson'. Duffen was a Spurs fan and Bartlett, who was a box holder at West Ham, had previously been behind bids for Cardiff and West Ham before the take over of City. there was no doubt that the money was available to take City forward. However, Duffen was keen to play down expectations. 'For this season, I am not going to make Phil Brown a hostage to fortune. However, I would want everybody to expect us to finish in the top half of the Division. Then, I would want us to do better the season after. There is no reason why this club can't compete in the Premier League . . . but all in good time.' Those words must have come as a relief to Brown, who was putting together his own plans for the new campaign. A key figure in those plans was Brian Horton, tempted back to City as assistant manager. Horton, one of the most respected figures in the game, was City's manager in the 1980s when he came desperately close to taking them into the top-flight. With coach Steve Parkin also on board, City's management team was in place. Meeting all three, you quickly sensed the balance was right – unlike the situation under Parkinson. Horton was a hugely popular figure. His return went down well with the fans. Horton was naturally delighted to be back. 'Look at the stadium and the training facilities,' he said. 'In my time, we were lucky if we got to train in a local park or what I called the vegetable patch – a piece of waste ground at the back of the main stand at Boothferry Park.' Horton's appointment was also a Pearson-led initiative before he'd handed over control of the club to Duffen. It was clear that the old and the new had already bonded. The atmosphere was a heady mix of trust and respect. And, although Pearson had handed over control, he looked for an influential role in City's affairs. He announced he was going to stay on and work alongside the new board of directors. Duffen said: 'Adam has a lot of knowledge and experience that we can only benefit from.' However, at the end of July – just days before the start of the season – Pearson resigned. It was the end of an era, arguably the most successful seven years in the club's history. Pearson wanted to buy a new club. 'I think it's best for all parties that I move aside and let the new chairman have the space. I don't want to be seen hanging around in the past. It's time the club went forward without me. The last few weeks have been difficult. When you're used to running the place, then it is potentially a bit awkward for the new directors and the new chairman.' Pearson was immediately linked with Huddersfield Town and Leeds. In the event, he settled on Derby.

It is almost impossible to sum up the impact he made at City. Without him, the club would have folded. The Premier League would have remained a distant dream. He was ambitious, committed and, at times, ruthless. He lived and breathed Hull City Football Club. No one defended City's corner more passionately. Somehow, I still expect him to emerge from his office at the KC Stadium, his arm extended, that firm wave that would 'invite' you into his domain and then the words: 'John, fellah . . . what is that crap you've printed in the paper?' We didn't always see eye-to-eye. I can still recall one rollicking in particular on the phone that went on for what seemed like 30 minutes. It was in the middle of the dispute between the club and the paper over KCFM. Pearson thought I should have backed the club against my then employers, and told me so in no uncertain terms. An hour later, he was back in the phone: 'I was out of order. Call in to see me tomorrow.' It was as though our argument had never even taken place. In another development during a dispute, I was threatened with being banned from a home game against Bristol Rovers. Finally I was allowed in after paying for a ticket. I couldn't use the press facilities or the press box. Instead, I was marched from once section of the West stand to another. At half time, I was even accompanied by two stewards when I went for a pee. It was stupid and unnecessary, and Pearson later apologised. I wasn't there when he drove away from the KC stadium for the last time. He wasn't an emotional person. I bet, though, that there were a few tears in his eyes. Pearson's sudden and surprise departure was accompanied by wave of rumours that he'd fallen out with the new regime. That wasn't the case. Nevertheless, it increased cynicism in some quarters surrounding the new ownership regime. City went on an all out PR offensive, though there was a mixed response to the club's audacious attempt to try to sign Brazilian star Juninho. When news of City's interest first leaked out, everyone seemed to be sceptical: 'Juninho, coming to Hull? Never.' Then Juninho was spotted coming out of a hotel with Duffen and Brown. At one stage, the deal looked certain to be completed before collapsing much to the annoyance of the player's agent. A similar move for Italian striker Christian Vieri also failed to materialise. When new signings did arrive, they were of a rather more modest variety: Brian Hughes, Richard Garcia, Wayne Brown and Dean Windass on a permanent basis. The 38-year-old joined for a fee of £150,000. There was an additional payment due if City won promotion. No one paid too much attention to that.

City's start to the season hardly smacked of the top six. They lost 3-2 at home to Plymouth. Henrik Pedersen, who had played under Brown at Bolton, arrived to add some much needed experience. Pedersen was at the latter end of his career, but was a model professional. Whenever you rang him, he seemed to be in Starbucks reading some book or other. City did beat Crewe 3-0 in the first round of the Worthington Cup and picked up their first League win against Norwich, thanks to second half goals from Windass and Garcia. The crowd for that game – 15,939 – was a cause for concern. The draw for the second round of the Worthington-backed event took Brown's team to Premier League Wigan. Rightly or wrongly, the competition is treated with disdain by many top flight managers, and some in the Championship. City, though went for the jugular that night and Elliott's clinical strike earned them a 1-0 victory. Wigan's side included striker Caleb Folan. A couple of days later, he became City's first £1m signing. Folan had spent time at the club before on a short loan spell from Leeds when Little was in charge. Back then, he was a quiet, almost shy figure. His father did most of the talking. The older Folan was much more confident. 'Bit different now, isn't it?' he said in his first interview as he looked around the club's training ground. The stewards on the gate were an indication of the changing times. Access to players was now strictly controlled and the local paper could no longer wander into a session and speak to whoever they wanted. Even fans had to apply for a ticket to watch training. No ticket, no admittance. Folan won't forget his 'second debut' for City in a hurry either. It was a League game at Blackpool on September 3. He suffered a nasty head injury and was rushed to a local hospital where he was detained overnight. 'It wasn't exactly what I'd planned,' he said. City lost at Blackpool; ironically Burgess scored the winning goal. It seemed a long journey home and conversation centred around increasing concerns that the club was heading for another battle against relegation.

Brown needed help, which came from an unlikely source: the Middle East. That's where Jay-Jay Okocha had spent the previous 12 months. Okocha was one of the best players ever to emerge from Africa. He'd captained Nigeria and led his country in the World Cup. Like Pedersen, he'd played for the Sam Allardyce/Brown regime at Bolton and was one of the major factors in establishing them as a respected Premier League force. Jay-Jay Okocha – so good they named him twice. When he left Bolton to move to Qatar, it was assumed his career was over. Only Brown hadn't forgotten the skills and style that had made the player such a favourite at the Reebok Stadium. Within days, Okocha had answered City's SOS and swapped the sandy shores of the Gulf for Hull. His signing took everyone by surprise. There was no doubting his class. However, there were genuine fears Okocha would struggle to settle – both in Hull and in the Championship. Cynics said it was a horribly similar scenario to the period in which Whitmore and Goodison had joined City. Okocha took everything in his stride, including his debut in a reserve team game at Scunthorpe. He was simply brilliant at Glanford Park. Even Scunthorpe's supporters applauded him. He made a big impression on everyone, not least when it came to his favoured mode of transport. He drove either a Ferrari or a Bentley. I interviewed him just hours after he arrived at the club. He was immaculately dressed: pale blue shirt, cream-coloured trousers, black shoes. I half-expected him to be aloof. He wasn't. Two things hit home immediately: his humble beginnings and his deep religious beliefs. As a youngster, he'd started playing football in Nigeria with his friends, kicking a ball made out of old rags around the dusty back streets. If he and his friends couldn't find any rags, then a battered old tin can would do. If he hadn't travelled to see a friend who was playing in Germany, his skills would probably have been lost to a world-wide public. While in Germany, Okocha played in what amounted to no more than a pre-season kick-about and was promptly signed. 'So, why Hull?' I asked him. 'Why not?' he said, a huge smile on his face. In fact, he always had a smile on his face . . . even when he was injured. 'When I went to Bolton, I knew nothing about the place. It's the same now. I know nothing about Hull. I always ask God if it is His will for me to do something. If so, then let it be.' Some people suggested Okocha's only reason for joining Hull was money. Those people didn't know him. He told me: 'If I'd wanted money, if I'd wanted lifestyle, I'd have stayed in Qatar. But that's if you are a lazy person. I am not lazy. True, I am 34, but I want a new challenge and I will give Hull everything I can. Of course, I know the team is struggling but hopefully I can help. The potential is here. We can get in the play-offs this season.'

Given City's faltering start to the season most fans probably laughed at his last comment. For survival was still the name of the game. Okocha made his debut in a 1-1 draw at Stoke and was given a standing ovation by both sets of supporters. The following week, he inspired City to a 1-0 victory at Wolves after a truly majestic display. The verdict of Wolves fans was: 'How the hell did you sign Okocha? He's brilliant.' It was a promising start but not even Okocha – the biggest signing in City's history – could perform miracles. Defeat at Sheffield Wednesday was followed by a humbling in the Worthington Cup – 4-0 at the hands of Chelsea at the KC. Avran Grant had just taken over as Chelsea's manager. The final whistle at the KC was one of the few times anyone had seen him smile. In the build-up to that tie, City had been reliably informed that Chelsea's billionaire owner Roman Abramovich would be attending the game. Some smart Alec even thought it would be a good idea to interview him.' 'So,' I said in a meeting of City's press staff, 'I just stroll up and talk to him.' 'Yes,' came the reply. 'Does anyone know if he even speaks English?' I asked. 'Of course he does,' was the answer. 'Just smile and ask him if he likes Hull.' Fortunately, he and his gang of burly minders never arrived. No one was surprised by the result against Chelsea and the Worthington Cup was low on Brown's list of priorities.

He desperately needed performances to pick up in the League. However, to suggest City struggled for consistency in October is probably an understatement. They won just one game. Brown's presence had helped clinch the signing of Okocha. Now the City manager pulled off another coup after persuading Manchester United to loan him a promising young striker, Fraizer Campbell. Few people outside of Old Trafford had heard of Campbell. Those that had said he looked certain to join the long list of United products to shine at youth team level and then slip off the radar. Campbell had spent the previous season on loan at Royal Antwerp, managed by Warren Joyce. So

I put in a quick phone call to Joycey for the inside information on City's new player. 'He's quick, and he'll score goals,' said the former City boss, who was drinking Stella in a market square when I rang. 'In fact,' he added, 'if Fraizer does well, you could finish in the top six.' I thought Joyce was being wildly over-optimistic. 'Have you looked at the table recently?' I asked. 'I tell you,' he answered. 'If Fraizer gets into double figures with goals, you'll get into the play-offs.' I nearly dropped the phone. Surely Joycey had tucked away too many Stellas? I asked him if I could use that quote about the top six. 'Why not?' he said, 'You've no need to make it up this time either.' When Campbell arrived at City, he was everything you wouldn't expect of a Manchester United player. He was quiet, unassuming. I travelled down to City's training ground to interview him soon after he'd signed. He was polite, but I was left with the distinct impression he'd have preferred to have avoided the interview all together. It's no secret that United's young players are coached in how to handle the media. I wanted to ask him about his time at United, and what Sir Alex Ferguson was really like. 'Err, I'd prefer to talk about something else,' said Campbell. Fair enough. The article that appeared was along the lines of: 'It's great to be here.' Fortunately, Campbell was a little more expressive on the pitch. He scored his first goals for City with a double in a 3-0 win over Barnsley in a Monday night live TV game. So much for that Sky Sports jinx. It was the only success in a worrying run that left City perilously close to the relegation positions. And a 2-0 defeat at QPR in November led to one of the few occasions Brown criticised his team in public. He labelled the performance at Loftus Road as 'uncharacteristic and unacceptable.' He added: 'We looked as though we were out-worked and that is why I felt sorry for our fans. They travelled a long way to watch us, but they didn't get the normal levels of work-rate and commitment. After the first goal went in, I thought one or two heads went down. That is unacceptable in my book.' Okocha was recalled to the side for that game at Loftus Road, but struggled in midfield. He wasn't the only disappointment. On the long trek back from the capital not too many fans were dreaming of the top six.

Brown demanded an improvement and his players responded superbly, reeling off a hat-trick of wins against Burnley, Preston and Scunthorpe. Turner clinched the first of those victories with a last minute winner at Burnley. Windass and Campbell were among the goals in the following two games. Windass scored twice in City's 2-1 derby win at Scunthorpe and, as ever, was ready with the quotes afterwards. 'Playing up front with Fraizer is like playing up front with my little boy,' said the veteran striker. When I ever so kindly pointed out to Windass that he was actually old enough to be Campbell's dad – Windass was born in 1969, Campbell in 1987 – I'd swear it's the first time I'd known him lost for words. City drew their next two games at home to Bristol City and Cardiff. The Cardiff result was hard to take because a deflected shot from Roger Johnson in the third minute of injury time kept them out of contention for a place on the periphery of the play-off zone. Still, City were unbeaten in five games. Brown was cautious and warned: 'It's a building block process. We have to be patient with these players. We've got to remember most of them are playing at the highest level they've ever played at.' His words seemed somehow prophetic as City duly lost their next couple of matches: 3-0 at Preston and 4-0 at Southampton. Neither the fans nor the boss were content. As he reflected on the heaviest defeat of his reign, he admitted he was 'disgusted' with the second half performance at St Mary's. 'We've not collapsed like that since I've been at the club. It won't happen again.' The loss of Turner at half time in that game with a hamstring injury was a hammer blow. The centre half had been one of the most consistent players in recent games. Brown was also staggered the referee did not award City a penalty for a foul on Windass when Southampton were only 1-0 ahead. Suddenly everything seemed to be conspiring against him. What followed was a five game unbeaten run, stretching from December 15 to January 5. That sequence included a 1-0 win at home to Sheffield Wednesday on December 30 with Windass on target. City had moved up to eighth; just one point adrift of the play-off pace. Windass' verdict? 'Things are going along nicely at the moment but no one is talking about the play-offs.' The following week, there was another encouraging result – a 1-1 draw at Stoke.

Dreams of an FA Cup run were dashed after a 3-2 defeat at Plymouth. There were a few raised eyebrows when back-up goalkeeper Matt Duke failed to take his usual place on the subs' bench for that tie. A few days later, City confirmed the player had undergone surgery for testicular cancer. Just before Christmas, I'd shared a joke with Dukie at the training ground and offered him a few tips on how he could oust Myhill from the first team. Suddenly I realised there are more important things in life than football. As Duke started his recovery, he sent a message to City fans, stressing he would be back – and as quickly as possible. He was right on both counts. There were changes to the playing staff as the injury-plagued McPhee and Coles left to join Blackpool and Bristol Rovers respectively. Delaney also moved on to Championship rivals QPR in a deal reported to be worth around £650,000. 'It seems like the end of an era,' said the genial Irishman, scorer of that last ever City goal at Boothferry Park. 'I will miss Hull. I've met some fantastic people during my six years there. People I'm sure I'll stay in touch with. Hull will always hold a special place in my life.' Few people blamed Delaney for moving on. He'd increased his wages and supposedly joined a bigger club; a club, moreover, capable of climbing into the Premier League. If only he'd known.

When City were beaten 3-1 by top-of-the-table West Brom at the KC, Brown was far from downhearted. 'The big positive for me was the battle I had with the players in the dressing room after that game because they were genuinely disappointed not to get something from it. When you compare the dressing room to last season, there is a massive difference. It's now full of men, full of characters – and characters who want to do well for Hull City.' City's next challenge should have been at Colchester. The game was postponed at the last minute because of a waterlogged pitch. A few days later Brown praised his players for an 'ugly' 1-0 win at home to Coventry, Folan scoring in the final minute. A crowd of fewer than 15,000 illustrated that not everyone in Hull shared the growing belief that City could claim a top six place. The month ended with another round of departures from the club: Sam Collins joined Hartlepool, Livermore moved to Oldham on loan and Elliott joined Doncaster on a temporary basis until the end of the season. It was genuinely sad to see Elliott move on. His goals had done so much to clinch those back-to-back promotions under Peter Taylor. He played as he approached everything in life – with a smile. Unfortunately, he was unable to consistently bridge the gap between League One and the Championship. Elliott had proved in City's first season in the Championship that he could score goals. However, a problem with asthma, which took a long time to diagnose, meant he was never the same player under the Brown regime. Of all the players who have left City, Elliott is the one I feel deserved a crack at the big time. With typical modesty, Elliott always played down his role in the club's success story. Jan Molby didn't get too much right during his time as City manager. Signing Elliott, though, was a master-stroke. As Elliott headed to Doncaster, he admitted: 'I don't really want to leave, but I need to play more games.' He suffered the same fate at Doncaster as he had at City. He never pulled on a black and amber shirt again. There were a couple of new arrivals: Mark Tyler as cover for Duke and Simon Walton, who joined on loan from QPR. Walton, who broke into Leeds' first team as a teenager, was looking to re-launch a promising career that had ground to a halt. His versatility promised to be an asset for City. So did the fact he had a Page Three girlfriend. Sadly, it wasn't something he was keen to talk about.

City went into February at the cross-roads of their season. The play-offs were a tantalising target. However, did they have the ability to challenge for the top six? Or would they slip back towards the relegation battle? Amazingly, the fans' message boards at the time were full of Brown doubters. It proved to be a good month: two wins, three draws and no defeats. The best result was undoubtedly a 2-1 win at West Brom, Campbell grabbing a superb goal after a 25-yard strike and Folan firing an equally impressive winner eight minutes from the end. 'All wins are satisfying,' said Brown, 'but none more so than against the team who are favourites for automatic promotion – and on their own ground. There was a lot of scepticism around before the game. I don't know why because we'd lost only once in ten games. Now we needn't fear anyone.' With eight games in 29 days, March was always going to be a crucial period. The first test was at Bristol City. City lost 2-1 and slipped to ninth in the table. They were, though, just two points off the top six. 'Another game has gone by but we're still confident we can get into the play-offs,' said Brown. 'We've got ourselves into a great position and we don't want to let things slip now.' City bounced back to beat Burnley 2-0 in a game that saw Okocha sent off for the first time in his career. Folan suffered the same fate. Mike Riley was the referee. Enough said. Ashbee declared the first 45 minutes against Burnley was 'the best we have played all season.'

Reinforcements were needed. They arrived in the familiar shape of Fagan, signed on loan from Derby with a view to a permanent deal. 'It's great to be back,' he said and added (to a somewhat muted response from his team-mates), 'I bet you've all missed me.' After leaving City the previous season, Fagan had helped Derby into the Premier League. However, he'd been unable to stop them sliding back towards the Championship after one of the worst top flight campaigns on record. City also welcomed another loan signing – Neil Clement from West Brom – and soon highlighted their play-off potential with a 2-0 win against Scunthorpe. Four days later, they lost 1-0 at Cardiff but recovered to thrash Southampton 5-0 at fortress KC. Brown's reaction after that Southampton game was pure delight. 'You know what?' he said. 'The most pleasing thing about the result is the clean sheet.' Who was he trying to kid? Five goals at home, and against a team that had been tipped for promotion at the start of the season. City faced a tricky trip back to Colchester in midweek in the re-arranged fixture. There was no love lost between the two clubs following a verbal spat after the Layer Road pitch was ruled unfit late on. In truth, the ill feeling probably carried over from the furore surrounding Phil Parkinson's appointment. Parkinson's City had been thrashed at Colchester. How things had changed. Under Brown, City were one of the form teams in the Division and reinforced that reputation with a 3-1 victory with Campbell (2) and Folan on target. It wasn't Colchester's night. They were reduced to ten-men after just 14 minutes when Phil Ifill was sent off. People whispered it quietly . . . but could this be City's season after all?

Largely happy to take a back-seat role, Duffen admitted he believed that a top six position was feasible; perhaps, he added, even automatic promotion. Another win followed – 2-0 at Leicester. City had climbed to third place. With six games to go, they were two points off a top two position. Long suffering fans probably had to glance twice when they checked the latest standings. Brown stressed he wasn't even looking at the table. 'I know this sounds like a cliché, but to be brutally honest, I've no idea what it (the table) looks like. All season our aim has been to get into the top six and we've probably arrived a bit early, but now that we're there, it's our intention to stay there.' What about a top two finish. 'It hasn't come into my thoughts,' added Brown. 'All I'm thinking about is winning the next game.' City had turned the pressure on their rivals; so much so that West Brom suddenly decided to recall Clement, who had been a tower of strength in defence during his short stay at the KC. 'I'd have done the same in their position,' said Brown. 'Neil had failed a few medicals at other clubs and I don't think West Brom believed he could play three games in a week, but he's done that for us.' Two City players made their international debuts following that Leicester victory – Campbell for England Under-21s and Myhill for Wales. Myhill, actually born in America, appeared to be eligible for most countries under the FIFA umbrella due to the various rules for qualification. He joined Sam Ricketts in the Welsh team. Both of them are about as Welsh as Yorkshire pudding. 'Did you sing the National Anthem?' was the question when they returned from Welsh duty. 'Err no,' said Myhill. 'There's a slight problem in that we don't know the words. We hummed the tune, though.'

Top six rivals Watford were next on the agenda at the KC. A few weeks previously not too many people outside Hull would have backed City to win. In the event, they coasted to a 3-0 success; Turner's first minute goal put them on the way to three points that clinched the Manager of the Month award for Brown. City were scheduled to play Barnsley. The game was called off because their opponents had reached the semi finals of the FA Cup. Although disappointed City's momentum had been halted, Brown acknowledged the week's rest had come at a perfect time. Ashbee, Wayne Brown and Windass were among the players carrying injuries. Despite having the weekend off, City held onto to third place. Bristol City headed the table, despite losing 2-0 at Southampton. Stoke held second place and Watford had clawed themselves level on points with City after beating Coventry 2-1. West Brom, Wolves, Charlton and Plymouth still harboured play-off hopes. With five games to go, City were in a strong position – just two points off the top of the table. It was time to start to dream. The sizeable presence of Delaney – and his QPR team-mates – arrived at the KC Stadium on April 12, determined to derail City's promotion charge. They left with a 1-1 draw after a tight game played out in front of almost 22,500. Rangers led until Turner grabbed an equaliser in the last seconds of the game. Brown admitted: 'When you're not at your best, it's vital you take something. We'll take the point.' The tension was increasing. Could Brown and his players handle it? They headed to Barnsley for a midweek derby, desperate to keep their promotion challenge alive. More than 5,000 fans made the trip and there were plenty of anxious faces around before the kick off. They needn't have fretted. City won 3-0 with Ashbee chipping in with a rare goal to support efforts from Marney and Windass. City were second for the first time in the season. Rumour had it the last time they were in such an exalted position, the bowler-hatted Ambrose Langley was the manager in 1910. First, there had been talk of the play-offs, then automatic promotion. Now it was the title. Brown said: 'If the opportunity comes round to win the title then that will be our next challenge.' That battle was a complicated one. Bristol City slipped back; West Brom were the new leaders; City were ahead of Stoke on goal difference.

On Saturday, April 19, City visited Sheffield United, West Brom faced a trip to Norwich and Stoke met Bristol City. Having lost only one of their last ten games, Brown's side produced a below-par performance at Bramall Lane and paid the price with 2-0 defeat. Brown refused to put the performance down to pressure, or nerves, or the fact he had to play Livermore as an emergency centre half. He said: 'Sheffield United deserve some credit. Their fans were goading us towards the end and if their players had played like that all season, they would have been in the top six and the top team in Yorkshire but they're not . . . we are.' It was defiant stuff and just what the fans wanted to hear. Seven days later and City were back in the promotion race after a 2-1 success against Crystal Palace at a packed KC. Ashbee scored the winning goal with eight minutes to go. Brown tried to convince everyone he'd enjoyed the game. The look of relief on his face in the post-match press conference told the true story. City were still very much in the race for the top two. However, West Brom made certain of one of the automatic promotion places after a 1-1 draw at Southampton on a Monday night.

One game to go. City trailed Stoke by three points, but boasted a superior goal difference. Even though second place was still a possibility, the omens did not look good. City needed to win at Ipswich and Stoke had to lose at home to already relegated Leicester. Ipswich's Portman Road ground seemed to be invaded by black and amber fans. It was impossible to get a ticket, for love or money – or both. Over 5,000 City fans watched the game on a live 'beam-back' at the KC. Inside Portman Road, eyes were focussed on the pitch, radios were tuned to Stoke v Leicester. In the event, City lost 1-0 and Stoke drew 1-1. Third place was still an outstanding achievement. At Christmas, you'd have got pretty good odds on City being relegated. Still, having come so close to promotion only to fall at the final hurdle, it felt as though City had failed.

Watford were waiting in the play-offs. But first Brown had to pick his players up off floor. 'I've never seen so many disappointed faces in a dressing room,' said Ashbee after that Ipswich defeat. There was no need for the nightclub City had booked for the celebrations just a few hundred yards away from Portman Road. The champagne stayed in the car boots of the staff who had ferried crates of it to the ground. Brown pulled off a masterstroke on the way back from Ipswich. He stopped the team coach at a hotel, sat the players down and told them how proud he was of them. He told them they were good enough to beat Watford. He reminded them that they were just three games away from the Premier League. There were only a few days for them to recover and repair morale. Brown and his backroom team worked wonders.

The first leg was at Watford. Brown had hammered home the message of how important it was to make a positive start. Barmby scored after just six minutes; Windass after 23. Myhill and his defenders then survived everything Watford could hurl at them. Leading 2-0, fans thought they were already in a Wembley final. Brown brought them back to earth. 'There's still everything to play for,' he said. 'We can't take anything for granted and there will be no complacency on our part. There's another 90 minutes to play and it's going to be one hell of a game.' And so to the KC. This time, it was Watford who made the positive start. They scored early on with a neat finish from Darius Henderson: 2-1 on aggregate. Game on. City looked awkward, unhappy and uncertain. Somehow they held out. Then, two minutes before half time, they struck a vital blow. Dawson's header caused havoc in Watford's penalty area. Leigh Bromby failed to clear, Garcia headed towards goal and Barmby forced the ball over the line. The KC erupted. It was probably the scruffiest goal Barmby had ever scored in his entire career. It was also the most important. City led 3-1 on the night, which became 4-1 after 70 minutes when Folan struck and then Garcia and Doyle grabbed late strikes to seal an empathic win. Cue a pitch invasion and some amazing celebrations. The 6-1 aggregate victory meant City were heading to Wembley for the first time in their history. So much for Hull being a rugby league city.

While the celebrations raged on in the bars and pubs surrounding the KC, the dressing room was surprisingly quiet. It was as though the players couldn't quite take in what they'd achieved. In truth, they hadn't won anything. Try telling that to Windass. The former frozen pea-packer was positively buzzing. 'Wembley. Bring it on.' And Doyle had scored his first goal for the club on the very day he'd become a dad for the first time. 'Can it get any better?' he asked.

Oh yes, it could.

Chapter thirteen:

Wembley, Wembley

May, 2008

'It was a fantastic night for this football club – but the job isn't done yet.' That was how Phil Brown reacted matter-of-factly to the win against Watford. Pragmatic? Certainly. Realistic? Definitely. With a Wembley final looming, Brown knew there was no other way to respond. Paul Duffen, however, was more emotional. 'For days after that win I was left with the sound of chanting fans in my ears and with the hairs on the back of my neck frequently tingling,' he said. 'There were almost continual flashbacks of what was a truly momentous occasion.'

Just think. When Duffen was finalising the takeover 12 months previously, most City supporters would have settled for pure survival. Now the club was preparing for the biggest match in its history: 90 minutes from the Premier League. It was hardly believable. It seemed to me that the whole of Hull – in fact, make that the whole of the East Riding – had gone City crazy.

The clamour for tickets was astonishing. For years, Hull's football fans had been forced to ensure the taunts that they lived in a rugby league city. Now, instead of Hull FC or Hull KR, it was Hull City who were heading for Wembley. Hull City. When the tickets went on sale to the general public, many camped out with sleeping bags and deck-chairs. The queues snaked around the KC Stadium several times and out into West Park. Emma Steele was one of the supporters in that queue. 'I'd been out the night before with my friends in Hull. The plan was to go to the KC the next morning and buy our tickets. Then I got a text message telling me there were already hundreds of people starting to queue. It was ten o'clock at night. I dashed out of the night-club and straight to the KC. I was still wearing a short skirt, a crop-top and my heels. I must have looked a right sight. Everyone was giving me funny looks, but I wanted a ticket. I'd only missed two games that season and I wasn't going to miss Wembley, no matter what. I remember it was bitterly cold and I started worrying I was going to freeze. Fortunately my boyfriend turned up with some extra clothes, a sleeping bag and a flask of soup. It was brilliant of him – and we got married six months later. Unfortunately, he's still a Middlesbrough fan. I haven't been able to convert him. He did come to Wembley, though.' As Duffen said: 'Suddenly, we seemed to have about 50,000 people who'd supported the club for years, and had been to every game that season. It was an impossible situation. We had staff working around the clock and everyone did the best they could in the circumstances. People did criticise us for a lack of planning – even a lack of foresight. However, three months earlier and how many of those people actually thought we'd stood a cat-in-hell's chance of getting to Wembley?'

Obtaining a ticket was one thing; securing transport to Wembley was quite another. Every single train and coach was booked solid. In the latter stages of the scramble, fans were splashing out around £100 for a top seat and then paying twice as much again for a hotel room. Long-time supporter Paul Ogden revealed: 'I regularly travelled to London on business and nearly always stayed at the same hotel just off the M1. It was convenient for Wembley. Rooms were usually £60 and sometimes they'd throw in a full English breakfast at that price. I rang them to book a room for the Wembley weekend. Suddenly it was £150 – without the breakfast.' Somehow money didn't seem to matter.

Bristol City stood between the City and the Premier League. Unlike Hull, Bristol had a top flight pedigree. They had been among the frontrunners for most of that season. Gary Johnson was widely recognised as one of the most under-rated managers in the Division and their key players included striker Lee Trundle and winger Michael McIndoe. Ominously, both of them had decent records against The Tigers with their former clubs Swansea and Barnsley respectively.

A Premier League place would guarantee the winning club £60m from TV income alone. As Anne Robinson would say, the losers would leave with nothing. It was – and still is – the richest game of football on the planet. City's players were totally relaxed in the build-up. I met strikers Windass, Campbell and Folan at the club's training ground. What seemed like the world's entire media had descended at the beginning of the week. This day, though, was quiet. The cameras had disappeared. The three players were stretched out on the lush grass, enjoying the early summer sun. By now, Campbell had come out of his shell. 'Will you have any problems sleeping before the final?' I asked him. 'Nah,' he said. 'I've got a copy of

Deano's autobiography . . . a signed one, of course. I read a couple of lines every night and then fall fast asleep.' Folan added, half seriously: 'I've learned a lot from playing alongside Deano. He's a top bloke, a great guy. There again, I'll say anything for a fiver.' In just four days' time, City would walk out in front of a packed house at Wembley. But the laid-back approach of the trio summed up the mood in the camp. The bookies couldn't separate Hull and Bristol. Having seen the players close-up, I always thought City would win it. Barmby was one of the few members of the squad who had previous experience of playing at the famous old stadium. Now he'd be experiencing the 'new' Wembley too. 'It's a special place,' he said. 'It generates such an atmosphere and it will be a special day for everyone. The richest game in the world for my hometown club, and to see all our fans at Wembley where we've never been before. Brilliant.' As of the game itself, he said: 'We know it will be difficult because Bristol are a good side, a footballing side. But we want to go there and win. If we manage to get through it and get into the Premier League, it would mean everything to the people of Hull, especially the young kids. To see the likes of Ronaldo coming to the KC next season, and going to places like Anfield and Old Trafford, would have a positive effect on the whole city.'

City opted to travel on the Thursday, two days before the match. The endless round of interviews had been completed. Now it was time to re-focus on football. Brown said: 'The players just need to get away from all that now and think about a big game of football.' City used Arsenal's training facilities. Brown added: 'To have Premier League surroundings can help create a Premier League mentality and that could be a key factor.' I, along with City's press office staff, travelled down on the Friday in time to meet up with Brown and the players at the stadium. The media were hovering, but there was a strict policy of no interviews. It was my first visit to 'new' Wembley. The twin towers may have disappeared, but the giant arch was truly an awe-inspiring sight. Walking out of the players' tunnel and looking up at steepling banks of red seats is something I'll never forget. The place looked massive. It was eerily quiet. Individual voices echoed around the place. I was taken up to the Royal Box and given a guided tour of the dressing rooms. They were enormous and fitted out like a five-star hotel. There were plush wash basins, whirlpool baths, an assortment of hairdryers mounted on the walls and countless mirrors. The toilets had slow-closing lids. There were dispensers for soap, toothpaste and deodorants. A couple of corners were dominated by huge fridges containing soft drinks; the sporting variety, of course. We'd heard various reports about the state of the pitch. It looked magnificent. 'Not bad this, eh,' said Windass. 'I wouldn't mind a bit of this turf in the back garden at home.'

As the players started to look around, we sat in the dug-out that had been assigned to City. Twenty-four hours later and Brown and his staff would be watching the drama unfold from here. Now only a couple of pigeons occupied one of the penalty areas. Deano strolled up, his hair dyed bottle blonde. He looked like Eninem. It was as though he didn't have a care in the world. 'I think I prefer Boothferry Park,' he said. While the players 'tested' the pitch, we collected our various passes: one each for the 100 or so check-points we seemed to need to get through on the day itself. It was a bit different to Torquay, I thought. So were the prices: £18 to park your car at the stadium – on the day before the game. I ignored the clamping warnings and stuck it across the road outside B&Q. Even though the stadium was impressive, majestic even – all tinted glass and white stanchions – the surroundings were still the same. I still find it hard to believe that the nation's premier sports stadium is slap bang in the middle of an industrial estate where every single unit seems to be fronted by abandoned white vans and unwanted pallets. It's a disgrace. Our city centre hotel was rather more palatial. We booked in at the same time as two Middle Eastern businessmen were booking out. They paid for their month-long stay in cash. I've never seen so many £50 notes. Apparently, a host of celebrities (well, Dale Winton anyway) were staying at the same hotel and were dining in the Garden Court restaurant. 'Do Sirs want to reserve a table?' asked the receptionist, handing over a menu. We looked at the prices and decided on a burger instead. If we'd eaten at the hotel, it would have taken up a hefty chunk of that £60m Premier League windfall. The following morning, we thought we'd head off to the stadium on the underground. The station was about 100 yards away. It was a big mistake. The queues were amazing. Fortunately, the players' wives and girlfriends were staying at the same hotel. I blagged a lift on their coach. Arriving at Wembley, I piled off the coach first. The camera crew from BBC North were not impressed. 'Ladies,' quipped the sound-man, 'you could have had a shave.'

Wembley wasn't even half-full at this stage. Two hours until kick-off. A lot of people were milling around on the various concourses. Again, it was an amazing sight: a sea of black and amber at one end, and red and white at another. Before the game, I stood in the players' tunnel. The atmosphere more than matched the weather. It was red-hot. City fans were away to our left and kept leaning over a barrier – cameras in hand – asking when the players were coming out. In the event, Brown kept his squad in the dressing room. It was a tip gleaned from Sir Alex Ferguson, who had warned City's management about the dangers of players being distracted at the last minute. 'You let them see their families and the fans and there's a danger their minds aren't on it,' was his message. Fair enough.

When the game kicked off, at exactly three o'clock, the noise was deafening. Up in the press box, one of the reporters from a Bristol paper almost started scrapping with some of the club's fans sitting in front of him. Their balloons drifted into his lap-top and then up into his face. They thought it was funny. He didn't. Brown patrolled the touchline in his lucky brown suit. Apparently, he'd worn it for the first time in that all-important win at Cardiff at the end of the previous season. It had seen better days, but try telling that to the man himself. He'd had a couple of buttons sewn back on for the big day. He also wore his 'lucky' tan shoes and yet he claims he's not superstitious.

Everyone said it would be a close contest. They weren't wrong. City had the first chance, but Richard Gracia's shot flew high into the Bristol fans packed behind the goal. Those fans taunted Garcia with the chant: 'Premier League? You're having a laugh.' Bristol might have scored seconds later when Dele Adebola – all 14 stones of him – turned like a ballet dancer inside the box only for Wayne Brown to get in a timely challenge. The ball trickled harmlessly through to Myhill. Windass was roundly jeered by Bristol's supporters in the 13th minute when he attempted a shot, but fell flat on his backside. The tension was incredible . . . and that was just in the press box. Would it by City's – and Deano's – day?

There was a scare for the Tigers in the 18th minute when midfielder Skuse surged to the edge of the area, but stuck a low drive a couple of yards wide. City countered and Windass's cross to the far post almost picked out Barmby. Full back Orr made a brave clearing header. From the resulting corner, Turner headed narrowly off target as 40,000 black and amber fans thought he'd scored. City pressed again. Campbell's shot was easily held by Basso, and Barmby shot wide. At the other end, a crunching Ashbee tackle halted Skuse in his tracks, and Dawson produced two vital defensive headers. Genuine chances were few and far between. Then City – and Windass – struck.

The 38th minute. Ashbee breaks up another attack and Barmby's through ball picks out Campbell, who is forced to the left edge of the penalty area by the covering Carney. Campbell is hemmed in, but looks up. He spots Windass in space and chips the ball to his strike partner 20 yards from goal. There's just one thought on Windass's mind. He lashes an unstoppable volley past Basso and into the back of the net. One half of the stadium goes wild. The other is deathly quiet. Windass has probably never run as far – or as fast – as he sprints away to celebrate. Brown punches the air and then hugs Steve Parkin: 1-0.

There were four of us from City's media team in the Press Box. We all leapt into the air and danced down an aisle. Our rivals from Bristol were not best pleased. We took our seats again. There was a long hold up as the unfortunate Orr was stretchered off, struggling after that earlier accidental clash with Barmby. As the half ended, Bristol piled forward. Turner and Wayne Brown stood firm. Noble shot over from 20 yards, Trundle hooked an effort well wide and Myhill clawed away a corner. Half time came and went. Could City hang on? Could they score again? A Wembley press officer told us they didn't normally allow dancing in the press box. I think she was joking.

The second half was less than a minute old when Skuse drilled a low shot wide with Myhill at full stretch, diving to his left. City tried to counter but passes were going astray. The heat was taking a toll on the older players such as Barmby. In the 54th minute, Noble shot straight at Myhill. City swept upfield and Campbell had a clear shot at goal, but scuffed his effort straight at a relieved Basso. Myhill clawed away a teasing corner under pressure from Adebola and then made a routine save from Trundle, whose close-range effort lacked real venom. City's fans tried to lift the players with chants of 'We are going up.' Campell attempted to tee Windass up again in the 74th minute. This time, the veteran could not hit the target.

The inevitable calls for the final whistle started in the 81st minute. No fan from either club left their seat. The tension grew. The noise increased. Brown appeared to be counting down the seconds. The fourth official produced a board which showed three minutes' stoppage time. It was the turn of Bristol's fans to explode into life. City's fans were hoping – and praying. Byfield looked a certain scorer, but somehow headed over from six yards and then shot wide from slightly further out. Gary Johnson buried his head in his hands. He knew the last chance had gone.

The final whistle. The impossible had happened. After 104 years, City were in the Premier League.

As the players performed their lap of honour, I rushed down to the dressing room area, passes hanging around my neck. Sure enough, a burly steward barred my way. 'You haven't got the right pass,' he growled. 'But I came down before the game,' was the reply. 'That was then,' he said. 'This is now. No pass, no entry.' I showed him about six different passes. The barrier remained. One of Wembley's own press staff intervened. She pointed at one of my passes and suggested I turned it round. 'Ah,' said the steward. 'Now, you are showing the right coloured sticker.' The press officer quickly apologised. 'Sorry about that but he (the steward) was only doing his job. He's used to dealing with the press at big matches.' Thanks. I didn't hang around to argue that this was the biggest match in City's history. Soon I was standing at the end of the players' tunnel watching the celebrations. The hairs on the back of my neck were standing up. It is true what they say. Wembley is no place for losers. Bristol's players filed dejectedly into their dressing room. There were tears in the eyes of their captain Louis Carey. Out on the pitch, City's players were still celebrating. For a few seconds, my mind drifted back to those dark, old days a Boothferry Park and all those 'last ever' matches. Now I looked out on the most famous arena in the world. I hadn't felt such emotion since my dad died. Suddenly I was joined by members of City's back-room staff, coach Steve Parkin, conditioner Sean Rush, physio Simon Maltby and kit-man Barry Lowe. We all shook hands, slapped each other on the back. They'd lived, eaten and breathed every pass, every tackle that season. Yet, here I was in the mix. It was just like the old days in the dressing room with Joycey. Back then, I almost felt like I was intruding. I felt the same now. A half full bottle of champagne was thrust into my hand. 'Have a swig,' said Rushie. 'You deserve it.' Really. What had I done? I felt as though I should be back on the other side of the barrier with the assembled ranks of the press. Then, another bottle of champagne was poured over my head. The players didn't want to leave the pitch. The fans didn't want to leave the stadium.

Beaten Bristol boss Gary Johnson walked by and spotted my City tie. We shook hands. 'Well played. You deserved it. Good luck for next season.'

Eventually the players returned to the dressing room and the doors were thrown open. The first face I spotted was Brown's. No doubt he'd have liked to have savoured a truly monumental victory, preferably with a pint of Guinness in his hand. His tie was askew. His lucky suit jacket and shirt were drenched in champagne. More champagne flowed down his forehead. He looked exhausted. He shook my hand before admitting: 'You know what? This is the best day of my life without a shadow of a doubt. But don't tell the wife I just said that. She'd kill us both.' He looked around the dressing room and added: 'People say that automatic promotion is the only way to go up. That would have saved us all a few grey hairs. But today . . . well it has been absolutely fantastic. There is a lot to be said for team spirit and togetherness. These players have put their bodies on the line mentally and physically – not just today – but all season. I'm proud of them. Proud of what they've achieved and how they've achieved it.' With that, he headed off. I remember worrying that he already appeared to have lost his voice, and he hadn't yet done a single interview.

It was pandemonium. Deano appeared, larger than life, bottle of beer in one hand and his winners' medal in the other. He wasn't wearing any socks. He'd chucked his shirt and his boots to some fans in the crowd. Fortunately, he'd kept his shorts on. His face was beetroot red. With the bleached blonde hair, only his mother and tens of thousands of City fans could love him. He made straight for me, shaking the can of beer before tipping it all over me. 'I'll let you into a secret,' he said. 'I told the gaffer before the game that I'll score you the winner to get us up. I honestly believed that. Now it's happened, it's a fairytale. I should have bought a fucking lottery ticket as well because someone up there obviously likes me.' I asked him about the goal. Another swig of beer, and then the answer. 'Hey, you know me. I just decided to smash it. It's instinct really. You do it every day in training – and usually the ball ends up in the canal or the top of a tree. I've stunned a fair few crows in my time. I'd like to say I placed it, but . . . ah . . .what's it fucking matter. To come back to this club and score the goal that takes us into the Premier League is amazing. Amazing. If you'd told me about it when I was 17 or 18 – running up and down the terraces at Boothferry Park – I'd have laughed in your face. If you'd said it a couple of years later when I was packing peas in the Birds' Eye factory, I'd have laughed even more. You know. I'd just like to say thanks to Terry Dolan. If it wasn't for him, I'd still be packing those peas and still playing for Gipsyville Tavern on a Sunday morning with dog shite all over the pitch.' There were tears in Deano's eyes. 'Here,' he said to me. 'Have the bottle. I'll go and get another.'

The emotion was also written all over Brian Horton's face. His eyes were red raw. Perhaps it was the champagne. Perhaps he'd been crying. 'Brilliant,' he said. 'We're in the Premier League. Takes some believing, doesn't it? No one can say we don't deserve it, though. I've got to admit that when I came back to the club, I didn't think it would happen as quickly as it has done. There was the ambition – and the potential – but it was a three year plan. If you sat down and looked at what happened the previous season, then we were only being sensible. Sometimes, though, plans are there to be broken.'

Dawson, one of the survivors from the club's days in League Two, was the next to appear. He said: 'My debut was on a Monday night at Doncaster. Now we've won at Wembley and we're in the Premier League. It's an amazing feeling. It's not just the players who have come all the way. The fans have as well. They've been brilliant. We've done it for them.' By now, I was sitting on an old plastic table, just inside the tunnel. Turner joined us. 'If you'd sat down with me at the start of the season and said all this would happen, I'd have thought you were mad. But we've done it and there's no feeling in the world like it. I'm looking forward to a holiday and then – just think - Man United, Liverpool, Arsenal, Chelsea.'

With that, there was a massive slap on my back. I almost disappeared into Bristol's dressing room. It could only be one person: Ashbee. A city scarf was draped around his neck. His socks were around his ankles. His shin-pads stuck out at right angles. His eyes were a tell-tale red-raw. 'Not bad is it? I just feel so emotional. I've been here for six years. To cement my name in Hull City's history was something I wanted to achieve. The Premier League is going to be a massive challenge for me, but the manager has said he thinks I can play in it. If he says that, then it's good enough for me.' Ashbee moved off, hugging Campbell on his way. The Manchester United loan star had been a key figure in that final – and in the season as a whole. Fifteen goals and a vital partnership with Windass. But what of the future? 'Was this my last game for Hull City?' he said. 'I honestly don't know. Would I come back to Hull? What do you think? Anyway, what would Deano do without me?'

It was well over an hour before the players made their way back to the team coach. The final words that afternoon went to

Duffen. 'In football terms, the result of winning this game is bigger than winning the Champions League or the UEFA Cup. It doesn't just mean a trophy and another entry on the roll of honour. It will change the lives of hundreds of thousands of people and have a lasting impact on the entire city. Each member of the squad has played his part and the credit is shared by the players, the coaching staff, the back-room staff and, of course, the manager and his assistant. They have written their names in Hull City folklore and will never be forgotten.'

There was a party for the players back at their hotel. I didn't go. I decided to head back up the M1 that night. There was work to do: a 50-odd page Wembley special for the City magazine. The deadline was 48 hours away. Just about every car I passed on the M1 seemed to be decked out in black and amber. Like everyone else, we were talking – and thinking – about the Premier League. Then, near to Sheffield, the traffic eased off. My mind drifted back to those earlier years: to Torquay, to Macclesfield, to Rushden and Diamonds, Lloyd, Buchanan, Hinchliffe, concrete coffins. I half expected someone to wake me up and tell me Wembley had just been a dream. I decided to ring Joycey. There was no answer from his mobile. I thought about ringing some of the leading characters I'd met down the years. Somehow, though, the timing didn't seem right.

After all, even if he had answered his phone, what could David Lloyd have said?

Chapter fourteen:

The boy from Brazil

May, 2008 - August 2008

The start of June: two weeks after Wembley. It felt strange as I drove into City's training ground. There's not a player in sight. They are all away, sunning themselves on a foreign beach. I know Deano is in the Algarve. As I park up, I can picture him boring the pants off someone at the next dining table as he talks about 'that' goal and how he's going to terrorise Premier League defences. Hull City in the Premier League. I still can't quite believe it.

I've pulled in next to a battered old white van. The paint splashed sign on the side shows it belongs to a local decorator. I walk though the main doors and I am greeted by a sea of dust-sheets. The whole place is getting an up-date, part of a £100,000-plus programme of improvements. The players' lounge will feature black leather sofas, coffee tables and a giant plasma-screen TV. Oh, and don't forget the pot plants. Hopefully, there will still be space for the dart-board. I notice a side-room is already full of dozen or so computers with the latest wi-fi connection. Ten years ago, Joycey and his players used to share a few sandwiches in the back of his people carrier. I recall they popped round to my house on one occasion. Fortunately, Brabs wasn't that hungry. An impromptu training session on my front lawn was cut-short when David Brown crashed the ball into a neighbour's window. He never could shoot straight. The neighbour, 'old' Frank, was not amused. 'You're worse than the flamin' kids,' he growled. He was a Leeds United season-ticket holder. Today, and the transformation of City's training complex is part of creating that all-important Premier League image.

Usually, the complex is a hive of activity, but it is eerily quiet. An empty champagne bottle lies on the kitchen counter, gathering dust. Suddenly, the silence is broken. Brian Horton emerges from the manager's office, which is hidden behind a step-ladder and pile of old paint pots. 'Can't keep away?' he says. 'Didn't see you at the reception,' he adds. 'Mind you, I can't remember much myself. Good day, wasn't it?' Two days after that Wembley triumph, there was a civic reception and open top bus tour. Apparently the chairman came within inches of being decapitated. Smiling and waving to the crowds lining the route, he didn't spot a very low railway bridge, but fortunately ducked a split-second before the bus passed under it. I was in the city square, along with around 5,000 fans. I'll never forget Deano – tears streaming down his face – singing the Tigers' anthem From Boothferry To Wembley while standing on the balcony – 60 feet of fresh air between him and the ground and John Cooper desperately clinging onto his ankles to stop him falling. He's a real stickler for health and safety. Horton and I share a few other recollections. Then he's off, heading for the exit. He trips over the handle of a roller brush. He kicks it and it leaves a huge, great mark on a freshly painted wall. 'The gaffer's in there,' he says, recovering his composure and pointing in the direction of the manager's office.

After Wembley, everyone thought Phil Brown would head straight for a holiday. However, he's not stopped working. There is a season of Premier League football to plan for. I knock on his door and walk in. Brown looks relaxed in cut-off shorts and black training top. He issues his catchphrase 'how are you' welcome at the same time as shifting a pile of papers off the only chair not covered by a dust-sheet. The conversation soon turns to the last couple of weeks. Brown says: 'I don't know about you, but it doesn't seem like five minutes since Wembley. There's been a lot going on since then, a whole range of emotions. First, there was the excitement, then the expectation and finally the realism. People might say, hold on a minute, 104-years of history and never been in the Premier League. Suddenly, we'd realised it. Straightaway, I knew there was a job to get on with. We've got an even bigger challenge, and as much as I'd like it, I can't prepare on a beach somewhere. There will be time for that later.'

Brown had already made some difficult decisions. Not all his promotion winning heroes will be gracing the Premier League. Okocha, for example, has been released. 'He wanted to stay,' adds Brown, 'and he was disappointed when I told him but he understood why we let him go.' Okocha didn't play at Wembley. He didn't play in as many games as he – and City – had hoped. There were tantalising glimpses of the form that made him one of the greatest players ever to come out of Africa. But that's all they were – glimpses. Okocha was a big influence on the rest of the squad. The fact a player of his stature signed for City reinforced the club's credibility at a time when there were plenty of cynics around. But, as Brown says, what would a 35-year-old Okocha have offered City in the Premier League? Manager and player went back a long way to their days together at Bolton. There was a deep-rooted mutual respect. However, sentiment plays no part in modern-day football. I can still remember the day Peter Taylor told Whittle he could leave. Whittle looked shell-shocked. Hull City was his life. I wanted to give him a hug. Blokes don't do that. Instead, I shook his hand. A few weeks later and Whittle was kicking lumps out of Alan Shearer in a Worthington Cup tie between Grimsby and Newcastle United. Now he is a part-time postman, playing for a few quid a week at North Ferriby United. His wife used to nag him to start his coaching qualifications. He never did. Okocha won't be delivering letters for a living. He'd already returned to his family in some oil rich country in the Middle East, talking about the possibility of opening a chain of football schools. City fans probably weren't surprised to see him go. Now they are focussing on who will replace him. Ever since that win at Wembley, City have been linked with just about every player in the western hemisphere and various others beyond it.

Depending on which tabloid paper you read, Brown has a war chest of anywhere between £10m and £40m to spend. He's been spotted speaking to so many big name players in so many restaurants, I'm surprised those cut-offs fit. He adds: 'Apparently, I've been to China, Chile and Russia. I can promise you, I haven't been any further than Bolton. No, wait a minute, I took the wife and kids to Blackpool for the day. It rained.' Brown is perched on his desk, surrounded by a mountain of files that have spilled over from a window sill. He explains the files contain the detailed profiles of players. 'See that one there,' he says. 'It's a dossier on the African Nations Cup. The tournament was in January and every single player who played in that tournament is included. I can tell you what he likes for tea, what he wears in bed.' Brown drops his voice and looks out of the window. Perhaps he's worried that The Sun has already sent a reporter to track his every move. The manager admits he and the chairman had been discussing potential signings for weeks – possibly months – before that Wembley final. But Brown didn't know whether he could offer new players Championship or Premier League football or Championship or Premier League wages. He's very aware City's fans are clamouring for as many new signings as possible. He also knows that, unlike the majority of their top flight rivals, City still haven't recruited anyone yet. Duffen repeatedly stressed that the club was adequately funded to support the purchase of new players. However, paying for players isn't even half the battle. First, Brown has got to convince them to come to Hull. He throws me a tabloid paper. 'Look at that,' he says, pointing to an article, ghost-written for an ex-Premiership player who thinks City will survive in the Premier League for four seasons: summer, autumn, winter and spring. It is the type of cheap 'shot' Brown can expect. It also highlights the size of the task he faces.

It isn't just that people think City won't survive in the Premier League. There's the place itself. 'A lot of people have made reference to the inner city (of Hull), but you show me an inner city anywhere in this country that doesn't have problems. Hull's no different to Manchester, Newcastle or Liverpool,' says Brown. 'I love it here,' he adds 'and it's not that bad. You live here,' don't you?' I grimace and tell him that I've just moved across the River Humber after buying a house in Lincolnshire.

HAPPY CHIMES: Chairman Paul Duffen (left) and manager Phil Brown ring a bell to announce the club's first-ever season of top flight football. The ceremony took place just before the kick off of the first game against Fulham but was very nearly cancelled . . . after the bell fell apart.

SAMBA STAR: Brazilian star Geovanni is somewhere in the middle of this huddle of City players after his stunning goal against Fulham. Coach Steve Parkin (second left) rushes to join the party.

Previous page: THE BIG TIME: Andy Dawson (right) walks out of the players' tunnel at the KC Stadium ahead of his several of his team-mates as City prepare for their first ever Premier League fixture against Fulham. Dawson is one of four players to have represented City in all four divisions.

I CAN FLY: Caleb Folan wheels away in triumph after scoring City's winning goal against Fulham.

OUT-GUNNED: Michael Turner (centre), Marlon King and goal-scorer Daniel Cousin leave shell-shocked Arsenal with that sinking feeling during City's remarkable 2-1 victory at The Emirates.

THAT WINNING FEELING: The outstanding Michael Turner celebrates City's win at Arsenal. Turner came desperately close to an England call-up after a tremendous season. The club's one - and only - England international was Edward Gordon Dundas Wright back in 1905.

LOOK AT ME: Loan signing Marlon King salutes the fans after scoring in Hull City's 3-0 win at Premier League rivals West Brom. King played a major role in City's early season successes before he left the club following a bust-up with Phil Brown.

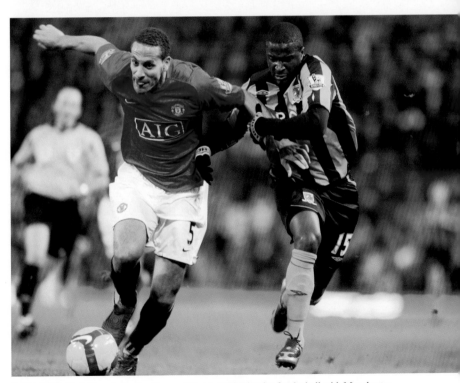

IT'S MINE: City's French signing Bernard Mendy (right) battles for the ball with Manchester United's Rio Ferdinand at Old Trafford. Mendy was one of City's goal-scorers in a pulsating 4-3 defeat at the home of the Premier League champions.

HEAD-TO-HEAD: Andy Dawson tussles with Manchester United and England star Wayne Rooney for possession at Old Trafford. For Dawson, the game was a far cry from his debut for City in the slightly less glamorous surroundings of Belle Vue, Doncaster.

DRESSING DOWN: Phil Brown gives his players a very public rollicking after a nightmare first half performance at Manchester City. Some critics suggested this marked the turning point of the Tigers' season.

WAIT FOR IT: Ian Ashbee (centre) and Michael Turner prepare to compete with Liverpool stars Stephen Gerrard and Jamie Carragher in the Premier League game at Anfield. City stunned their illustrious hosts by grabbing a 2-0 lead before being pegged back to a 2-2 draw.

OH YES: Manager Phil Brown punches the air in triumph after Manucho's late, late goal secured an important 1-0 win at Fulham on March 4. Brown, though, didn't have too much to celebrate in the second half of the season.

JIMMY, JIMMY: Record signing Jimmy Bullard meets the fans after his £5m move from Premier League rivals Fulham. The England international suffered a season-ending knee injury after less than 20 minutes of his debut at West Ham United.

CENTRE OF ATTENTION: Assistant manager Brian Horton who found himself embroiled in the 'Spit-gate' saga following the club's controversial exit from the FA Cup at Arsenal.

UNDER PRESSURE: Phil Brown shows visible signs of anguish during City's defeat at relegation rivals Middlesbrough. In the background is Middlesbrough manager Gareth Southgate. Brown labelled his side's performance that day as 'unacceptable' but he was still smiling at the end of the season . . . unlike Southgate.

LOOKING WORRIED: The expression on the face of this City fan at Sunderland says it all. A 1-0 defeat at The Stadium of Light had the cynics rushing to write off the club's chances of staying in the Premier League.

YOU'RE OFF: A distraught Caleb Folan is sent off during the latter stages of City's Premier League game against Liverpool at the KC Stadium. The decision delivered the final blow to any hopes of a fight-back.

FEELING THE HEAT: A steward has to hold back Brian Horton as he berates the officials following the crushing defeat against Stoke at the KC Stadium. The game was billed as a must win match for City but they were well-beaten.

Opposite: SO PRECIOUS: Craig Fagan celebrates scoring one of the most important goals in City's history, the equaliser at Bolton that did so much to clinch the club's place in the top flight. In the background is Manucho, a loan signing from Manchester United who made a limited impact on the Tigers' desperate battle for survival.

WE'RE SAFE: Paul Duffen (left) and Phil Brown just seconds after the final whistle against Manchester United confirmed City were safe . . . and the fact Newcastle were relegated along with Middlesbrough and West Brom.

SAYING IT ALL: First-team coach Steve Parkin (left) and an injured Jimmy Bullard don't need to say anything as the banner proclaims City are staying in the Premier League.

WE'VE DONE IT: Fans rush on to the pitch at the KC Stadium to celebrate Hull City's dramatic escape from relegation on the final day of the season against Manchester United. Newcastle's defeat at Aston Villa meant that the result - displayed on the giant electronic scoreboard in the background - was insignificant.

THE RELIEF: Chairman Paul Duffen hugs Craig Fagan at the end of that Manchester United game.

OFF KEY: Phil Brown proves he's no match for Susan Boyle as he belts out a tune immediately after the Manchester United game.

RUBBISH EVERYWHERE: The West Stand - and players' car park - before the demolition men moved in at Boothferry Park. This is where Peter Taylor and I were almost crushed by the reversing Rochdale team coach. All that remains today are the floodlight pylons.

GONE BUT NOT FORGOTTEN: The wreck of the West Stand . . . and the weeds on the pitch at Boothferry Park. This photograph was taken just before the start of the club's first season of Premier League football.

Over: TODAY: All that remains of the West Stand at Boothferry Park. I used to report on games from the Press Box which was tucked away at the back of the second tier. On a clear day, you could just about see the site of the KC Stadium a mile of so down the road.

He shakes his head but presses on. "There's some beautiful countryside around here. There's loads of good things happening about the place. It's about telling players that, telling them that this is a club and an area on the up.' I point out – gingerly – that the three aforementioned cities have an established Premier League pedigree. Before Brown can answer, his mobile rings. It's another agent, trying to sell another player. 'Here we go again,' says Brown. 'If you hear a name, it doesn't go any further than this room.' He borrows my pen and scribbles down a few details on the back of a telephone directory. I can't help but feel that directory is somehow fitting. Add the transfer fee and the likely wage packet together, and you are talking telephone numbers.

In fact, on the car radio on the way into the training ground, I'd been listening to how much Manchester United were willing to pay Ronaldo to fend off reported interest from Real Madrid: £140,000-a-week. It seems only yesterday that Colin Alcide was telling me he was content to sign for City for £650-a-week. It was £200 more than he was getting at Lincoln. In previous seasons, City had always been one of the best paying clubs in their Division, the proverbial big fish in a small pond. Now, they were competing with some of the biggest clubs in the country. As Brown continued his conversation, I couldn't help but imagine that if I was a player, what would I do with a choice between Hull and, for example, Bolton? Not even the local tourist board could match Brown's enthusiasm for Hull. And, his phone conversation over, he returns to the topic of the Premier League. 'I've been in this position before – at Bolton, not as manager but as assistant. We'd just gone up from the Championship and everyone thought we'd go straight back down. We stayed up the first season, re-built and where are Bolton now? Exactly. I know what we need to do.' A few minutes later and my interview ends. 'The signings will come,' he says. 'They might not be the number one or number two targets, but we will strengthen. Just tell people to be patient.' I stop off on the way back to the KC Stadium to buy a national newspaper. There are tiny headlines on City, four pages in from the back, next to the speedway and basketball columns. A report says Harry Kewell is definitely set to sign, though I'd read the previous day that he'd packed his bags and headed off to play in Turkey. Two other names mentioned are Newcastle's Alan Smith and Manchester United's Paul Scholes. As if . . .

Smith has been linked with City for days now. The fans on the message boards are convinced he will sign after he'd been seen leaving City's offices. True, there was a blonde-haired visitor on that very day, but he was a plumber who had fixed a blockage in the ladies' toilet. Brown and Duffen are keeping their cards close to their chest. The one player City had confirmed an interest in was Frazier Campbell. However, he was still very much a Manchester United player and the Old Trafford giants had a few striking problems of their own. City had offered around £7m and enquired about re-signing the player on loan. The response was lukewarm. United wanted Dimitar Berbatov. Until they sign him, Campbell can't go anywhere. Apart from signings, the big talking point was a potential increase in capacity at the KC Stadium from 25,000 to around 35,000. The club had already sold almost 20,000 season passes leaving very few actual match-day tickets available for sale. It was public knowledge that a second tier could be added to the East Stand. I'd been writing stories along those lines when I was still at the

Hull Daily Mail. However, Duffen said the cost of adding a second tier was more than the £34m it had taken to build the entire stadium. And if City's stay in the top flight was only going to be for one season, what was the point of a 35,000 capacity ground in the Championship? So, an extension would have to wait. It was July before the signings started to arrive. The first, Fagan, was predictable. The second, Geovanni, was stunning. Geovanni's former clubs included Barcelona and Benfica. He had spent the previous season at Manchester City and scored in a derby win against United at Old Trafford. Like everyone else, I was caught up in the euphoria. City had signed a player from Brazil, albeit on a free transfer. Amid all the headlines, it was easy to overlook the fact Geovanni had been unable to hold down a regular place at Manchester City under ex-England boss Sven-Göran Eriksson. Even so, when news of his arrival started to leak out, no one quite believed it. At first, people said it was another red-herring; another Juninho. Then, the Samba star actually put pen-to-paper. 'This signing,' said Duffen, 'highlights our ambition. We aren't just going into the Premier League to make the numbers up. We intend to compete.' It was what the fans wanted to hear.

I met Geovanni on the day he signed. He had a smile on his face. Perhaps that went back to his first job after leaving school, selling ice-creams on some sun-kissed Brazilian beach. His signing meant another first at the club: the presence of an interpreter. Geovanni spoke very little English, but his 'minder-cum-chauffer-cum-car-washer' did and was soon on hand to help out. I'd ask Geo a question and his burly accomplice would translate and then give the reply in English. The system just about worked. Mind you, I was a little suspicious. Geo always seemed to provide a rambling answer to even a simple question. The translator would then provide the answer that usually contained three words: he, is and 'happee.'

'So,' I asked, 'why has Geo come to Hull?'

'Because he is happee,' came the reply.

I wanted to know his opinion of Eriksson. The accomplice asked the question. The answer seemed to cover a couple of minutes. Then, the translation: 'He says he is a very nice man.' The big names continued to be linked with City. From a purely selfish point of view, I hoped – and prayed – some of them would speak English. Bernard Mendy arrived in Geovanni's slip-stream. The Frenchman was a free transfer recruit from Paris St Germain. Mendy and had played under Brown at Bolton. He also spoke English. Then, three signings were announced in one day: George Boateng, Peter Halmosi and Tony Warner. Boateng, the snappiest dresser I've ever met, had spent almost a decade playing in the Premier League. He cost a reported £1m from Middlesbrough and arrived for his press conference driving a Bentley. Brown also spent a record £2m-plus to persuade Hungarian international Halmosi away from Plymouth. Warner, or Denzil as he was known because of a striking resemblance to the character in the TV comedy *Only Fools and Horses* arrived on a free from Fulham. City now had three senior goalkeepers. Boateng was a delight to interview, polite and articulate. He spoke better English than the majority of Hull's home-grown players. With his long hair and angelic looks, Halmosi looked like a little boy lost. However, he could make himself understood in English. Of the three new signings, the most difficult to understand was Warner – a broad Scouser.

The new signings settled in. We were promised more would

follow as Brown whisked his players away to Italy for a pre-season training camp. 'It was a lucky venue last year,' said Brown, 'so why change it?' When City returned, their programme of matches included friendlies against Belgian side KV Oostende. Spaniards Osasuna visited the KC Stadium in the final warm-up game. My 'beefed-up' job description didn't feature trips to Italy or Belgium. However, I did watch the Osasuna game and a 1-0 defeat hardly inspired confidence. City looked lightweight up front and one-paced in midfield. Campbell continued to be linked with the club, but joined Spurs on loan as part of the deal that took Berbatov to Old Trafford. Still, I sensed the fans were satisfied with City's recruitment – even though Brown still looked to be at least a couple of players short. Immediately after that Wembley final, he said he intended to stay loyal to the majority of the squad that won promotion. In fact, four players – Ashbee, Dawson, France and Myhill – were poised to join a very select band who had appeared in all four Divisions with the same club. Ash was Ash; always proud, always abrasive, always good value in interviews. As the season approached, he smarted at the suggestion that he was lucky to have progressed from the former Division Four to the best League in the world. He said: 'There's been managers come and managers go at this club and I've been one of the players they wanted to keep. Is that luck? I don't think so. I think it is justice. There's been a lot of hard work, a lot of blood and sweat and a few tears, and I don't think you can be lucky over six years. I'm proud of what I've achieved.'

I can recall looking back with Ash at some of the team-mates he'd played alongside on his debut for City: August 10, 2002, a home game against Southend in front of 10,000 fans at

Boothferry Park. As we peered at the team-sheet, five of those players were no longer at Football League clubs. Former record signing Dudfield was at Notts County; Green was at Blackpool; Elliott at Doncaster. No one could come close to matching Ash's record. A measure of the man is that perhaps no one ever will. Ash was certainly looking forward to rubbing shoulders with Rooney and Ronaldo, even though they promised to present a rather different challenge to Southend. Ashbee said: 'Ronaldo? Yeah, he's quality, but you tell me, how does John Terry play against him? I can't worry about who I am playing against. I never have, never will. As a team, you've got to respect the best teams and the top players, but we're not going into this to roll over and die. We'll compete against everybody.' Few people outside Hull realistically thought City could survive.

The fixture list had been kind to City in the respect that their opening games were against Fulham, Wigan, Blackburn and Newcastle. Some fans, the majority of them no doubt first-time season ticket holders, were a little disappointed that they would have to wait to see the likes of Manchester United and Liverpool at the KC. In United's case, they would visit Hull on the very last day of the season. Fulham were first up, and Brown looked forward to realising his ambition of managing in the top Division. 'It is something I've been waiting for all my life. We've got 38 games this season . . . 38 Christmas Days coming up. At the moment, it is a bit like Christmas Eve for us. We're all excited. We know what we want, but we don't quite know whether we'll get it. The confidence is high. I know the players and I know they will be trying the best they can. I can't ask for any more than that. You know what? I'll be 50 next summer. I hope I can say that I'll still be a Premier League manager.'

Brown was speaking at a press conference, a week before the Fulham game. Hull City staying in the Premier League? The reporter from The Mirror just managed to stifle a laugh.

Chapter fifteen:

The big time - at last

August, 2008 - December, 2008

It had taken 104 years, so the build-up to Hull City's first-ever game in the top flight of English football was predictably chaotic. As the Fulham game approached, the training ground was invaded by the national and even international media. The paint-splattered decorator's van had gone and in its place were row upon row of shiny new BMWs and Audis owned by the players. I felt embarrassed parking my 02-reg Ford Focus in the same place. A TV crew from Japan had flown in, especially to interview Phil Brown and Geovanni. At the training ground, one of the Japanese reporters approached me and said they wanted to take a couple of players to a Japanese restaurant. 'Err, there's just one problem,' I said. 'There isn't one. There's a decent Chinese, just down the road in Cottingham. Will that do?' The response was venomous. If looks could kill . . . In the end, the crew settled for the Humber Bridge which, contrary to what Deano would have everyone believe, was still the most iconic and recognisable thing about Hull. We headed off. Unlike previous years, the sun shone and even the Humber looked an inviting shade of blue (well, almost). The cameraman was none too happy when a black mongrel cocked its leg on a tripod. The Japan crew eventually left. They managed an interview with Geo without an interpreter. I never did catch the broadcast. It must have made interesting viewing. They handed me a memento: a chewed pen with 'Welcome to London' inscribed on the side.

Brown dealt with every single media inquiry that week, even though it was often the same question over and over again. 'How will you survive?' He'd smile, grit his teeth and answer ever so politely. The final press day was Thursday, 48 hours before the Fulham game. There were more than 60 media representatives at training. Three years earlier it had been Radio Humberside and me, plus Monty, my labrador. He used to fetch the stray balls from an adjoining wood. He was very busy. Now, as I looked at the melee, it was a different world to the days when I was interviewing Joycey in the bath at Boothferry Park. The club went out of its way to help the visiting press. Probably not one of them gave City a prayer of staying in the top flight. Brown and his players made it clear they didn't care what anyone thought.

City's starting eleven against Fulham contained just four new signings: Anthony Gardner, Boateng, Geovanni and Marlon King. King had been brought in from Wigan on a season-long loan. With all due respect to King, City had not been able to attract a big name striker. At £2.5m, ex-England defender Gardner (he'd won one cap a few years ago) had replaced Halmosi as the club's record signing, having turned an initial loan move from Spurs into a longer-term deal. Gardner had an impressive pedigree, but a worrying injury record. The entire summer seemed to have swept by, but somehow the last few hours before the Fulham game took an age to come around.

I had a new travelling companion to games: Steve Searby. Having moved to a remote village in the heart of the Lincolnshire Wolds, almost 50 miles from Hull, one of the first people I bumped into was Steve. He was wearing a replica City top. My heart dropped. 'I'd seen you walking by,' said Steve, 'and I said to the wife, that's John Fieldhouse . . . you know, the bloke who used to report on City for the Hull Daily Mail.' Steve, a seed salesman, was a City nut, a season-ticket holder for longer than he could remember. He suggested we share lifts to games, a round trip of around 100 miles. 'We can stop off at a pub on the way back,' he added. That swung it. Steve is tall, bald and totally laid back. The only two things that stir him into life are City and the price of wheat. At least travelling with me meant a place in the club car park and the occasional free lunch in the press room. That press room had been moved. It was now well away from the players' tunnel. The actual press box was still high in the West Stand, but it had been extended and, in line with Premier League regulations, could accommodate more than 80 journalists, who all had to have access to a computer point and a TV screen. Again, it was a different world to Boothferry Park. Back then, you could forget about a free lunch, computer points or TV screens. There were rarely enough reporters to fill the dozen or so rickety old seats. I wasn't the only person who moaned about the one problem we faced: those seats faced the pitch. In the lead up to the Fulham game, I'd been bombarded with requests for tickets from friends and family I hadn't seen or heard of in years. Premier League mania had gripped Hull. I couldn't believe the number of kids I'd seen kicking a ball about in the streets and parks while wearing a replica City jersey rather than one from Manchester United.

The match finally arrived. The atmosphere was incredible. An hour before kick-off and the stadium was filling up fast. Fans had travelled from far and wide. I bumped into Mark Lamb, an old golfing colleague. He'd flown to the game from Hong Kong, where he now lived and worked. Apparently, he'd convinced his wife that it was the 'perfect time' to visit his family. He'd paid over £200 for his ticket from a tout in a city centre pub. It had a face value of £28. He'd had to shell out for two return flights, rail fares from London to Hull, spending money and what seemed like half the stock of the club shop. In all, he reckoned he'd spent a couple of grand. He told me: 'Hull's first game in the Premier League. I wouldn't have missed it for the world.' To me, it seemed like it had cost him the world. 'Nah,' he said, 'it's worth it. Anyway, I've just met a bloke and he's flown here from Sydney. He got here yesterday and is flying back tomorrow. At least, we're here for a few days.'

Fulham might not have been the biggest draw in the Division, but were still an established Premier League force. When they took the lead early on, it was only what many people had expected. City had spent around £10m on new signings; Fulham about the same on one player, Andrew Johnson. The Tigers responded superbly. Geovanni equalised in the 21st minute with a spectacular strike. He cut in from the touchline and curled a shot into the bottom corner of the net. From then on, it was nip and tuck. Chances came and went. With nine minutes to go, Caleb Folan climbed off the subs' bench to score the winning goal. City – and 20,000-plus fans – were ecstatic. Fulham were shell-shocked.

The impossible had happened. The dream had come true. City had won their first-ever match in the Premier League 2-1. As the fans celebrated, it was like Wembley all over again. I caught up with Lambie after the final whistle. His verdict? 'That was worth flying half way round the world for.' Whether they lived in Hong Kong or Goole, no one wanted to go home. The press wanted to talk to both City goal-scorers. The club rule was just one player for interview after matches. Geo escaped. Folan was on duty. He said: 'A dream day? You bet. It was important to get the three points and to get the winning goal. It doesn't get much better. We're not getting carried away, though. We know there's a lot of hard work to be done.' Watching City on Match of the Day that Saturday night was a new experience. Gary Lineker looked straight into the camera at the end of the programme and said: 'Hull City . . . the only side in the history of the Premier League with a 100 per cent record. Goodnight.' One game down. Thirty seven to go.

The big three, Brown, Horton and Parkin, kept everyone's feet firmly on the ground during the next few days. The players told me they'd never trained as hard in their entire lives. On a couple of stamina-sapping mornings, the smile even disappeared from Geo's face. The reaction of the media to that opening win was along the lines of a 'flash in the pan' or 'it was only Fulham.' City's second game was at Blackburn Rovers. Ewood Park is not one of my favourite grounds. Why is it that so many modern stadiums are soulless places, miles from anywhere and surrounded by waste-land or carpet stores? Around 5,000 travelling black and amber fans at least created a cracking atmosphere, and the general feeling was that City could get something from the game. Blackburn's manager was Paul Ince, who had taken his former club MK Dons to promotion from League Two the previous season. He, like City, was new to the Premier League. Brown made a couple of changes and City recovered from conceding an early goal to grab a 1-1 draw, Richard Garcia's looping header cancelling out Jason Roberts' opener. Brown was all smiles and said: 'I'm delighted with the point. If we can continue to play with this type of passion and commitment, then we'll be okay.' Garcia, meanwhile, had a difficult job convincing everyone that he meant to guide his header into the top corner of the net. TV replays showed the Australian had headed the ball with his eyes completely closed. Luck might have been on Garcia's side. Still, who was complaining? Four points from the opening two games. As one fan commented on a local radio phone in: 'Premier League – why all the fuss?' The 100 per cent record had gone and this time Lineker rounded off Match of the Day with the comment: 'Hull City, the only club never to have lost a Premier League game.'

Brown made 11 changes for a mid-week Carling Cup tie at Swansea. He handed a debut to 16-year-old defender Liam Cooper. City lost, 3-2 in extra time. I didn't go. In my book, the best thing about Swansea is the M4 leading out of Wales. Windass played in that Swansea tie, but was back on the bench for the visit of Wigan to the KC the following Saturday. It was the first sign that all was not well between the management and City's veteran Wembley hero. Wigan were next up – at the KC – and after encouraging results from the opening two League games, the fans turned out genuinely expecting to see a home win. What happened was a sobering experience. Wigan gate-crashed the party and romped to a 5-0 win in an amazing game. Brown's verdict? 'We didn't deserve that. Still, we now know what this League is all about. If you don't bring your best game to the table, you'll get punished.' The match stats showed City actually had more shots on target than Wigan. However, some of City's defending was sub-standard. Emile Heskey looked world class. Wayne Brown, who had replaced the injured Gardner in City's line-up, was pretty much the scapegoat. He didn't get another chance to prove his Premier League pedigree.

Brown promised new signings. Within 48 hours of that Wigan debacle Paul McShane, Kamil Zayette and Daniel Cousin arrived just before the transfer window closed at the end of August. Republic of Ireland international McShane joined on loan from Sunderland. Guinea-born Zayette and Gabon-born Cousin added to the United Nations' set-up in City's dressing room. Zayette signed on loan from Swiss side FC Young Boys; Cousin cost in excess of £1.5m from Glasgow giants Rangers. I met Zayette and Cousin at the training ground. Having being assured by Horton that they could speak English, I discovered they spoke French. So City arranged for Mendy to act as an interpreter. There was just one problem. Mendy's English is just about passable, but even he struggled to understand the two new signings, who appeared to speak in different dialects. The result was chaos. It was the longest – and craziest – interview I'd ever conducted; and that is saying something. At one stage, I'm sure Mendy seemed to suggest Zayette was married to Cousin's brother. Then, I thought they were discussing swimming pools, but Cousin was only enquiring whether there was a decent fish restaurant in Hull. Slowly, but surely, we made progress. It emerged Cousin was married to a well-known African-born model. When I prompted Mendy to ask for a few details, Cousin just shrugged his shoulders and smiled. 'Come on,' said Mendy, 'let's talk football.' He then lapsed into a conversation with Zayatte about French music. My head still ringing with various accents and phrases, I headed off to interview the Portuguese/Spanish speaking Geovanni and his minder. City's magazine wanted a feature on how Geo relaxed at home.

'So, what does Geo like to do away from football?' I asked.

'Ah,' said his minder, 'he loves watching TV.'

But, hang on a second, how does a person who doesn't speak English understand English TV? 'Does he like the soaps?' I asked. 'Soaps?' replied the minder. 'What are they? He has a washer of dishes.'

'Programmes like Coronation Street,' I said.

The minder seemed confused. He eventually added: 'I think Geo likes this programme. He thinks it is funny.'

I included that snippet of trivia in an article for the magazine. A week later, a tabloid paper picked up on it and suggested the Brazilian was one of Coronation Street's biggest fans and that Vera Duckworth was his favourite star. To this day, I'd swear Geo hasn't watched a single episode, let alone understood one. Geovanni did reveal he would love to play for Brazil again – his last appearance was seven years ago – and his early season form suggested he might well earn an international recall. There was a break in the Premier League fixtures during the first week of September and City's foreign legion duly headed off to all four corners of the world. I used to get excited when Jamie Wood was picked for the Cayman Islands. Now City had players representing Gabon, Guinea, Australia and Hungary, and two boys from the Valleys, Myhill and Ricketts, were a little further on learning the words to the Welsh national anthem.

City returned to League action with a 2-1 win at crisis-hit

Newcastle, who were reeling from owner Mike Ashley's 'I will sell, I won't sell' declarations. King scored both goals, the first a penalty and the second a sublime shot that beat Shay Given. Newcastle were poor. I went to the game with a long-time friend, Trevor Bailey, a Geordie season-ticket holder for almost 20 years. On the way home, he was all doom and gloom. 'If we can't beat Hull, we're going down,' he said. 'We need to get Ashley out and get someone in who knows what they are doing.' In the post match press conference, Brown had admitted he was 'ecstatic.' Ashbee, who looked like he'd been performing at this level all his life, gave a stoic response. 'People keep saying the bubble will burst. But why should it?' he said. City were in the top five – ahead of Manchester United.

A week later, the Tigers had a great chance to add Everton to their list of early scalps. They led 2-0 at the KC only to be pegged back to a 2-2 draw. Incredibly, some fans moaned that it was a case of two points dropped rather than a point gained – against an Everton side that had finished in the top six the previous season. Brown said: 'Two-nil up, 20 minutes to go. Should we have won? What do you think?' On the way back to Lincolnshire, my seed-selling mate Steve pointed out that had City won, they would have been in the top three.

With all respect to City's early season opponents, it was a visit to Arsenal's Emirates Stadium on September 27 that really brought home the enormity and scale of the Premier League. I've always loved the KC, but the Emirates is a class apart. I arrived in good time and was allowed a brief tour of the stadium. The place sparkled – all glass and marble. The pitch looked an impossible shade of emerald green. Visiting the trophy room was an eye-opening experience. I'd never seen so much gold and silver; so many honours collected by so many international players. I stood in the middle of that room thinking that just three years ago, City couldn't find the key to their own trophy cabinet after beating local rivals North Ferriby United to win the Billy Bly Memorial Cup. Now here I was: Arsenal, the Emirates. One of the first people I bumped into was Terry Neil. An Arsenal legend, he had come as close as anyone to leading Hull into the top flight when he was appointed player/manager in the early 70s. In fact, rumour has it that when City's directors tempted Neil to Hull by buying him an E-type Jaguar, it was the start of the Tigers' financial problems. Neil told me: 'I always hoped Hull City would get in the Premier League, but I was never sure it would quite happen in my life-time.' City's odds on winning at Arsenal were 16-1 against. They were still 15-8 to go down.

If Neil was surprised to see City in the top flight, then he – and the rest of the football world – was truly astounded by the result that afternoon. City won 2-1, again after staging another stunning fight back. I'd watched Arsenal's players arriving. They were laughing and joking. To me, it appeared they thought they only had to turn up, pull on a pair of boots and stroll to three easy points. They were a little too smug. Still, Arsenal went ahead and you could almost see them preening themselves. City, though, stormed back. In the 62nd minute, Geovanni scored a truly spectacular equaliser – a swerving, dipping shot from all of 30 yards that found the top corner of the net. I was surrounded by Arsenal fans, but leapt out of my seat to celebrate. Four minutes later, I was on my feet again as Cousin rose above Arsenal's dithering defenders to head in the winner. It was Cousin's first goal for the club. What a time and place to record that particular feat. Cousin duly agreed to a couple of interviews afterwards and to my surprise spoke in perfect English. 'I have scored in the Rangers v Celtic derby,' he said, 'but this is the best.' He then smiled – and winked – at me. Arsenal manager Arsene Wenger was definitely not smiling at the post-match press conference. He said: 'We did not play well but we did not deserve to lose.' Ashbee trotted out to meet the media and gave an insight into the reasons behind City's amazing second half recovery. 'A few of the lads weren't exactly happy with the gaffer. He owns a horse (European Dream) which was running today and he told us it was a cert to win. It was terrible. We found out at half time that it didn't finish the race. He's cost us a few quid. Seriously, he had a pop at us at half time because he said we didn't believe enough. If the boss thinks that, then he certainly has the belief in us. No one gave us a hope in hell of winning here so it is a momentous day. We've gone and proved people wrong.'

City had only ever beaten Arsenal once before in the League – in the old Second Division in 1915. Herbert Asquith was the Prime Minister; the Women's Institute was founded; and beer was 3d a pint. Ashbee and his team-mates had 11 points from six games. Before the start of the season, they were 2-5-on to go down. Now they were 6-5 to stay up. Lineker had run out of things to say. The media descended on the club after that win, and Duffen produced one of the quotes of the entire season. He said: 'Winning at Arsenal was not beyond my wildest dreams because they involve Elle McPherson.' Duffen and Brown headed off to Bahrain a day or so later and that sparked speculation the club was about to be taken over by mega-rich Arab businessmen. The chairman and manager were actually checking facilities for a mid-winter training camp. When they returned, everyone was asking whether City could complete a remarkable North London double and beat Spurs.

A quick glimpse of Spurs' team-list before the kick-off at White Hart Lane showed they had spent around £100m. However, they were in free-fall under Juande Ramos, whose coaching methods hadn't been universally welcomed by everyone, not least his own players. And City sensed all was not well in the Spurs' camp. Perhaps it was the inside knowledge Andy Dawson gleamed from his brother Michael, who played for the opposition. The Tigers won again. Geovanni scored another contender for goal of the season, this time from a free kick. 1-0 to City after just nine minutes. Their goal led a charmed life as Spurs missed chance after chance. The look on Ramos's face after the match said it all. It was as though he knew he'd be sacked; and he was, 48 hours later. 'We're in dreamland,' admitted Brown. 'Now comes the big test. I have got to get the players' minds back on the next game against West Ham because reality is kicking in. You have got to remember we are only seven games into a 38 game campaign.' And what about Geovanni? Brown added: 'It is a pleasure to work with him, though it has not always been plain sailing. You have to understand that, when you play for Hull City, you have to do certain things every week. Every player has to understand what their role is when we don't have the ball, Geo included. Tottenham had 23 or 24 attempts, but I think you will find the best chances fell to us. People will talk about Geo because of that goal. Personally, I thought Ash was outstanding. He is like my coach on the field. He has big players around him but he has taken to the Premier League like a fish to water.'

By now, it was almost impossible to switch on a TV or radio

and not see, or hear, a City-related story. The press office was inundated with requests for interviews from TV crews from all over the world. Positive publicity is fine, but the early season success story was threatening to spiral out of control. Everyone wanted to know the secret behind City's success. Brown explained: 'Our game plan is simple – we play, our opponents don't play. That may not always be possible in the Premier League and if you'd said to me a fortnight ago that we'd win at the Emirates and White Hart Lane, I'd have thought you were crazy. But we will continue to work hard. We're in a great position. Can we stay there? Come back in a few weeks and ask me that again.' All this was happening almost six years ago to the day that City had lost 3-1 at home to Macclesfield in one of Jan Molby's final games in charge. Four years before that, Warren Joyce was about to take over from Mark Hateley as manager with City ten points adrift at the bottom of the Football League. Now they were within touching distance of the top of the Premier League. Brown was everywhere. Could he appear on a Question of Sport? Of course. What about Match of the Day 2 on Sunday night? No problem. Back in Hull, he posed naked in the club magazine to fulfil a promise. He said he'd do so – or alternatively bungee jump off the Humber Bridge – if a City supporter won a Coca-Cola competition, worth £250,000, that involved all League clubs. When it duly happened, Brown chose to strip in preference to dangling over Humber. 'I'm not totally mad,' he explained.

Against West Ham, Brown urged his players to stay focussed. He was remarkably honest (and fully clothed) in the build up. 'Of course, you worry about it going tits up,' he said. 'There again, there is no expectation on us. We are the no hopers, just up for a brief visit, a magical mystery tour to Old Trafford, the Emirates and Anfield.' The media loved Brown, dubbing him 'tan man' because of his apparent love of sun beds. 'I swear I have never been on one in my entire life,' he said. Brown's popularity was about to get another boost. City beat West Ham 1-0 at the KC. The fact no one seemed surprised by that result highlighted the staggering progress the club had made. That win made it London 0, Hull 4. Mike Turner scored the only goal of the game and there were chants of 'Turner for England' from the KC faithful. The always modest Turner looked embarrassed, and so did Hammers' boss Gianfranco Zola. Eight games, 17 points: the second best start to a Premier League campaign ever behind Nottingham Forest. Brown won the Manager of the Month award for September. Earlier in the season, a trip to West Brom had promised to be a decisive battle between two of the sides surely destined for a quick-fire return to the Championship. Not any longer. However, West Brom had targeted this one game to turn their faltering season around. City won 3-0. Lineker's verdict this time? 'Incredib-hull.' Who writes his scripts?

I thought the bubble had to burst at some stage. I wasn't the only one who sensed City were getting carried away on the back of all the headlines, welcome as they were. City had built their success around a fantastic team spirit. They positively thrived under the tag of perennial under-dog and an attitude of 'no one likes us but we don't care'. Articles started to appear about the possibility of City playing in Europe the following season. The chairman and the manager were both 'guilty' of talking about a possible top six finish. Even the normally restrained Ashbee appeared to have caught the bug, admitting: 'Wouldn't it be great – leading Hull out at Roma next season. It would not so much be the icing on the cake but the hundreds and thousands on top of that. I remember playing at Rochdale on a wet Tuesday night. There were about 2,200 fans there. There had been a pile-up on the motorway and we got there about ten minutes before kick off. It was silly things, like we had to buy our own drinks to have on the coach. Now we're playing Manchester United, Arsenal, Chelsea. If you said that to me when I was leading the side out at Rochdale, I'd have said,"no, never."' It wasn't just Ashbee. In fact, it's easy to understand why City were caught in the spotlight. The club and the players had never been in such an exalted position before. Suddenly they were everyone's second favourite team. They were even invited to a tournament in China the following summer. However, with all the talk of the top six, City were in danger of losing their focus.

City had allowed themselves to be built up by the media. In the best of British traditions, the very same people were waiting and only too willing to shoot them down. Predictably, Chelsea put an end to a four game winning run with a 3-0 victory in mid-week at the KC. Frank Lampard scored the opener with a superb finish – Geovanni-esque almost – and Phil Scolari's side hammered home their superiority. They were different class. City spent the entire night chasing shadows. I don't think they managed to tackle Lampard once while he was in possession. For the first time, Brown faced some awkward questions from the London-based reporters, who had turned out in force for the Chelsea fixture and had expected a much better and much more in-your-face performance from the Tigers. 'The bubble hasn't burst,' said Brown. 'You are talking about one game – one game against one of the best teams in the world.' On the drive back home to Lincolnshire that night, my mate Steve was a little worried. 'I know it was Chelsea,' he said, 'but do you think we got a bit carried away by some of those early results? I honestly thought we might win tonight.'

City didn't have too much time to dwell on that Chelsea result. Three days later, they were heading for Old Trafford. I'd been looking forward to something like this for years. Hull City at Old Trafford in the Premier League. Unthinkable. Stupidly, I locked myself out of my car on the morning of the game. Three hours before kick off, and I was watching a very helpful man from the AA break into my car in a Lincolnshire park. Why hadn't I used the spare key? It was locked inside the glove compartment. I thought about rushing to Old Trafford. It was a good two hours away – and more. I rang my press office colleagues and thought about a thousand excuses. I told them the truth. They killed themselves laughing. 'We'll get you a programme,' said Brendon Smurthwaite. He did, and promptly demanded the five-and-a-half quid before he'd hand it over. I would have loved to have been at Old Trafford. But some things aren't meant to be. I was in good company. Ashbee also missed that game through suspension. I listened at home on the radio. I almost took the dog for a walk when United romped into a 4-1 lead early in the second half. However, a dramatic fight-back – featuring goals from Mendy and Geovanni – had the Premier League champions on the ropes. United hung on for a 4-3 win. Still, City had won tremendous praise. Sir Alex Ferguson admitted: 'Four-one up, we started playing in the comfort zone. We should have won by ten and we ended up scrambling a victory. You've got to give credit to Hull, they don't give up and that's the nature of their team. They had two chances and managed to score three goals – that's amazing.' Brown said: 'We paid them far too much respect in the first half. You cannot sit off them, otherwise they will show you what they are capable of. In the second half, we got in their faces. The game became feisty and we got some pride back in the shirt. Unfortunately, that's all we got. We can take a lot of positives. What we've got to do is get away from all the back-slapping and the plaudits and stop believing our own press. Maybe the last two games have been a timely reminder of that.'

Back-to-back defeats against Chelsea and Manchester United were hardly a shock. Forthcoming games against Bolton, Manchester City, Portsmouth and Stoke appeared to offer a more realistic chance of points. City, though, failed to win any of those next four games. They were unlucky to come up against a Bolton side inspired by goalkeeper Jussi Jaaskelainen. His brilliant performance helped Bolton steal a 1-0 win at the KC. Brown and Jaaskelainen were and remain good friends. Their children attend the same school. The pair are co-owners of a racehorse. The Bolton game marked three defeats in a row. Ashbee sounded the rallying call. 'I know the characters in the dressing room so I am not worried. I never got carried away because we won at Arsenal, so I am not going to get down because we've lost three games.' City did stop the rot, drawing 2-2 at home to Manchester City, Robinho and all. Again, there was a feeling the Tigers could have taken all three points against the out-of-sorts visitors whose manager Mark Hughes was under intense pressure. Despite the mini slump, City were still sixth and Geovanni had scored his sixth goal of the season. Brown admitted: 'I wouldn't swap Robinho for Geovanni, mainly because my Brazilian was free and theirs cost £32m.'

City headed to Portsmouth the following weekend. It's not a

trip I was scheduled to make, car keys or not. Brown recalled Windass for a rare start. The man who had scored the winning goal at Wembley had been a bit-part player in the Premier League and had made his feelings known in a series of newspaper columns and internet blogs. Ominously, the columns weren't the only time Windass had appeared in the headlines. Earlier in the month, he'd become embroiled in an altercation with team-mate King at a casino in Scarborough during a three-day team training break. All the information suggested it was a classic case of handbags at six paces. The headlines said it all: 'Premiership stars in casino punch-up.' Read the article and it sounded like World War Two. According to City, it wasn't anything of the kind. The publicity, though, demonstrated the profile the players were under. I'd witnessed a few bust-ups among team-mates in my time as a reporter. In fact, I'd almost come to blows myself during the Joycey era after a row with Gareth 'Gripper' Williams. He took exception to being given five-out-of-ten in the Hull Daily Mail after one particularly unmemorable performance. Williams tried to push me and failed. I shoved him down a grass bank and he fell flat on his backside. That was the end of it. End of story. He slunk off. Had it been Brabs, I'd have been worried. In Divisions Three and Four, no one bothered. No story of a bust-up ever appeared on page five of The Sun. The furore soon died down, not least after Windass scored a late equaliser in a 2-2 draw at Portsmouth. The smile was back on his face. He said: 'I am one for knocking the manager's door down when I'm not in the team, and I don't think there are any more to knock down. I've ruined a few in the last few weeks. I have told Phil Brown how it is. I have told him I want to be involved and now he has food for thought.' Windass was back on the bench the following week.

Stoke were next up. Geovanni was struggling to re-capture his best goal-scoring form but he did declare he was in love with Hull. There were rumours Geo wasn't happy with his role in the side; rumours he quickly dispelled in an interview with me for the club magazine. He said: 'I've played for some big clubs – Barcelona and Benfica – but I've never felt more loved. I am very happy. In the story of my career, Hull is a special time.' City followed that point at Portsmouth with another draw: 1-1 at Stoke. It was a controversial clash and Brown claimed his side had been 'robbed' after Stoke striker Ricardo Fuller earned a controversial penalty that led to the equaliser. Brown said: 'I felt it was a very theatrical dive. A referee has to be 100 per cent right when he makes decisions like that.' Apart from the penalty, and another King goal for City, the clash featured one of the more unusual bookings in Premier League history. Windass was shown a yellow card after warming up directly in front of Rory Delap, just as the Stoke midfielder was preparing to deliver one of his trademark long throw-ins. City were unfortunate to leave Stoke with only a point. A week later, though, and they were lucky to beat Middlesbrough at home. The visitors were leading 1-0 with just ten minutes to go. Somehow Mendy squeezed in an equaliser. Middlesbrough then had David Wheater sent off for allegedly hauling down Geovanni, who looked suspiciously off-side. King stroked home the penalty. Three points in the bag. Sixth place in the table. The start of December. Not bad.

The bandwagon was rolling again, so much so that Brown was strongly linked with the managerial vacancy at Sunderland following Roy Keane's resignation. Brown had supported Sunderland since childhood, but ruled himself out of the running. Nick Barmby urged his manager to stay and said: 'You look at what the gaffer and his staff have done and they have been fantastic. To nearly go out of the Championship two years ago and to get promoted and do what he is doing in the Premier League is tremendous. From a greedy point of view, we want him to stay, the chairman wants him to stay and the fans want him to stay.' Brown enhanced a growing reputation after City drew 2-2 at title-chasing Liverpool. The Kop was stunned when the Tigers led 2-0 after just 22 minutes, but a Steven Gerrard inspired comeback salvaged a point for the hosts. City claimed both Liverpool's goals should have been disallowed for fouls by Gerrard on Turner. Brown said: 'All we are asking for is a level playing field, regardless of whether you are little old Hull City or one of the big boys. Michael Turner was fouled in the build up to both Liverpool goals and the referee was ball watching. At 2-0 up, there was a handball in their area, but I don't think we were allowed to go 3-0 up here. One of City's most effective players at Anfield – and in recent weeks – was King. In the week leading up to the Liverpool game, he'd been arrested for an alleged assault on a woman in a London nightclub. With a hefty driving ban also looming, his off-the-field problems were threatening to overshadow his efforts on it.

Draw at Anfield or not, City had won just one of their last eight games and it quickly became one from nine when Sunderland romped to a 4-1 win at the KC Stadium four days before Christmas. To be fair, the result could have gone either way but after Sam Ricketts had been sent off, City collapsed and two late goals earned Sunderland a flattering win. City needed reinforcements. The transfer window was due to re-open in a couple of weeks and Brown admitted he wanted to make changes. He certainly wasn't happy with the Sunderland display and said: 'We lost 3-0 at home to Chelsea but at least we competed in that one. Maybe we forgot how good Sunderland can be. We can't allow ourselves to take the foot off the gas, no matter who we are playing.' There were high hopes City could bounce back at Manchester City on Boxing Day. Their opponents were hardly flourishing, despite the massive investment that followed a takeover by a Middle East-based consortium. The Tigers lost 5-1 and Brown was so unhappy with their first half performance (City were losing 4-0) he delivered his half-time pep talk on the pitch in front of the travelling City fans. It was an amazing scene, more reminiscent of a local Sunday League game than a Premier League match. Brown was roundly criticised afterwards by several pundits, who effectively claimed he was getting too big for his own boots and was in danger of losing the respect of his players. Some of the London-based national press wrote that the season was fast becoming about Phil Brown and not his team. Knives were being sharpened. The manager defended his decision. 'It wasn't a knee-jerk reaction. It was definitely the right thing to do. If it meant bruising one or two egos then so be it.'

City were beaten again in their last match of the year. Zayette's own goal gifted the points to top-four chasing Aston Villa at the KC. Again, the match was shrouded in controversy after the referee awarded City a penalty in the last minute only to change his mind. There were allegations from within the Tigers' camp that the referee had been influenced by a fellow official, who had the benefit of seeing a TV replay. That replay clearly showed the ball had struck the Villa bar, and not the hand of Ashley Young – as the referee initially ruled. It was the correct decision. Brown, though, wasn't happy and became embroiled in a frivolous dispute with a reporter in the post-match press conference. The pressure was mounting. City had now won just once in 11 games and were sliding down the table. Still, eighth place going into the New Year. Why worry? While Brown attempted to strengthen his squad with a top class striker, Duffen reflected on the drama of the previous year. He admitted: 'It has been a truly amazing last 12 months, a real year of the Tiger in every sense. How do you sum it up? Simple. Twelve months ago, no one gave us a prayer of winning promotion. Now we are sitting in the top half of the Premier League.'

Chapter sixteen:

The fight for survival

January 2009 - May, 2009

At the start of the year, the Premier League table made comfortable viewing for Hull City. The club was in eighth place. That, though, masked the overall picture. On the one hand, City had won just one of their final eleven games of 2008. On the other – as Brown pointed out – they had done far better than anyone had a right to expect. 'Now, though, is when the battle starts,' warned the manager There was mounting concern about City's performances, particularly the heavy defeats against Sunderland and Manchester City. Had Brown 'lost' the dressing room after that on-the-field team talk at the City of Manchester Stadium? What about the future of Windass? And what of new signings during the January transfer window?

I didn't have to read the fans' message boards to know Brown was under increasing pressure. He was still a popular figure with the majority of supporters. Others, though, were calling for his head. The national media kept harking back to events at Manchester City. Perhaps Brown could have reacted differently.

There's no doubt the likes of Geovanni were stunned by their very public dressing down. But I knew the players. I knew they were still behind the manager. Any criticism was partially diverted by all the latest transfer speculation. The goals had dried up and City desperately needed a new striker. Kevin Davies emerged as a target but Bolton, fighting for their Premier League lives themselves, would not sell. Attention switched to James Beattie who, I was told, was ready to move to the KC Stadium. Apparently his wife took one look at Hull and he signed for Stoke instead. Given the respective positions of the two clubs, it hardly seemed the right choice. And, I could be wrong, but the streets of Stoke are not exactly lined with designer boutiques and swanky wine bars.

City's first match of 2009 was an FA Cup tie against Newcastle United at the KC. The game ended in a tame 0-0 draw. Newcastle, now managed by Joe Kinnear, were poor; City a shadow of the positive side that had won at St James' Park earlier in the season. Seven days later, City were soundly beaten 2-0 at Everton. Brown claimed with some justification that Everton's first goal was off-side, but didn't mention his side scarcely mustered a half-decent shot in the entire 90 minutes. The manager had shown terrific loyalty to his squad, but he accepted there had to be changes. The transfer window was open. West Ham's Luis Boa Morte and former Liverpool full back Steve Finnan, now playing in Spain, held talks, but did not sign. Brown did recruit Kevin Kilbane in a near £750,000 deal from Wigan. Kilbane boasted tremendous experience and could play at either left back or in midfield. Windass joined Division One promotion hopefuls Oldham on loan. He was frustrated by the lack of first team chances at the KC and still sniping at the club in his various columns. City had taken seven points from a possible 36. Brown summed up the position with typical honesty. 'In the first ten games opposing teams and players didn't know what Hull City were about. Now they do. There are 14 teams in a relegation battle and we are one of them.' City did win the Cup replay 1-0 at Newcastle. Cousin scored in a tie overshadowed by a touchline bust-up between Brown and Kinnear. Both managers were sent to the stands and subsequently fined by the FA.

Finally, Brown recruited a long-awaited striker. Manucho – an Angolan-born forward – arrived on loan from Manchester United. Manucho – or Mateus Alberto Contreiras Goncalves to give him his full name – had shot to prominence in the previous year's African Nations Cup. Ominously, he'd struggled to make an impact at Old Trafford. Brown appeared confident that the gangling, raw-boned Manucho would make a similar impact to Campbell's 12 months ago. The need for a goal-scorer increased after Arsenal won 3-1 at the KC on January 16. The headlines were dominated by reports of a pre-match row between Brown and King. Apparently, King had arrived late and then stormed out of the dressing room – and the stadium – after being told he was substitute. City tried to play down the incident. There was no turning back. It was the end of King's loan stay, and he was soon on his way to Middlesbrough. A very good player had become a liability. I'd always found King to be helpful and friendly. A few days before his sudden exit, I'd met him at the KC where he was reminiscing about a recent trip back to Jamaica for a World Cup qualifier. At a beach-front bar in Montego Bay, he'd been stunned to see a replica Hull City shirt hanging between one from Real Madrid and another from

Liverpool. The bar owner was asking the same price for all three. When King asked for a cut-price deal, the bar owner offer to reduce the price of the Real Madrid and Liverpool shirts, but not the City one. King had always led the Tigers' attack with commendable spirit. He'd scored some important goals. However, off-the-field events had shown there was another side to his character. Many people saw Manucho as a direct replacement, though that was asking a lot of a player who had hardly any Premier League experience. Manucho might have won a penalty on his debut in that Arsenal game. The referee waved away City's claims. At the time, Arsenal were winning 1-0. Wenger was in a much happier mood than the one he showed after City's win at the Emirates earlier in the season. Asked whether he thought City would stay up, he shrugged his shoulders and replied: 'I am here to talk about my players, my team.'

City had taken just seven out of a possible 39 points. Brown promised a major signing was on the way. Forty-eight hours later, Fulham's Jimmy Bullard arrived for a record fee of £5m. Reports indicated the England midfielder had signed a three-and-a-half year contract, worth a mind-boggling £40,000-a-week. That made him City's best-paid player by some distance. Bullard was introduced to the fans before the FA Cup fourth round tie at home to Millwall on January 24. He received a standing ovation as The Undertones' hit *Jimmy, Jimmy* blared out over the PA system. 'I've joined a very ambitious club,' he said. 'They have worked so hard to get into the Premier League and I intend to help them stay there.' The fact City had spent £5m on one player again highlighted the astonishing progress the club had made. As I watched Bullard salute the fans, I remembered the day supporters were goggle-eyed when Adam Pearson wrote a cheque for just over £200,000 to sign Lawrie Dudfield. The whole of Hull had gone Bullard crazy. Amid the euphoria, people forgot the fact the player had battled back from a career-threatening knee injury at Fulham – an injury that had sidelined him for 18 months. Bullard's arrival coincided in a change of fortune. City saw off Millwall 2-0. The win was marred by trouble between rival fans. The scenes inside the stadium were like a throwback to the 1960s and 70s. Seats were ripped up and used as missiles. It was sad to see a line of police horses on the pitch at the end of the game. Duffen immediately condemned Millwall's supporters and announced he'd be seeking compensation for the damage caused. The police and the FA launched investigations. Several offenders were quickly identified by CCTV and handed life bans. Three days after that game, Bullard made his debut as a second half substitute in a League game at West Ham. His signing had lifted the entire club, but his debut was a disaster. City lost 2-0 and their expensive new recruit suffered a knee injury after just six-and-a-half minutes. It was, everyone was assured, nothing to worry about. Two weeks later, and City were forced to admit Bullard was in America undergoing a career-saving operation. The diagnosis was not good. Bullard would be out for the rest of the season. Critics had a field day. City's handling of the affair was not good. After Bullard's previous problem at Fulham, speculation mounted that he might not play again. Some newspapers claimed City had signed Bullard, even though they had been warned about his dodgy knee. Others claimed they could not understand how the injury had not shown up on the medical. The Hull Daily Mail's headline, 'Bullard a £14m gamble,' certainly ruffled a few feathers at the KC. To be honest, City couldn't expect anything else.

Even without Bullard, the Tigers were backed to beat rock-bottom West Brom at home, but were held to a 2-2 draw. Mendy and Fagan scored for City, but that result and the whole Bullard episode hardly improved the increasingly sombre mood among fans. Things weren't expected to get any better with a trip to Chelsea at the start of February. City nonetheless came away with a creditable 0-0 draw. Matt Duke – selected ahead of Myhill – pulled off some fine saves. City could have won if Fagan and Dean Marney had made more of second half chances. Chelsea reacted by sacking Phil Scolari. Despite that draw, Brown found himself having to defend his selections and his tactics. He had become, some suggested, too cautious, too negative. He countered by saying: 'You're not after plaudits as a manager, you are just trying to get decisions right.' Centre half Turner, tracked by England manager Fabio Capello, suggested the 0-0 draw was a 'step in the right direction.' He added: 'Going there and getting a point is good for everyone's confidence. I'm sure it can help kick start our season. We are back on track.'

Amid the continuing fall-out from the Bullard fiasco, City drew 1-1 at Sheffield United in the FA Cup, Zayatte scoring the equaliser. That meant a replay at the KC during a hectic spell of five games in 13 days. Brown admitted: 'It's a big ask but I've every confidence in the players.' The sequence started with a Monday night home game against a Spurs' side still struggling in the relegation zone, despite a huge investment in players under Harry Redknapp. Brown sprang a surprise by pairing Cousin and Garcia up front with Geovanni on the bench. Spurs took a 1-0 lead through Aaron Lennon before Turner scrambled in an equaliser. City were good value for a point at the very least until Jonathan Woodgate stole victory for Spurs with a late header. It was becoming the story of City's season. Again Brown was in the firing line for what fans believed was an over-cautious approach. Why had Geovanni been left on the bench? Why was Garcia selected as a striker? Redknapp didn't help matters when he said City had 'picked a side not to lose the game.' He also said that had City won, they would have been almost certain to stay up. Brown, as ever, came out fighting. 'It was a positive performance and a positive selection. We didn't deserve to lose.' The inquest went on. City had taken nine points from a possible 51. If that type of return carried on, they would pick up only six points from their remaining 12 games.

Fortunately, there was a welcome reprieve in the shape of the cup replay against Sheffield United. City won 2-1, but their Championship opponents were left fuming after the Tigers' controversial first goal. TV replays clearly showed the ball had not crossed the line. Halmosi, fast becoming the forgotten man of City's Premier League campaign, scored the winning goal in the second half. City's reward was a sixth round tie at Arsenal, but before then attention switched back to the League. The game against fellow strugglers Blackburn on March 1 was always going to centre on the two managers: Brown and Sam Allardyce. They'd worked together for almost a decade at Bolton and were still good friends. With both sides desperate for points, there was no chance of any favours. City lost 2-1 with Blackburn's goals coming in a three minute spell in the first half. A mistake by Duke led to the first and ex-Tiger Keith Andrews slotted in the second after more rank defending. Down on the touchline, Allardyce danced with delight and punched the air in triumph.

Brown buried his head in his hands. Ashbee did pull a goal back but it was too little, too late. Marney was sent off and it was hardly a surprise afterwards when a grim-faced Brown admitted: 'I'm facing the biggest test of my career. We're in the mire. There are 11 games to go and we've got to be positive.' At Christmas, City had been a dozen points clear of the relegation positions. Now the margin was down to three.

City faced a trip to Fulham the following Wednesday. Few people gave them a chance against the surprise team of the Premier League. Duke performed heroics, Manucho scored with virtually the last kick of the game and the Tigers left London with a 1-0 win. Manucho's goal celebrations said it all. He was mobbed by delighted team-mates. Brown's reaction? 'Everybody was going on about the fact we'd won once in 18 games, but we had 13 or 14 good performances in that. In fact, tonight wasn't a good performance.' City now had 32 points and a better than reasonable chance of adding three more the following Saturday when Newcastle visited the KC Stadium. Driving to that game, you could almost feel the tension in the streets. About half-a-mile from the stadium, I joined the queue in the outside lane at a set of traffic lights. A car pulled up on the inside and the driver gave me a V-sign. I was just about to return the gesture when I realised it was Windass. His loan spell at Oldham had been cut short; by mutual consent, apparently. 'I'm back,' he shouted across at me, a huge smile on his face. He knew the terms of his loan meant he couldn't play first team football for City but there was talk of a coaching position. The hero had returned. The Newcastle game finished 1-1. Looking down Newcastle's team-sheet it was hard to imagine why they were struggling with names like Butt, Geremi, Bassong, Smith,

Gutierrez, Owen, Martins, Duff. That was before they started playing. They were totally devoid of idea and confidence. City weren't much better. Although Geovanni gave them the lead with a well-taken header – his first goal since November – they missed a great chance to gain a win that would have probably made them safe. Brown said: 'We're still clear (of the relegation positions) but I think ten or 11 teams are involved. I think the battle will go right down to the last day of the season.'

City faced their FA Cup quarter final tie at Arsenal three days later. The players were busy talking up the prospect of a Wembley appearance either in the semi finals or even the final. Geovanni said: 'Everyone knows the FA Cup. My dream is to be at Wembley.' I suspected several of his team-mates were just relieved to escape the pressure of the increasingly desperate relegation fight. City had embarrassed Wenger and Co to win 2-1 at the Emirates earlier in the season, but few pundits thought they could repeat it . . . until Barmby gave them the lead with a first half strike that he swears to this day wasn't a miss-kick. Barmby also had another effort ruled out for offside. City suffered a blow when Ashbee was forced to limp off with a hamstring injury just before half time. Arsenal piled forward in the second half. Their pressure had to tell. Robin Van Persie equalised and, ten minutes later, William Gallas headed the home side in front from a blatantly offside position. City were beaten 2-1. They were out of the cup, but no one could predict the storm of controversy that followed. Brown slated referee Mike Riley for allowing Gallas' goal to stand and then accused Arsenal captain Cesc Fabregas of spitting at his assistant Brian Horton. The reporters couldn't write down Brown's quotes fast enough. 'He (Fabregas) spat at my assistant in the tunnel. That's their club captain. I hope he's proud of himself. He spat at his (Horton's) feet.' Fabregas wasn't even playing that night, but went onto the pitch to celebrate Arsenal's victory. He denied spitting. Wenger said he hadn't seen the incident and was about the only person inside the Emirates to claim Gallas was on-side when he scored. On the subject of that Gallas goal, Brown was asked whether he felt cheated. He replied: 'You said the word (cheated). I can't use the word I'm afraid but that is the case. The lad (Gallas) is two yards offside. In the first half, Nick Barmby is a yard offside, sticks the ball in the back of the net, but the flag goes up. As it is, that's why we are out of the FA Cup. Ask Mr Riley how much that is going to cost Hull City and I don't think he'd understand. I don't even think he'd care. When you come to the Emirates, I understand you are not going to get the rub of the green but it's hard to take.'

All hell broke loose over the spitting allegations. City pledged to support Horton and stressed they intended to report Fabregas to the FA. City duly submitted their evidence; Arsenal their defence. It was the final week of the season before the FA ruled Fabregas had no case to answer. Brown's outburst was understandable, though many people felt he should have made his complaint behind closed-doors to Arsenal first rather than speaking out on TV. His standing in the national media went down another couple of levels. Reporters who, earlier in the season, were praising his every move now labelled him as arrogant and aloof. Brown remained steadfast. 'I don't think I need to change. I'm me and that is what you get. If there are people out there who don't like me, then so be it. I'm more bothered with keeping this club in the Premier League and what the people of Hull think and what my chairman thinks.' The person I felt most sorry for in all this was Horton, as honest a person as you could wish to meet. He seemed bemused by the whole affair. In the aftermath of what became known as 'Spitgate', Brown claimed the affair would galvanise his team. He also admitted the injury-plagued Gardner would miss the rest of the season after fracturing his back in the very last seconds of that cup tie at the Emirates – following an illegal challenge that went unnoticed by the officials. Gardner had only just returned to action after a lengthy thigh injury.

A few days later and a 1-0 defeat at Wigan plunged City fans into even deeper despair. The match kicked-off on a Sunday lunch-time and was played in what seemed like a half-full stadium. The atmosphere was as flat as City's League position. The winning goal came late on from a City error. Brown's players leapt to his defence. Fagan proclaimed: 'He is a strong personality but that's because he cares about this club and his players.' City were still three points above the bottom three and there was finally some better long-term news about Bullard. He announced the surgery on his knee had been successful and said he hoped to be back in action early next season, with City still a Premier League side. I listened to those last few words and wondered how many people shared Bullard's optimism. Brown reckoned City needed three wins from their final eight games to be certain of safety. Most pundits thought 40 points was the minimum requirement. Portsmouth were in relegation trouble themselves and when they visited the KC on April 4, there was genuine hope of a home win. However, City were held to a 0-0 draw in another poor quality clash. David James briefly stirred himself from his slumbers to deny Fagan. Pompey hit the post with a header deep into stoppage time when most fans were already on their way home. On the positive side, it was another point. City were edging towards safety. It could have been three, but the players looked like a side under pressure, short on confidence – and, more importantly, goals. Brown was content with the draw and described the next two games at Middlesbrough and Sunderland as six-pointers. Middlesbrough were below City in the table and seemingly on course for the Championship. Sunderland were just above them, but still not safe and in free fall under Ricky Sbragia. Attention during the build-up to the Middlesbrough game was diverted by the announcement that Newcastle had appointed Alan Shearer as their new manager in what Brown described as a 'last desperate throw of the dice.' Newcastle also trailed City in the table, but the media portrayed Shearer as the Magpies' God-like saviour. Brown called for his players – and the fans – to focus on events at City and not at other clubs. 'Our fate is still in our own hands', he said. 'We just need one win, one good performance, to kick-start things.'

City lost 3-1 at Middlesbrough, where Marlon King predictably scored the third and final goal. The result was the low point of the entire season and driving back from the Riverside that night, I genuinely thought for the first time that City would be relegated. True, there were still another six games to play, but my head was full of negative thoughts: Would I still have a job if the club went back into the Championship? It didn't help when I reached home, popped into my local for a pint and some wag said: 'Don't worry, we need someone to cut the grass verges next year.' The mood around the club was grim. Brown had slammed his players after what he correctly described as an 'unacceptable performance' at The Riverside. The players admitted the manager was spot on. Ashbee said: 'The gaffer had every right to have a go. We let ourselves down.' As the Sunderland game approached, the smiles returned. With the media at the weekly Thursday press conference, Brown finished a training session with a light-hearted game of head tennis. He said: 'There's nothing wrong with the spirit here. Middlesbrough has been and gone. We can't do anything about it. Now it's Sunderland and we need to bring a much better game to the table. No matter how well we did at the start of the season, we were under no illusions that we wouldn't be in a scrap by the end of it.'

Brown did get that improved performance at Sunderland, but the result was worryingly predictable: a 1-0 defeat. The manager rallied his side. 'I'm confident we can still stay up,' he insisted. The pundits didn't share his view. Former England international Chris Waddle summed up the mood when he said: 'Hull are doomed. They have been found out. They are in free fall and I fear nothing will save them. For me, Newcastle and Sunderland will definitely stay up. Hull, Middlesbrough and West Brom will definitely go down.' On paper, City's previous eight League games had all seemed winnable. In the event, they served up one win (at Fulham), two draws (at home to Portsmouth and Newcastle) and five defeats. A grand total of five points and five goals. If that wasn't worrying enough, next up at the KC were Liverpool, who still harboured hopes of the title. On the way to the game, my mate Steve reckoned Hull could win. 'Gerrard isn't playing,' he said, hopefully. I wondered if he'd been on the home brew. Liverpool won 3-1 and perhaps the only surprise was that Torres didn't score. It was another improved performance by City but there was an air of inevitability about things. Liverpool were class. I asked Rafa Benitez after the game whether he thought Hull would stay up. He looked at my club tie, smiled and complained about the length of the grass on the KC pitch. It was more than a week until City's next match, which was a Monday night visit to Aston Villa. The game was broadcast live on Sky Sports. John Carew's first half goal gave Villa the lead. To add to City's woes, Ashbee was forced off the pitch with a season-ending knee injury. To their credit, City threw everything at their hosts in the last few minutes but missed a couple of glorious chances. Three games to go: Stoke (home), Bolton (away) and Manchester United (home). Brown reckoned the promotion fight would go right down to the wire. Ah well, Man United at home – no problems.

Stoke surely represented the best chance of three points. The visitors were virtually assured of survival themselves. Just think, before Christmas and they'd trailed City by 12 points. Now they were six points ahead. The KC was packed to the rafters and everyone expected a Hull win. Unfortunately, a Ricardo Fuller goal just before the break and a Liam Lawrence long distance strike in the second half meant the points were heading back to the Potteries. Andy Dawson's free kick in stoppage time was another classic case of too little, too late. Few City fans were left in the stadium to witness Dawson's impressive effort. As the layers trouped from the pitch, all I could hear was the Stoke fans signing 'Delilah' followed by 'Going down, Going down.' Brown was clutching at straws as he admitted: 'I thought we played some decent stuff and did enough to have had noses in front. They had two chances and scored twice. The big difference was in the quality of their strikers and our nerves.' One of those strikers was James Beattie. If only his missus had liked Hull. His eight goals had done so much to keep Stoke up. When City had expressed an interest in signing Beattie, many fans questioned a £5m price tag. Now those very same fans were moaning the club had wasted a great opportunity.

City were still above the bottom three – but perhaps only for 48 hours. That Stoke game took place on a Saturday. On the Monday evening, Newcastle entertained Middlesbrough at St James' Park. City would be dragged into the relegation positions for the first time in the season if Newcastle won. Brown admitted he was praying for a draw. That looked the likely outcome until Shearer threw on his 'super subs' Obafemi Martins and Peter Lovenkrands. Newcastle won 3-1. Middlesbrough were effectively doomed. Newcastle and Shearer had a lifeline. City were in the bottom three. The frown lines on Brown's forehead seemed to be getting deeper and in the week leading up to that Bolton game, he whisked his entire squad away to the Lake District for what he termed a 'team bonding experience.' There were no distractions. WAGS and mobile phones were banned. There was no Windass either. He'd been told to stay away from the club. The players yomped over the hills and fells, took part in clay pigeon shooting and raced kayaks on Lake Windermere. Apparently, now wasn't the time to practice set-pieces. Brown maintained similar trips had led to a positive impact when he was assistant manager at Bolton. City didn't need to read the newspapers to know the bookmakers had installed them as one of the three teams to go down. Former England international Ian Wright even reckoned they would finish bottom of the table as West Brom had staged something of a belated recovery. City had won just once in 18 games. They were struggling to score and were leaking goals at bad times.

The omens didn't look good. Duffen admitted City were drawing up plans for 'all possibilities.' The club had sold almost 20,000 season tickets, but he warned relegation would see around £30m of guaranteed Premier League revenue trickle away. Brown and his players returned from the Lakes looking happier and relaxed. 'There's no reason why we can't win at Bolton,' said the manager. The cynics pointed out they had heard it all before. There again, what could the manager say? What could he do? He could make changes, but by and large he was turning back to players who had already been found wanting at Premier League level. City's best hope seemed to be the fact Bolton were virtually safe. They didn't have anything to play for apart from pride. I travelled across to the Reebok Stadium with two members of City's staff who produce a monthly DVD to accompany the magazine. We arrived three hours before the game and already fans were gathering outside the ground. I spotted Don Jarvis who had stood beside me in that FA Cup tie at Salisbury all those years ago in one of Warren Joyce's first matches in charge. Since then, I've seen him at most games – from Canvey Island to Cardiff. He is black and amber through and through and even cut short his honeymoon in Blackpool to watch City in action at Torquay. 'I think we'll do it,' he said. 'I think we'll stay up. If we can get just a point today, it could be enough. We just need Fulham to win at Newcastle.'

Bolton's players started to arrive. They happily signed autographs and posed for photos. Two or three of them were discussing where they were spending their summer holidays. Suddenly I shared Don Jarvis's optimism. City were capable of beating Bolton. Inside the ground, the assembled media, many of who I'd known for a few years, tucked into their lunch and grilled me on just where it had all gone wrong for City. I tried to remain positive in what became rather a heated debate and pointed out City still weren't down. 'And, no,' I said, 'it wasn't that on-the-pitch team talk at Man City. There are various reasons – injuries, a few dodgy decisions, loss of confidence . . .' My audience shook their heads. Why bother trying to reason with them? They'd write what they wanted anyway, as Brown had already discovered to his cost. The match was unbelievably tense. I'd asked the man from Radio Five Live not to tell me what was happening at Newcastle. He duly passed on information every five minutes. 'Newcastle have scored,' he said. 'No, wait a minute . . . they haven't. It's still 0-0' Bolton did score, full back Gretar Steinsson thumping in a 25 yard shot before the break. The support at Bolton was truly outstanding, as it had been all season. City's 5,000 travelling fans raised the roof. Early in the second half, Fagan took advantage of a mistake by Danny Shittu to equalise. City's representatives in the press box leapt into the air and were told to sit down again. The man from the BBC couldn't see. By now, Fulham were winning at Newcastle. Suddenly, there was light at the end of the tunnel. It could have been even better if Brown's best 'mate' Jaaskeleinen hadn't produced two world class saves. The final whistle: 1-1 at the Reebok and Fulham had won at St James' Park. I didn't really listen to a report that said Newcastle had a legitimate equaliser ruled out.

Bolton's Gary Megson faced the media first. He could bore for Britain. Then, it was Brown's turn. He looked upbeat, even though he spilled half a bottle of fizzy water in his lap. As he made a joke about that, I could almost sense a huge weight had been lifted from his shoulders. 'Yeah,' he quipped, 'Jussi

Jaaskeleinen. That's twice he's done us this season. He used to be a good mate of mine.' Outside, City's fans didn't want to go home. When I headed for the car park, Don Jarvis rushed over. 'I told you we'd get a point,' he said. 'You should have believed me. I also put a tenner on Fulham beating Newcastle one-nil.' I asked Don whether he'd got any predictions for the last day of the season. 'Yeah,' he said 'We'll murder Man U.'

The scenario was simple. City were one point and one place ahead of Newcastle. They just had to equal Newcastle's result on the last day to stay up. While City had drawn at Bolton, West Brom's defeat at home to Liverpool meant they were down. Middlesbrough could still survive but had an inferior goal difference to City. Even if they won their last game at West Ham, they could only equal the Tigers' tally of 35 points. Sunderland were still in trouble but could afford to lose at home to Chelsea and still stay-up. So it was between City and Newcastle: City at home to Manchester United, Newcastle at Aston Villa. United were assured of the title, having drawn against Arsenal in their penultimate game of the season. Their visit to the KC was taking place three days before their Champions League final against Barcelona in Rome. Suddenly, the press was full of reports that Sir Alex Ferguson would play his youth team at the KC. It was claimed – wrongly – that the other clubs threatened with relegation would sue United if they went down in such circumstances. Brown distanced himself from the speculation and said: 'He (Ferguson) will do what he thinks is best. All we can do is concentrate on ourselves.'

Surprisingly, the atmosphere at City's training ground during the week was relaxed. With all the final fixtures being played on a Sunday, the players were given a couple of extra days off. They attended the club's annual awards on the Tuesday night and the outstanding Turner almost completed a clean sweep. The Chairman's Trophy went to Ashbee, who limped on to the stage to rousing applause. The following night Brown and his players visited the newly opened Hull Truck Theatre to watch Alan Plater's play *Confessions Of A City Supporter*. Generally, the days seemed to fly by . . . until Saturday. Then, time seemed to stand still. I couldn't even pop round to my mate Steve's house to talk about the game and the chances of survival. Incredibly, he would be missing the most important match in City's history. His wife had booked a cottage in Cornwall, starting that very Saturday. There was no escape. Steve had even checked on flights back from Newquay for the game. There weren't any. 'I'll watch it on TV,' he said, his face as long as a wet weekend in Worthing. I felt gutted for him. Then again, I wasn't going to tangle with his missus. All the final day fixtures kicked off at four o'clock. An hour-and-a-half before, I watched United's team coach pull into the KC. Among the waiting fans was a United supporter holding his young son in his arms. As the players stepped off the coach, the boy kept asking: 'Who's that dad? Each time the reply was the same: 'Err, I don't know son.' At last, there was a familiar face. 'That,' said dad, 'is Wes Brown. That's Gary Neville and that's Anderson.' Actually, it wasn't. It was Nani. United's squad was hardly crammed with household names. In fact, some of their players looked as though they'd had to get permission from their head-teacher to play. They were remarkably relaxed. Forty five minutes before kick off, I was standing outside United's dressing room. There was no sign of Ferguson. Brown and Danny Welbeck played a game of football-tennis in the corridor. Brown won 9-5. Then the dressing room door opened. Ferguson barked out something and Brown and Welbeck scuttled back inside. When the players emerged from the tunnel, the noise was deafening. Three-and-a-half sides of the stadium were a sea of black and amber. It was a year to the day since the Wembley play off final. I was in a seat next to the City dug-out. Brown, as usual, was dressed in a suit and tie. He couldn't stand still. I craned forward to see Ferguson take his seat in United's dug-out. Wait a minute. Was that a smile on his face? Even a friendly handshake for the fourth official. Anyone expecting a blood-and-thunder battle was disappointed. The game resembled a pre-season friendly. Just about everyone seemed to have a radio fixed to their ear, waiting for news from Villa Park and Upton Park.

Sitting along from me were Ash and Bullard. Ash had a 'mate in the crowd' at Villa and was relaying details of the game to City's bench. Bullard was doing the same regarding the West Ham v Middlesbrough game. It was tense. Ferguson left his seat midway through the first half. He'd been caught short and had to ask a steward in the tunnel to point him in the direction of the nearest loo. He returned just in time to see Darron Gibson put United ahead with the type of quality strike that would have delighted Ronaldo. City's fans were momentarily silenced. Then they found their voice. 'We are staying up, we are staying up.'

Suddenly a massive cheer echoed around the stadium. Villa had taken the lead over Newcastle, courtesy of a Damien Duff own goal. A couple of minutes later, and there was another cheer. Surely Villa had scored again. 'Nah,' said Ash. 'It's still 1-0.' Brown clasped his hands even tighter behind his back. Parkin looked to have aged ten years. Cousin, who was on substitute duty, yawned. The rest of the game was almost surreal. Rarely can such an important game have passed by with so little incident. City huffed and puffed but never looked like blowing United's house down. Brown kept looking at Ashbee. 'It's still 1-0 gaffer.' The minutes and then the seconds ticked away. The final whistle came. City had lost 1-0. The fans poured onto the pitch. There was still another minute to play at Villa Park. And then the news came through. Newcastle had been beaten. The agony was over. City were safe by one single point . . . one bloody point. Brown sprang into the air and hugged and kissed anyone within 30 yards. Horton and Parkin grabbed each other and danced in delight. The fans ignored the calls over the PA system to clear the pitch. City's players sprinted for the safety of the tunnel. They looked drained, physically and mentally, as they filed passed me. One win in 22 games. Just eight points from the last 63. Statistics like that didn't matter. City had 35 points; Newcastle had 34. 'We've done it,' said Fagan. 'We've fuckin done it.' Bo Myhill slapped me on the back. Geovanni shook my hand and said: 'I am very happee.' Dawson walked by. 'This,' he said, 'beats the three promotions.'

Eventually, the pitch cleared and the players summoned the energy for a lap of honour. There were smiling faces everywhere. Brown proclaimed staying up as the biggest achievement of his career; bigger than winning the play-off final. The overwhelming feeling, though, was one of intense relief. Brown hugged his daughter Sophie, who was dressed in a replica City kit and carried a huge toy Tiger. Anyone expecting the manager to celebrate quietly was disappointed. He grabbed the stadium announcer's microphone and led the crowd in a rendition of 'We are staying up' and then the Beach Boys' song *Sloop John B* with the lyric 'This is the best trip I've ever been on.' Nearby, an exhausted Barmby admitted: 'I hope to God he isn't leading the karaoke in the pub tonight.' Brown had just proved that when it comes to singing, not all Britain has got talent. Eventually the noise died down. The fans wended their way home.

An hour after the final whistle and I was outside Brown's office. The door opened and Ferguson stepped out. 'Right,' he said to one of United's burly security staff, 'are we ready to go?' 'Yeah gaffer,' came the reply. 'We've been waiting for ages.' Ferguson looked at my City tie and nodded his head. Then, he took a couple of strides along the corridor but suddenly stopped. He stepped backwards and placed his hands on the shoulders of someone leaning against the wall. It was Ashbee. The most successful football manager in British history had just met the most successful captain in City's history. 'Well done on this season son,' said Ferguson. It was the first time I'd ever seen Ash blush. 'Thanks,' said Ashbee. 'It's just a shame I can't seem to play against you. I've missed both games.' 'Never mind son,' added Ferguson. 'There's always next season.' With that, Ferguson headed off towards Rome and the final against Barcelona. First, though, it was Hartshead Moor Service Station on the M62, to drop off a couple of United's West-Yorkshire based players.

That brief meeting between Ashbee and Ferguson was wonderful. Somehow it summed everything up. There was time for one quick drink then it was time to leave. It was almost deserted outside the stadium. 'See you in July,' shouted Barmby as he headed for his car, his two young sons falling in behind him. I looked around. The KC Stadium shone in the bright sunlight. Hull City were still a Premier League club. An incredible journey. On the road out of Hull, I pulled into a lay-by outside Boothferry Park. I sat for a few minutes – alone with all those memories.

Then it was time to go home.

Acknowledgements

The last decade has been remarkable, even by Hull City's standards.

From the very brink of the abyss to the glamour and glitz of the Premier League. What a journey.

I owe so much to so many people for letting me be part of that journey.

I will never forget the help - and trust - I received from Warren Joyce. It's amazing to think he was appointed as player/manager on the very day I started writing about City for the Hull Daily Mail. As we sat in the dressing room after a defeat at Shrewsbury, if someone had told us City would be a top flight club within ten years, we'd have looked for the nearest straight-jacket and white van.

Since those early days, I've lost count of the column inches I've written . . . the friends - and the enemies - I've made.

My thanks have to go to the likes of Brian Little, Peter Taylor, Adam Pearson and - more recently - Paul Duffen and Phil Brown for letting me experience the world of professional football. Then, there is the endless list of players who have contributed to the story.

I wouldn't say covering City has always been a labour of

love. It was a factor in the collapse of my marriage. I also missed my dad dying. I was reporting on a match at Darlington instead.

Now, I'm actually working for City. There is 'life' on the other side. Like the Tigers, I've come full circle, from Boothferry to Wembley - and beyond.

Writing this book has brought back so many memories . . . some fond, some not so fond.

I'd like to thank City's Marketing Manager Rob Smith for the confidence he's shown in me. Thanks to John Cooper for helping plot a trail through the very complicated era of David Lloyd.

The list of others who have contributed is too long to mention. You know who you are.

Particular thanks to the patience of the library staff at the Yorkshire Post.

It would be very remiss of me not to pay tribute to the sheer professionalism of my editor Duncan Hamilton who never interfered but somehow kept me going through the most difficult days. Any mistakes are mine.

Finally, a word or two to my long-suffering partner Mandy who, over the last few months, has endured the moans, the groans, the sleepless nights and not even asked for a share of the royalties - yet.

Without her, I probably wouldn't be here to tell the incredible story.

Here's to the next decade.

John Fieldhouse, June, 2009.

Match by Match Record: Season 2008-2009

MATCH 1
Saturday, August 16, 2008
Barclays Premier League
KC Stadium
Hull City 2   **Fulham 1**
Geovanni 22   *Ki-Hyeon 8*
Folan 81
Hull: Myhill, Ricketts, Turner, Anthony Gardner, Dawson, Garcia (Fagan, 74), Ashbee, Boateng, Barmby (Halmosi, 62), Geovanni, King (Folan, 70). Subs not used: Duke, Windass, Mendy, Marney.
Fulham: Schwarzer, Pantsil, Hangeland, Hughes, Konchesky, Davies, Murphy (Andreasen, 85), Ki-Hyeon (Nevland, 85), Bullard, Gera, Zamora (Dempsey, 81) Subs not used: Zuberbuhler, Teymourian, Stoor, Kallio,
Attendance: 24, 525

MATCH 2
Saturday, August 23, 2008
Barclays Premier League
Ewood Park
Blackburn 1   **Hull City 1**
Roberts 38   *Garcia 40*
Blackburn: Robinson, Ooijer, Samba, Nelsen, Warnock, Reid, Mokoena (Tugay, 67), Dunn (Emerton, 46), Pedersen, Roque Santa Cruz, Roberts (McCarthy, 81). Subs not used: Simpson, Treacy, Derbyshire, Brown,
Hull: Myhill, Ricketts, Turner, Anthony Gardner, Dawson (Mendy, 58), Garcia (Barmby, 78), Ashbee, Marney, Fagan, Geovanni (Folan, 65), King.Subs not used: Brown, Windass, Duke, Halmosi.
Attendance: 23,439

MATCH 3
Tuesday, August 26, 2008
Carling Cup
The Liberty Stadium
Swansea 2   **Hull City 1**
Pintado 63   *Windass 11*
Gomez (p) 105
Swansea: De Vries, Painter, Monk, Collins (Rangel, 55), Serran, Orlandi, Gomez, Tudur-Jones, MacDonald, Allen (Pintado, 54), Bauza (Brandy, 81)Subs not used: O'Leary, Tate, Gower, Lawrence,
Hull: Duke, Brown, Mendy, Doyle, Cooper (Turner, 91), Barmby (Featherstone, 72), Hughes, France, Halmosi, Folan, Windass (King, 62). Subs not used: Atkinson, Garcia, Welsh, Warner.
Attendance: 8622

MATCH 4
Saturday, August 30, 2008
Barclays Premier League
KC Stadium
Hull City 0   **Wigan 5**
Rickets (og) 5
Valencia 13
Zaki 63
Heskey 68
Zaki 81
Hull: Myhill, Ricketts, Brown, Turner, Dawson (Mendy, 71), Fagan, Ashbee, Marney, Garcia (Barmby, 60), Geovanni (Windass, 56), Folan. Subs not used: Duke, Hughes, Halmosi, Cooper.
Wigan: Kirkland, Melchiot, Boyce, Bramble, Figueroa, Valencia, Palacios, Cattermole (Kapo, 79), Kilbane (Brown, 56), Heskey (Camara, 85), Zaki. Subs not used: Pollitt, Koumas, De Ridder, Kupisz.
Attendance: 24,282

MATCH 5
Saturday, September 13, 2008
Barclays Premier League
St James Park
Newcastle United 1   **Hull City 2**
Xisco 82   *King (p) 34*
King 55
Newcastle: Given, Edgar (Bassong, 68), Steven Taylor, Coloccini, N'Zogbia, Geremi, Butt, Guthrie (sent off 90), Xisco, Owen, Ameobi (Gonzalez, 61). Subs not used: Harper, Cacapa, Danquah, Doninger, Donaldson.
Hull: Myhill, McShane, Turner, Anthony Gardner, Dawson, Mendy (Folan, 73), Marney (Hughes, 78), Ashbee, Halmosi, King (Zayatte, 83), Fagan. Subs not used: Duke, Windass, Geovanni, Ricketts.
Attendance: 50,242

MATCH 6
Sunday, September 21, 2008
Barclays Premier League
KC Stadium
Hull City 2   **Everton 2**
Turner 18   *Cahill 73*
Neville (og) 50   *Osman 78*
Hull: Myhill, McShane, Turner, Zayatte, Dawson, Mendy (Garcia, 77), Ashbee, Marney, Halmosi, Cousin (Folan, 69), King (Boateng, 81). Subs not used: Duke, Geovanni, Hughes, Ricketts.
Everton: Howard, Neville, Jagielka, Yobo, Baines (Lescott, 46), Osman, Fellaini, Arteta, Castillo (Saha, 46), Cahill, Yakubu (Vaughan, 87). Subs not used: Nash, Nuno Valente, Rodwell, Baxter.
Attendance: 24,845

MATCH 7
Saturday, September 27, 2008
Barclays Premier League
The Emirates Stadium
Arsenal 1 **Hull City 2**
McShane (og) 51 *Geovanni 62*
Cousin 66
Arsenal: Almunia, Sagna, Toure, Gallas,
Clichy, Eboue (Bendtner, 69), Fabregas,
Denilson, Walcott (Vela, 77), Adebayor,
Van Persie. Subs not used: Fabianski,
Ramsey, Song Billong, Silvestre,
Djourou.
Hull: Myhill, McShane, Zayatte, Turner,
Dawson, Marney, Boateng (Garcia, 76),
Geovanni (Hughes, 72), Ashbee, Cousin
(Mendy, 80), King.
Subs not used: Duke, Halmosi, Ricketts,
Attendance: 60,037

MATCH 8
Sunday, October 5, 2008
Barclays Premier League
White Hart Lane
Tottenham 0 **Hull City 1**
Geovanni 9
Tottenham: Gomes, Gunter (Bentley, 55),
Corluka, Woodgate, Bale, Lennon
(Giovani, 74), Jenas, Zokora, Modric,
Pavlyuchenko (Bent, 35), Campbell.
Subs not used: Cesar, Dawson, O'Hara,
Assou-Ekotto.
Hull: Myhill, McShane, Turner, Zayatte,
Dawson, Marney, Ashbee, Boateng,
Geovanni (Halmosi, 71), King (Folan,
81), Cousin (Mendy, 60). Subs not used:
Hughes, Duke, Garcia, Ricketts.
Attendance: 36,062

MATCH 9
Sunday, October 19, 2008
Barclays Premier League
KC Stadium

Hull City 1 **West Ham 0**
Turner 51
Hull: Hull: Myhill, McShane, Zayatte,
Turner, Dawson, Marney, Ashbee,
Boateng (Hughes, 72), Geovanni
(Halmosi, 73), Cousin (Garcia, 82),
King.
Subs not used: Duke, Mendy, Folan,
Ricketts.
West Ham: Green, Faubert (Di Michele,
73), Neill, Upson, Ilunga, Behrami,
Parker, Noble, Etherington (Sears, 83),
Bellamy, Cole.
Subs not used: Lastuvka, Lopez, Boa
Morte, Mullins, Davenport.
Attendance: 24,896

MATCH 10
Saturday, October 25, 2008
Barclays Premier League
The Hawthorns
West Brom 0 **Hull City 3**
Zayette 47
Geovanni 62
King 66
West Brom: Carson, Zuiverloon, Donk,
Olsson, Robinson, Morrison (Moore,
80), Greening, Koren (Brunt, 80), Borja
Valero, Miller (MacDonald, 80), Bednar.
Subs not used: Kiely, Hoefkens, Cech,
Barnett.
Hull: Myhill, McShane, Zayatte, Turner,
Dawson (Ricketts, 10), Marney, Ashbee
(Hughes, 75), Boateng, Cousin, King,
Geovanni (Garcia, 78).
Subs not used: Duke, Mendy, Halmosi,
Folan.
Attendance: 26,323

MATCH 11
Wednesday, October 29, 2008
Barclays Premier League
KC Stadium
Hull City 0 **Chelsea 3**
Lampard 3
Annelka 50
Malouda 75
Hull: Myhill, McShane, Turner, Zayatte,
Dawson, Marney (Garcia, 71), Ashbee,
Boateng (Halmosi, 62), Geovanni, King
(Windass, 84), Cousin.
Subs not used: Duke, Hughes, Mendy,
Ricketts.
Chelsea: Cech, Bosingwa (Ivanovic, 86),
Carvalho, Terry, Ashley Cole, Deco
(Kalou, 78), Mikel, Lampard, Joe Cole
(Belletti, 54), Anelka, Malouda.
Subs not used: Cudicini, Di Santo,
Bridge, Alex.
Attendance: 24,906

MATCH 12
Saturday, November 1, 2008
Barclays Premier League
Old Trafford
Manchester United 4 **Hull City 3**
Ronaldo 3 *Cousin 23*
Carrick 29 *Mendy 69*
Ronaldo 44 *Geovanni (p) 82*
Vidic 57
Manchester: Van der Sar, Neville,
Ferdinand, Vidic, Evra, Ronaldo, Carrick
(Giggs, 72), Anderson (O'Shea, 88), Nani
(Tevez, 64), Berbatov, Rooney.
Subs not used: Foster, Park, Rafael Da
Silva, Fletcher.
Hull: Myhill, McShane, Turner, Zayatte,
Dawson, Marney, Hughes (Mendy, 59),
Boateng (Folan, 86), Geovanni, King
(Halmosi, 63), Cousin. Subs not used:
Duke, Barmby, Garcia, Ricketts.
Attendance: 75,398

MATCH 13
Saturday, November 8, 2008
Barclays Premier League
KC Stadium
Hull City 0   **Bolton 1**
                          Taylor 50
Hull: Myhill, McShane, Turner, Zayatte,
Dawson (Ricketts, 64), Boateng (Folan,
73), Ashbee, Marney, Geovanni, King,
Cousin (Mendy, 54). Subs not used:
Duke, Barmby, Garcia, Halmosi.
Bolton: Jaaskelainen, Steinsson, Cahill,
Andrew O'Brien, Samuel, Muamba,
Gardner, McCann, Taylor, Elmander
(Smolarek, 77), Kevin Davies.
Subs not used: Al Habsi, Helguson,
Shittu, Basham, Sissons, Obadeyi.
Attendance: 24,903

MATCH 14
Sunday, November 16, 2008
Barclays Premier League
KC Stadium
Hull City 2   **Manchester City 2**
Cousin 14   *Ireland 37*
Geovanni 60   *Ireland 45*
Hull: Myhill, McShane, Turner, Zayatte,
Ricketts, Boateng (Halmosi, 85), Ashbee,
Marney, Geovanni, Cousin (Barmby, 76),
King. Subs not used: Duke, Doyle,
Garcia, Folan, Giannakopoulos.
Man City: Hart (Schmeichel, 19),
Zabaleta, Richards, Ben-Haim, Garrido,
Wright-Phillips, Kompany, Ireland,
Benjani (Jo, 76), Robinho, Vassell.
Subs not used: Onuoha, Michael Ball,
Hamann, Elano, Evans.
Attendance: 24,902

MATCH 15
Saturday, November 22, 2008
Barclays Premier League
Fratton Park
Portsmouth 2   **Hull City 2**
Crouch 20   *Turner 54*
Johnson 63   *Paramot (og) 89*
Portsmouth: James, Johnson, Kaboul,
Distin, Pamarot, Diop, Davis, Hughes
(Nugent, 58), Belhadj (Traore, 58),
Crouch, Utaka (Kanu, 74). Subs not
used: Ashdown, Hreidarsson, Mvuemba,
Little.
Hull: Myhill, McShane, Turner, Zayatte,
Ricketts, Marney (Giannakopoulos, 82),
Ashbee, Boateng (Halmosi, 72),
Geovanni, King (Windass, 72), Cousin.
Subs not used: Duke, Doyle, Barmby,
Garcia.
Attendance: 20,240

MATCH 16
Saturday, November 29, 2008
Barclays Premier League
Britannia Stadium
Stoke 1   **Hull City 1**
Fuller (p) 73   *King 45*
Stoke: Sorensen, Griffin, Abdoulaye
Faye, Cort, Higginbotham, Soares
(Tonge, 62), Amdy Faye, Diao, Delap,
Sidibe, Fuller. Subs not used: Simonsen,
Olofinjana, Whelan, Cresswell,
Dickinson, Sonko.
Hull: Myhill, McShane, Turner, Zayatte,
Ricketts, Marney, Boateng (Cousin, 78),
Ashbee, Barmby (Halmosi, 69),
Geovanni (Garcia, 89), King.
Subs not used: Duke, Windass, Mendy,
Giannakopoulos.
Attendance: 27,500

MATCH 17
Saturday, December 6, 2008
Barclays Premier League
KC Stadium
Hull City 2   **Middlesbrough 1**
Turnbull (og) 82   *Sanli 79*
King (p) 85
Hull: Myhill, McShane, Turner, Zayatte,
Ricketts, Boateng, Ashbee, Marney
(Cousin, 61), Barmby (Mendy, 61),
Geovanni (Halmosi, 86), King. Subs not
used: Duke, Windass, Garcia,
Giannakopoulos.
Middlesbro: Turnbull, Hoyte, Wheater
(sent off 84), Pogatetz, Taylor, Aliadiere,
Arca, Digard (Hines, 87), Downing,
Sanli, Alves.
Subs not used: Jones, Emnes, Adam
Johnson, McMahon, Grounds.
Attendance: 24,912

MATCH 18
Saturday, December 13, 2008
Barclays Premier League
Anfield
Liverpool 2   **Hull City 2**
Gerrard 24   *McShane 12*
Gerrard 32   *Carragher (og) 22*
Liverpool: Arbeloa, Hyypia, Carragher,
Dossena, Mascherano (Lucas, 87),
Alonso, Benayoun (El Zhar, 74),
Gerrard, Riera (Babel, 82), Kuyt. Subs
not used: Cavalieri, Agger, Keane, Ngog.
Hull: Myhill, McShane (Marney, 27),
Zayatte, Turner, Ricketts, Mendy,
Ashbee, Boateng (Halmosi, 66),
Geovanni, Barmby (Windass, 77), King.
Subs not used: Warner, Garcia, Cousin,
Giannakopoulos.
Attendance: 43,835

MATCH 19
Saturday, December 20, 2008
Barclays Premier League
KC Stadium
Hull City 1   **Sunderland 4**
Barmby 19   *Malbranque 10*
                         Zayette (og) 78
                         Jones 84
                         Cisse 90
Hull: Myhill, Mendy, Turner, Zayatte,
Ricketts (sent off 81), Garcia (Cousin,
57), Ashbee, Boateng (Halmosi, 81),
Geovanni, Barmby (Giannakopoulos,
68), King. Subs not used: Duke, Doyle,
Windass, Marney.
Sunderland: Fulop, Bardsley, Nosworthy,
Ferdinand, Collins, Malbranque, Tainio
(Leadbitter, 79), Richardson (Edwards,
89), Reid (Whitehead, 74), Jones, Cisse.
Subs not used: Colgan, Murphy, Yorke,
Healy.
Attendance: 24,917

MATCH 20
Friday, December 26, 2008
Barclays Premier League
City of Manchester Stadium
Manchester City 5   **Hull City 1**
Caicedo 15   *Fagan 80*
Caicedo 27
Robinho 28
Robinho 36
Ireland 82
Manchester City: Hart, Zabaleta, Dunne,
Richards (Onuoha, 46), Michael Ball,
Wright-Phillips, Ireland (Fernandes, 85),
Kompany, Elano, Robinho, Caicedo (Jo,
46). Subs not used: Schmeichel, Vassell,
Garrido, Sturridge.
Hull: Myhill, Mendy, Zayatte, Turner,
McShane, Boateng (Doyle, 34),
Geovanni (Cousin, 70), Ashbee, Marney,
Windass (Fagan, 46), King. Subs not
used: Duke, Barmby, Hughes, Halmosi.
Attendance: 45,196

MATCH 21
Tuesday, December 30, 2008
Barclays Premier League
KC Stadium
Hull City 0   **Aston Villa 1**
                         Zayete (og) 88
Hull City: Myhill, McShane, Turner,
Zayatte, Ricketts, Mendy, Garcia (Fagan,
89), Ashbee, Halmosi, Barmby (Hughes,
85), Cousin (King, 69). Subs not used:
Duke, Doyle, Geovanni,
Giannakopoulos.
Aston Villa: Friedel, Reo-Coker, Knight,
Davies, Luke Young, Milner, Sidwell
(Gardner, 86), Petrov, Barry, Ashley
Young, Agbonlahor. Subs not used:
Guzan, Harewood, Delfouneso, Salifou,
Shorey, Osbourne.
Attendance: 24,727

MATCH 22
Saturday, January 3, 2009
FA Cup, third round
KC Stadium
Hull City 0   **Newcastle United
0**
Hull: Duke, Doyle, Turner, McShane,
Ricketts, Fagan (Halmosi, 73),
Giannakopoulos, Boateng, Marney,
Geovanni, Cousin (King, 73). Subs not
used: Ashbee, France, Zayatte, Warner,
Featherstone.
Newcastle: Given, Coloccini, Bassong,
Steven Taylor, Jose Enrique, Duff,
Guthrie, Butt, N'Zogbia (Gutierrez, 36),
Owen, Carroll. Subs not used: Harper,
Xisco, Geremi, Kadar, Edgar.
Attendance: 20,557

MATCH 23
Saturday, January 10, 2009
Barclays Premier League
Goodison Park
Everton 2   **Hull City 0**
Fellaini 18
Arteta 45
Everton: Howard, Hibbert, Jagielka,
Lescott, Baines, Osman, Arteta, Neville,
Pienaar, Fellaini, Cahill (Anichebe, 73).
Subs not used: Nash, Van der Meyde,
Castillo, Jutkiewicz, Gosling.
Hull: Myhill, McShane (Halmosi, 79),
Zayatte, Turner, Ricketts, Mendy,
Ashbee, Marney (Fagan, 54), Geovanni
(Cousin, 66), Barmby, King. Subs not
used: Duke, Doyle, France, Boateng.
Attendance: 37,527

MATCH 24
Wednesday, January 14, 2009
FA Cup, third round replay
St James Park
Newcastle 0   **Hull City 1**
                         Cousin 81
Newcastle: Given, Edgar, Bassong,
Coloccini, N'Zogbia, Gutierrez (LuaLua,
82), Butt, Guthrie, Duff, Owen, Xisco
(Carroll, 76). Subs not used: Harper,
Steven Taylor, Kadar, Donaldson,
Ranger.
Hull: Duke, Doyle, McShane, Zayatte,
Ricketts, Fagan (Mendy, 74), Halmosi,
Boateng (Ashbee, 67), France, Garcia,
Cousin (Folan, 86). Subs not used:
Warner, Featherstone, Giannakopoulos,
Atkinson.
Attendance: 31,380

MATCH 25
Saturday, January 17, 2009
Barclays Premier League
KC Stadium

Hull City 1   **Arsenal 3**
Cousin 65   *Adebayor 30*
                         Nasri 82
                         Bendtner 86

Hull: Myhill, Doyle, Turner, Ricketts,
Kilbane, Mendy, France (Fagan, 83),
Ashbee, Halmosi (Manucho, 53),
Geovanni (Garcia, 87), Cousin. Subs not
used: Duke, Dawson, Folan,
Giannakopoulos.
Arsenal: Almunia, Sagna, Toure,
Djourou, Clichy, Eboue (Bendtner, 69),
Diaby, Denilson, Nasri, Adebayor (Song
Billong, 87), Van Persie. Subs not used:
Fabianski, Vela, Ramsey, Gibbs, Merida.
Attendance: 24,924

MATCH 26
Saturday, January 24, 2009
FA Cup, fourth round
KC Stadium

Hull City 2   **Millwall 0**
Turner 15
Ashbee 84

Hull: Warner, Ricketts, Turner, Zayatte,
Dawson, Garcia, Ashbee, Marney,
Halmosi (Featherstone, 66), Cousin,
Manucho (Folan, 75). Subs not used:
Duke, Doyle, Geovanni, France, Mendy.
Millwall: Forde, Dunne, Robinson,
Craig, Frampton, Grabban (Hackett, 77),
Laird, Abdou, Martin (Grimes, 77),
Harris, McLeod (Alexander, 74).Subs not
used: Pidgeley, Kandol, O'Connor,
Fuseini,
Attendance: 18,639

MATCH 27
Wednesday, January 28, 2009
Barclays Premier League
Upton Park

West Ham 2   **Hull City 0**
Di Michelle 33
Cole 51

West Ham: Green, Neill, Collins, Upson,
Ilunga, Behrami, Parker, Collison
(Faubert, 71), Noble (Boa Morte, 84), Di
Michele (Nsereko, 86), Cole. Subs not
used: Lastuvka, Tristan, Tomkins, Sears.
Hull: Duke, Ricketts, Turner, Zayatte,
Dawson, Marney (Mendy, 73), Ashbee,
Kilbane, Geovanni (Bullard, 53), Cousin,
Manucho (Fagan, 53). Subs not used:
Myhill, Garcia, Halmosi, Folan.
Attendance: 34,340

MATCH 28
Saturday, January 31, 2009
Barclays Premier League
KC Stadium

Hull City 2   **West Brom 2**
Mendy 44   *Simpson 53*
Fagan 69   *Brunt (p) 73*

Hull: Duke, Ricketts, Turner, Zayatte,
Dawson, Mendy, Garcia (Folan, 81),
Ashbee, Marney, Kilbane, Fagan. Subs
not used: Myhill, Doyle, Geovanni,
Hughes, France.
West Brom: Carson, Zuiverloon, Donk,
Meite, Robinson, Morrison (Kim, 76),
Koren, Borja Valero (Pele, 88), Brunt,
Fortune (Bednar, 75), Simpson. Subs not
used: Kiely, Hoefkens, Cech, Filipe
Teixeira.
Attendance: 24,879

MATCH 29
Saturday, February 7, 2009
Barclays Premier League
Stamford Bridge

Chelsea 0   **Hull City 0**

Chelsea: Hilario, Bosingwa, Alex, Terry,
Ashley Cole, Mikel (Belletti, 57),
Quaresma (Drogba, 63), Ballack (Deco,
73), Lampard, Kalou, Anelka. Subs not
used: Taylor, Ivanovic, Di Santo, Stoch,
Hull: Duke, Ricketts, Turner, Zayatte,
Dawson, Garcia, Ashbee, Marney,
Kilbane, Geovanni (France, 81), Fagan.
Subs not used: Myhill, Doyle, Barmby,
Hughes, Halmosi,
Attendance: 41,802

MATCH 30
Saturday, February 14, 2009
FA Cup, fourth round
Bramall Lane

Sheffield United 1   **Hull City 1**
Halford 7   *Zayette 34*

Sheff Utd: Kenny, Jihai (Naughton, 60),
Morgan (Webber, 31), Kilgallon,
Naysmith, Cotterill, Montgomery, Quinn,
Hendrie (Howard, 73), Halford, Sharp.
Subs not used: Bennett, Walker,
Hull: Myhill, Ricketts, Turner, Gardner,
Dawson, Mendy (France, 88), Marney,
Zayatte, Garcia (Manucho, 79),
Geovanni (Barmby, 73), Folan. Subs not
used: Warner, Doyle, Halmosi,
Featherstone,
Attendance: 22,283

MATCH 31
Monday, February 23, 2009
Barclays Premier League
KC Stadium
Hull City 1   **Tottenham 2**
Turner 27   *Lennon 12*
           Woodgate 86
Hull: Duke, Ricketts, Turner, Gardner,
Dawson, Marney, Ashbee, Zayatte
(Geovanni, 87), Kilbane, Garcia
(Manucho, 79), Cousin (Mendy, 67).
Subs not used: Myhill, Doyle, Barmby,
Halmosi.
Tottenham: Cudicini, Corluka, Woodgate
(Dawson, 89), King, Assou-Ekotto,
Lennon (Zokora, 87), Jenas, Palacios,
Modric, Keane, Bent (Pavlyuchenko,
72). Subs not used: Gomes, Bentley,
Huddlestone, Chimbonda.
Attendance: 24,742

MATCH 32
Thursday, February 26, 2009
FA Cup, fourth round replay
KC Stadium
Hull City 2   **Sheffield United
1**
Kyle Naughton (og) 24   *Sharp
32*
Halmosi 56
Hull: Myhill, Doyle, Turner, Zayatte,
Ricketts, Mendy, France, Marney,
Halmosi, Barmby (Garcia, 73), Folan
(Manucho, 65). Subs not used: Warner,
Geovanni, Cousin, Featherstone,
Gardner.
Sheff Utd: Kenny, Naughton, Morgan,
Walker, Naysmith (Jihai, 88), Cotterill,
Howard, Stephen Quinn, Hendrie,
Halford, Sharp. Subs not used: Bennett,
Keith Quinn, Starosta.
Attendance: 17,239

MATCH 33
Sunday, March 1, 2009
Barclays Premier League
KC Stadium
Hull 1   **Blackburn 2**
Ashbee 79   *Warnock 34*
           Andrews 37
Hull: Duke, Doyle (Fagan, 67), Turner,
Zayatte, Dawson, Mendy, Ashbee,
Marney (sent off 64), Kilbane (Cousin,
53), Geovanni (Barmby, 53), Garcia
Subs not used: Myhill, Halmosi,
Manucho, Gardner,
Blackburn: Robinson (Brown, 46),
Ooijer, Nelsen, Samba, Givet, Diouf
(Mokoena, 83), Grella, Andrews,
Warnock, Pedersen (sent off 70), Roque
Santa Cruz (Roberts, 86)
Subs not used: Tugay, McCarthy, Treacy,
Villanueva,
Attendance: 24,612

MATCH 34
Wednesday, March 4, 2009
Barclays Premier League
Craven Cottage
Fulham 0   **Hull 1**
           Manucho 90
Fulham: Schwarzer, Pantsil, Hughes,
Hangeland, Konchesky, Davies, Murphy,
Etuhu, Dempsey, Johnson, Zamora
(Kamara, 89). Subs not used:
Zuberbuhler, Nevland, Gera, Dacourt,
Stoor, Kallio.
Hull: Duke, Zayatte, Turner, Gardner,
Kilbane, Mendy (Garcia, 89), Ashbee,
Ricketts, Geovanni, Fagan, Cousin
(Manucho, 76). Subs not used: Myhill,
Hughes, France, Halmosi.
Attendance: 23,051

MATCH 35
Saturday, March 14, 2009
Barclays Premier League
KC Stadium
Hull 1   **Newcastle 1**
Geovanni 9   *Steven Taylor 38*
Hull: Duke, Ricketts, Turner, Gardner,
Kilbane, Mendy (Barmby, 80), Ashbee,
Zayatte, Geovanni, Fagan (Garcia, 70),
Cousin (Manucho, 54). Subs not used:
Myhill, Dawson, Hughes, Halmosi,
Newcastle: Harper, Steven Taylor,
Coloccini, Bassong, Jose Enrique, Smith
(Ryan Taylor, 75), Butt, Geremi,
Gutierrez, Owen (Ameobi, 73), Martins .
Subs not used: Forster, Duff,
Lovenkrands, Edgar, Carroll.
Attendance: 24,914

MATCH 36
Tuesday, March 17, 2009
FA Cup, fifth round
The Emirates Stadium
Arsenal 2   **Hull 1**
Van Persie 74   *Barmby 13*
Gallas 84
Arsenal: Fabianski, Sagna, Gallas,
Djourou, Gibbs, Walcott (Eboue, 82),
Song Billong (Bendtner, 64), Diaby, Vela
(Nasri, 64), Van Persie, Arshavin. Subs
not used: Mannone, Toure, Denilson,
Silvestre.
Hull: Myhill, Ricketts, Gardner, Zayatte,
Dawson, Ashbee (Hughes, 46), Barmby
(France, 76), Geovanni, Fagan.
Manucho, Halmosi (Mendy, 67). Subs
not used: Duke, Garcia, Folan,
Featherstone.
Attendance: 55,641

MATCH 37
Sunday, March 22, 2009
Barclays Premier League
JJB Stadium
Wigan 1   **Hull 0**
Watson 84
Wigan: Kirkland, Melchiot, Bramble,
Boyce, Figueroa, Watson, Brown,
Scharner (Kapo, 77), N'Zogbia (De
Ridder, 46), Rodallega, Mido (Zaki, 72).
Subs not used: Kingston, Pollitt, Edman,
Cho.
Hull: Duke, Ricketts, Zayatte (Folan,
61), Turner, Dawson (Garcia, 38),
Mendy, Marney, Kilbane, Geovanni,
Manucho, Fagan (Halmosi, 82). Subs not
used: Myhill, Doyle, Barmby, France.
Attendance: 17,689

MATCH 38
Saturday, April 4, 2009
Barclays Premier League
KC Stadium
Hull City 0   **Portsmouth 0**
Hull: Duke, Ricketts (Folan, 85),
Zayatte, Turner, Dawson, Mendy,
Ashbee, Barmby (Marney, 74),
Geovanni, Manucho, Fagan (Kilbane,
71)Subs not used: Myhill, Garcia,
Halmosi, Featherstone.
Portsmouth: James, Kaboul, Campbell,
Distin, Hreidarsson, Johnson (sent off
80), Mullins, Hughes, Nugent (Kanu,
64), Kranjcar (Belhadj, 76), Crouch.
Subs not used: Begovic, Pennant,
Basinas, Pamarot, Utaka.
Attendance: 24,802

MATCH 39
Saturday, April 11, 2009
Barclays Premier League
The Riverside Stadium
Middlesbrough 3   **Hull 1**
Sanli 3   *Manucho 9*
Bates 29
King 90
Middlesbro: Jones, McMahon, Wheater,
Huth, Taylor, Bates, Aliadiere (Emnes,
89), Downing, Sanli, Alves (Adam
Johnson, 77), King. Subs not used:
Turnbull, Hoyte, Shawky, Riggott,
Walker.
Hull: Duke, Ricketts, Zayatte, Turner,
Dawson, Fagan (Boateng, 71), Mendy
(Marney, 46), Ashbee, Barmby (Folan,
62), Geovanni, Manucho. Subs not used:
Myhill, Halmosi, Kilbane, Featherstone.
Attendance: 32,255

MATCH 40
Saturday, April 18, 2009
Barclays Premier League
Stadium of Light
Sunderland 1   **Hull 0**
Cisse 45
Sunderland: Gordon, Bardsley,
Davenport, Ferdinand, Collins, Edwards
(Malbranque, 78), Leadbitter, Tainio,
Reid (Richardson, 76), Cisse (Murphy,
89). Jones. Subs not used: Fulop, Ben-
Haim, Yorke, McShane.
Hull: Myhill, Ricketts, Zayatte, Turner,
Dawson, Fagan, Geovanni (Mendy, 74),
Boateng (Barmby, 77), Marney (Folan,
68), Kilbane. Subs not used: Duke,
Doyle, Halmosi, Cousin.
Attendance: 42,855

MATCH 41
Monday, May 4, 2009
Barclays Premier League
Villa Park
Aston Villa 1   **Hull 0**
Carew 34
Aston Villa: Friedel, Luke Young,
Davies, Knight, Shorey, Milner, Petrov
(Reo-Coker, 89), Barry, Ashley Young
(Gardner, 89), Carew (Heskey, 86) . Subs
not used: Guzan, Sidwell, Delfouneso,
Clark.
Hull: Myhill, Ricketts, Turner, Zayatte,
Dawson, Garcia, Boateng, Ashbee
(Marney, 9), Kilbane (Manucho, 73),
Geovanni (Barmby, 46), Cousin . Subs
not used: Duke, Doyle. Halmosi,
Featherstone.
Attendance: 39,607

MATCH 42
Saturday, May 9, 2009
Barclays Premier League
KC Stadium

Hull 1   **Stoke 2**
Dawson 90   *Fuller 41*
               Lawrence 73
Hull: Myhill, Ricketts, Turner, Zayatte
(Geovanni, 67), Dawson, Garcia (Mendy,
60), Boateng, Kilbane, Barmby, Fagan,
Cousin (Manucho, 60) Subs not used:
Duke, Hughes, Halmosi, Marney.
Stoke: Sorensen, Wilkinson, Shawcross,
Abdoulaye Faye, Cort, Lawrence, Delap,
Whelan, Etherington (Pugh, 85), Beattie
(Cresswell, 78), Fuller (Kelly, 89). Subs
not used: Simonsen, Olofinjana, Camara,
Sonko.
Attendance: 24,932

MATCH 43
Saturday, May 16, 2009
Barclays Premier League
Reebok Stadium
Bolton 1   **Hull 1**
Steinsson 26   *Fagan 47*
Bolton: Jaaskelainen, Steinsson, Cahill,
Shittu, Samuel, Kevin Davies, Muamba
(Basham, 82), McCann, Mark Davies,
Taylor (Riga, 82), Elmander (Makukula,
89). Subs not used: Al Habsi, Hunt,
Puygrenier, Cohen.
Hull: Myhill, Ricketts, Turner, Dawson,
Kilbane, Fagan, Boateng, Garcia,
Barmby (Marney, 72), Geovanni
(Cousin, 77), Manucho (Halmosi, 83).
Subs not used: Duke, Doyle, Hughes,
Cooper.
Attendance: 25,085

MATCH 44
Sunday, May 24, 2009
Barclays Premier League
KC Stadium
Hull 0   **Man United 1**
            Gibson 24
Hull: Myhill, Ricketts, Turner, Kilbane,
Dawson, Garcia (Cousin, 81), Marney,
Boateng, Barmby (Mendy, 68), Geovanni
(Folan, 54), Fagan . Subs not used:
Duke, Hughes, Halmosi, Zayatte.
Man Utd: Kuszczak, Rafael Da Silva.
(Eckersley, 60), Neville, Brown, De Laet
(Possebon, 79), Nani, Fletcher, Gibson,
Welbeck (Tosic, 87), Martin, Macheda.
Subs not used: Amos, Corry Evans,
Drinkwater, James.
Attendance: 24, 945

Also by Great Northern

SWEET SUMMERS
The Classic Cricket Writing of JM KILBURN
Edited by Duncan Hamilton

WISDEN BOOK OF THE YEAR

Capturing a time when the true spirit of cricket existed. Through Kilburn's writing, some of the game's past legends are brought to life among them Donald Bradman, Fred Trueman, Jack Hobbs, Keith Miller, Garfield Sobers, Hedley Verity, Len Hutton and Walter Hammond.

For more than forty summers, J M Kilburn, the Yorkshire Post's cricket writer, captured the spirit and beauty of the game and the legends gracing it, among them Donald Bradman, Fred Trueman, Jack Hobbs, Keith Miller, Garfield Sobers, Hedley Verity and Walter Hammond. He writes of the days when 8,000 people watched Yorkshire's County Championship matches; when he travelled by ship on an Ashes tour with his friend Len Hutton; and of a bygone but beautiful period when one-day matches, coloured clothing and rampant commercialism in cricket simply didn't exist. Now you can explore these summer days in a richly satisfying collection of Kilburn's work gleaned from the *Yorkshire Post*, *Wisden* and *The Cricketer*. Kilburn is worth reading not only because he was a knowledgeable and respected interpreter of cricket – well balanced, tough-minded and scrupulously honest in his verdicts – but also for the valuable historical and social perspective that reading him provides. Most of all he demonstrably cared about cricket. His heart was in it – and belonged to it.
Hardback. Illustrated.

Visit www.greatnorthernbooks.co.uk